Jean-François Vilar
Theatres Of Crime

LEGENDA

LEGENDA is the Modern Humanities Research Association's book imprint for new research in the Humanities. Founded in 1995 by Malcolm Bowie and others within the University of Oxford, Legenda has always been a collaborative publishing enterprise, directly governed by scholars. The Modern Humanities Research Association (MHRA) joined this collaboration in 1998, became half-owner in 2004, in partnership with Maney Publishing and then Routledge, and has since 2016 been sole owner. Titles range from medieval texts to contemporary cinema and form a widely comparative view of the modern humanities, including works on Arabic, Catalan, English, French, German, Greek, Italian, Portuguese, Russian, Spanish, and Yiddish literature. Editorial boards and committees of more than 60 leading academic specialists work in collaboration with bodies such as the Society for French Studies, the British Comparative Literature Association and the Association of Hispanists of Great Britain & Ireland.

The MHRA encourages and promotes advanced study and research in the field of the modern humanities, especially modern European languages and literature, including English, and also cinema. It aims to break down the barriers between scholars working in different disciplines and to maintain the unity of humanistic scholarship. The Association fulfils this purpose through the publication of journals, bibliographies, monographs, critical editions, and the MHRA Style Guide, and by making grants in support of research. Membership is open to all who work in the Humanities, whether independent or in a University post, and the participation of younger colleagues entering the field is especially welcomed.

ALSO PUBLISHED BY THE ASSOCIATION

Critical Texts
Tudor and Stuart Translations • *New Translations* • *European Translations*
MHRA Library of Medieval Welsh Literature

MHRA Bibliographies
Publications of the Modern Humanities Research Association

The Annual Bibliography of English Language & Literature
Austrian Studies
Modern Language Review
Portuguese Studies
The Slavonic and East European Review
Working Papers in the Humanities
The Yearbook of English Studies

www.mhra.org.uk
www.legendabooks.com

RESEARCH MONOGRAPHS IN FRENCH STUDIES

The *Research Monographs in French Studies* (RMFS) are selected, edited and supported by the Society for French Studies. The series seeks to publish the best new work in all areas of the literature, language, thought, history, politics, culture and film of the French-speaking world and to cover the full chronological range from the medieval period to the present day. Proposals are accepted for monographs of up to 85,000 words, while proposals for 'short' monographs (50,000–60,000 words), a traditional strength of the series, are still welcomed.

Editorial Committee
Diana Knight, University of Nottingham (General Editor)
Robert Blackwood, University of Liverpool
Jane Gilbert, University College London
Shirley Jordan, Newcastle University
Neil Kenny, All Souls College, Oxford
Max Silverman, University of Leeds

Advisory Committee
Wendy Ayres-Bennett, Murray Edwards College, Cambridge
Celia Britton, University College London
Ann Jefferson, New College, Oxford
Sarah Kay, New York University
Michael Moriarty, University of Cambridge
Keith Reader, University of Glasgow

PUBLISHED IN THIS SERIES

20. *Selfless Cinema? Ethics and French Documentary* by Sarah Cooper
21. *Poisoned Words: Slander and Satire in Early Modern France* by Emily Butterworth
22. *France/China: Intercultural Imaginings* by Alex Hughes
23. *Biography in Early Modern France 1540–1630* by Katherine MacDonald
24. *Balzac and the Model of Painting* by Diana Knight
25. *Exotic Subversions in Nineteenth-Century French Literature* by Jennifer Yee
26. *The Syllables of Time: Proust and the History of Reading* by Teresa Whitington
27. *Personal Effects: Reading the 'Journal' of Marie Bashkirtseff* by Sonia Wilson
28. *The Choreography of Modernism in France* by Julie Townsend
29. *Voices and Veils* by Anna Kemp
30. *Syntactic Borrowing in Contemporary French*, by Mairi McLaughlin
31. *Dreams of Lovers and Lies of Poets: Poetry, Knowledge, and Desire in the 'Roman de la Rose'* by Sylvia Huot
32. *Maryse Condé and the Space of Literature* by Eva Sansavior
33. *The Livres-Souvenirs of Colette: Genre and the Telling of Time* by Anne Freadman
34. *Furetière's* Roman bourgeois *and the Problem of Exchange* by Craig Moyes
35. *The Subversive Poetics of Alfred Jarry*, by Marieke Dubbelboer
36. *Echo's Voice: The Theatres of Sarraute, Duras, Cixous and Renaude*, by Mary Noonan
37. *Stendhal's Less-Loved Heroines: Fiction, Freedom, and the Female*, by Maria C. Scott
38. *Marie NDiaye: Inhospitable Fictions*, by Shirley Jordan
39. *Dada as Text, Thought and Theory*, by Stephen Forcer
40. *Variation and Change in French Morphosyntax*, by Anna Tristram
41. *Postcolonial Criticism and Representations of African Dictatorship*, by Cécile Bishop
42. *Regarding Manneken Pis: Culture, Celebration and Conflict in Brussels*, by Catherine Emerson
43. *The French Art Novel 1900-1930*, by Katherine Shingler
44. *Accent, Rhythm and Meaning in French Verse*, by Roger Pensom
45. *Baudelaire and Photography: Finding the Painter of Modern Life*, by Timothy Raser
46. *Broken Glass, Broken World: Glass in French Culture in the Aftermath of 1870*, by Hannah Scott
47. *Southern Regional French*, by Damien Mooney
48. *Pascal Quignard: Towards the Vanishing Point*, by Léa Vuong
49. *France, Algeria and the Moving Image*, by Maria Flood
50. *Genet's Genres of Politics*, by Mairéad Hanrahan
51. *Jean-François Vilar: Theatres Of Crime*, by Margaret Atack
52. *Balzac's Love Letters: Correspondence and the Literary Imagination*, by Ewa Szypula
53. *Saints and Monsters in Medieval French and Occitan Literature*, by Huw Grange
54. *Laforgue, Philosophy, and Ideas of Otherness*, by Sam Bootle
55. *Theorizing Medieval Race: Saracen Representations in Old French Literature*, by Victoria Turner

www.rmfs.mhra.org.uk

Jean-François Vilar

Theatres Of Crime

Margaret Atack

Research Monographs in French Studies 51
Modern Humanities Research Association
2020

Published by Legenda
an imprint of the Modern Humanities Research Association
Salisbury House, Station Road, Cambridge CB1 2LA

ISBN 978-1-78188-703-5 (HB)
ISBN 978-1-78188-390-7 (PB)

First published 2020

All rights reserved. No part of this publication may be reproduced or disseminated or transmitted in any form or by any means, electronic, mechanical, photocopying, recording or otherwise, or stored in any retrieval system, or otherwise used in any manner whatsoever without written permission of the copyright owner, except in accordance with the provisions of the Copyright, Designs and Patents Act 1988, or under the terms of a licence permitting restricted copying issued in the UK by the Copyright Licensing Agency Ltd, Saffron House, 6–10 Kirby Street, London EC1N 8TS, England, or in the USA by the Copyright Clearance Center, 222 Rosewood Drive, Danvers MA 01923. Application for the written permission of the copyright owner to reproduce any part of this publication must be made by email to legenda@mhra.org.uk.

Disclaimer: Statements of fact and opinion contained in this book are those of the author and not of the editors or the Modern Humanities Research Association. The publisher makes no representation, express or implied, in respect of the accuracy of the material in this book and cannot accept any legal responsibility or liability for any errors or omissions that may be made.

Trademark notice: Product or corporate names may be trademarks or registered trademarks, and are used only for identification and explanation without intent to infringe.

© Modern Humanities Research Association 2020

Copy-Editor: Charlotte Brown

CONTENTS

	Acknowledgements	ix
	List of Abbreviations	xi
	Introduction	1
1	Black is Black	9
2	Murder in the Art World	29
3	Paris Crime Scenes I: The Imaginary City	47
4	Paris Crime Scenes II: History and Memory	65
5	Criminal Art	79
6	All That is Solid Melts into Air	93
7	Memento Mori	113
	Conclusion	131
	Bibliography	135
	Index	147

To
Aaron, John, and Chantelle
and
in loving memory of
David Macey (1949–2011)

ACKNOWLEDGEMENTS

I owe an enormous debt of gratitude to Diana Knight and Graham Nelson at Legenda. Diana has been rigorous, exacting, stoically patient, and unfailingly encouraging. Graham's good-humoured, supportive patience has also been exemplary. I cannot thank them enough. I am also very grateful to Charlotte Brown for her excellent work on the typescript.

I would like to acknowledge the generosity and encouragement of Jean-François Vilar who, although already very ill, too ill for us to meet, took the time and energy to write to me at some length.

I am indebted to many for their generous gifts: to Paule Monory for her kind permission to use one of Jacques Monory's extraordinary paintings for the cover image; to Sonia Zannettacci who helped me enormously by sending copies of exhibition catalogues of the work of Jacques Monory, Antonio Seguí, and Jacques Villeglé, hosted at her gallery in Geneva, including those to which Vilar contributed the text; to Pascale Hassoun, for the volume of essays in memory of her husband the psychoanalyst Jacques Hassoun to which Vilar contributed a short story; to Louise Lamé and Corsaire Sanglot, the brilliant writers of the blog *Passage Jean-François Vilar*, a *flânerie* through and around the works of Vilar that is both erudite and creative, for their hospitality, copies of otherwise unobtainable works, and kind encouragement.

The holdings of the following libraries have been indispensable: the Brotherton Library of the University of Leeds, including the very special Special Collections, the Bibliothèque nationale de France at Tolbiac, and BILIPO, the Bibliothèque des Littératures policières in Paris. I am grateful to them all, and to the immensely helpful librarians.

It is also a pleasure to thank the friends, family, and colleagues who have read, advised, helped, supported, or encouraged in a host of different ways: Elizabeth Brunazzi, Caroline Deneuville, Moira Dick, Claire Gorrara, Vee Harris, Diana Holmes, Jim House, Abi Macey, Marni Macey, Zak Macey, Daniel Pegg, Sophie, Leo, Oliver and Connor Pegg, David Platten, Marie Quenel, Keith Reader, Christine Reddaway, Nigel Saint, Max Silverman, Andy Stafford, Marion and Dick Toy, Richard Williams, Sarah Wilson.

Needless to say, any omissions or errors are mine alone.

This book is dedicated to my children, Aaron, John, and Chantelle, whose love and support are a constant joy and source of strength, and to the memory of David Macey. No one who knew him would be surprised to learn that time and time again while working on this book, I would come across something I should read

— art, philosophy, politics, literature, history — and find it already on our shelves. It is such a shame I have not been able to discuss the book with him as it evolved, but his intellectual projects and intellectual curiosity are woven into its pages, and it is all the better for it.

M.A., Leeds, May 2020

LIST OF ABBREVIATIONS

Quotations from the following, frequently-cited works by Vilar are taken from the following editions and are referenced in the main text with the abbreviations below and a page number. Unless otherwise stated, all translations are my own.

BT   *Bastille-Tango* [1986] (Arles: Actes Sud, 1998)
CTA   *C'est toujours les autres qui meurent* [1982] (Paris: J'ai Lu, 1986)
D   *Djemila* (Paris: Calmann-Lévy, 1988)
E   *Les Exagérés* [1989] (Paris: Seuil, coll. Points, 1990)
EU   *État d'urgence* [1985] (Paris: J'ai Lu, 1987)
MM   'Memento Mori', in Jacques Monory, *Memento mori*, exhibition catalogue (Geneva: Galerie Sonia Zannettacci, 2014)
NC   *Nous cheminons entourés de fantômes aux fronts troués* (Paris: Seuil, 1993)
P   'Poses', in Jacques Monory, *Come-back*, exhibition catalogue (Geneva: Galerie Sonia Zannettacci, 1990)
PN   *Paris la nuit*, photographs by Michel Saloff (Paris: ACE éditions, coll. Le Piéton de Paris, 1982)
PS   *Passage des singes* [1984] (Paris: J'ai Lu, 1985)
SH   *Sherlock Holmes et les ombres*, photographs by Christian Louis (Paris: Du Collectionneur, 1992)
T   'Tandem', *Tango*, 3 (July–September 1984), 32–37

INTRODUCTION

Jean-François Vilar came to public attention when his first novel, *C'est toujours les autres qui meurent*, written at speed in response to a competition, won the Télérama Prix du roman noir in 1982.[1] It is a witty, clever novel that combines serious themes with a virtuoso use of Marcel Duchamp and contemporary political, contestatory art. It struck a very different tone within the crime fiction corpus, and with a photobook and two further novels published in quite quick succession — *Paris la nuit*, in collaboration with the photographer Michel Saloff, *Passage des singes*, and *Etat d'urgence*[2] — he was soon recognised as one of the key figures of the new generation of crime writers, appearing on *Apostrophes* alongside Didier Daeninckx and Thierry Jonquet in 1985.[3] In 1998 he received the Grand Prix Hammett, awarded every five years in recognition of an entire body of work.[4]

Vilar's crime novels, short stories, and non-fictional writings on Paris are self-reflexive texts that play with referentiality at the level of plot and theme, involving representations and reproductions of political and historical crimes and events; multiple identities; characters working in art, film, photography, journalism, and television; violent plots of war, terrorism, and revolution, from the Revolution, the Commune, the 1930s, the German Occupation, the Algerian War, and beyond. His work intersects with that of other writers using the crime genre or a knowing awareness of textuality to write about the violent politics and history of the twentieth century, such as Didier Daeninckx, Pierre Siniac, Frédéric Fajardie, Jean-Patrick Manchette, Jorge Semprun, Georges Perec, Patrick Modiano. Vilar stands out, however, by his particular insistence on the political and aesthetic conflicts of the nineteenth and early twentieth centuries, his carnavalesque theatricality, at once exuberant and melancholic, and his exploitation, both thematically and structurally, of avant-garde art.

It is often said that he wrote very little, but a brief glance at the bibliography of his works at the end of this volume will quickly dispel that notion. From 1982 to 1993 he was very prolific, publishing short stories, essays, and articles, and contributing to art works, in addition to his novels which were all very well received. After 1993 his publications became more occasional, but included several short stories and substantial texts for catalogues of exhibitions by Antonio Seguí and Jacques Monory. Pierre-André Sauvageot made a film about his work, *Jean-François Vilar: 95% de réel*, in 1997, where Vilar spoke of the development of a novel set in Prague, but it never appeared. Jean-Christophe Brochier, who published a personal memoir, *Petits Remèdes à la depression politique*, which is in part a tribute to Vilar, described him as 'a revolutionary activist, a fiercely determined, intensely committed ('enragé')

Trotskyist, sincere to the point of bad faith; a dedicated journalist who combined a messianic passion for culture with revolt and their immediate implementation'.[5] Vilar's last work of fiction was his contribution to the catalogue of Jacques Monory's exhibition *Memento mori* in May 2014. He died the following November.

This book focuses primarily on Vilar's seven novels, the photobooks, and the two Jacques Monory exhibition catalogues. It is the first full-length study of his writing, and aims to give an overview of its range as well as arguing for the literary and cultural importance of his work for post-war social and cultural history. His best-known novels, *C'est toujours les autres qui meurent*, *Bastille-Tango*, and *Les Exagérés*, are regularly if briefly cited in studies of crime writing and Paris.[6] There is some interesting, if not extensive, critical work on him, particularly his use of Marcel Duchamp.[7] Kristin Ross considers his work from the angle of 1968, and also the politics of his representation of Paris;[8] Annie Collovald and Eric Neveu look at the political implications of the move into crime fiction by several former militants, including Vilar.[9] The importance of photography, his use of the Paris of the surrealists, and the aesthetic and political configuration of contestation in his representation of Paris, have also received some detailed attention.[10] The aim of this book is to elucidate the coherence of the political, thematic, generic, and textual dimensions of his writing, to establish its wider significance, and to contribute to debates about fiction, politics and history; philosophy, narrative and art; text and image. It concentrates on the portrayal of cities: Paris, but also Venice, Djemila, and Prague; on history and memory; and on writing, narrative, and art, for art and reflexion on artistic practice is woven into the fabric of all Vilar's novels.

He famously said that his three guardian angels were Dashiel Hammett, Leon Trotsky, and Marcel Duchamp, bringing together Hammett's political crime fiction of the 1930s, Trotsky's political reading of the world as well as a commitment to action and change, and, in Duchamp, an artist famous for his fairly aggressive dismantling of the mechanics of representation, and of Art and the Artist.[11] To these one might add Walter Benjamin, André Breton, Léo Malet, famous figure of the French *roman noir*, and Jacques Monory, leading artist of the *Figuration narrative* movement from the 1960s onwards. Julio Cortázar and Eugène Atget also take their place in this pantheon, and in Paris Vilar has a huge cast of literary *flâneurs*, as well as artists, writers, photographers, and performers of all kinds.[12] His novels bristle with references, allusions, and citations. They were also universally praised in reviews for their elegant, precise, nonchalant, and irreverent sense of style.

The central topos of Vilar's fiction is the street as theatre of crime, around which operates a constellation of key themes: photography, the city, *roman/film noir*, and politics. In the programme for the seventh Festival du roman et du film policier in Reims, he wrote a short introduction to the exhibition of his photographs: 'Quelques images en quête du crime' [Some Images in Search of a Crime]:

> Dans sa 'Petite Histoire de la Photographie', Walter Benjamin explique: 'Ce n'est pas sans raison qu'on a comparé les vues d'Atget à celles d'un théâtre du crime. Dans nos villes, est-il un seul coin qui ne soit un théâtre du crime, aucun passant qui ne soit un criminel? La photographie ne doit-elle pas, sur ces images, découvrir la faute et désigner le coupable?' Ailleurs le même Benjamin

suggère que la photographie n'est rien d'autre que l'inconscient de la vue. De là à penser que *le crime est l'inconscient de la rue*, il n'y a qu'un menu écart. Sanctionné justement par la photo. Amplifié, développé, par quelques romans noirs.[13]

[In his 'Little History of Photography', Walter Benjamin explains: 'It is no accident that Atget's photographs have been likened to those of a crime scene. But isn't every square inch of our cities a crime scene? Every passerby a culprit? Isnt it the task of the photographer to reveal guilt and to point out the guilty in his pictures?' Elsewhere, the same Benjamin suggests that photography is nothing else than the optical unconscious. From there to think that *crime is the unconscious of the street*, there is only a small step. Authorised by photography itself. Amplified and developed, by some crime novels.][14]

The street here is a kind of stage, waiting for its crime and its assassin. Benjamin has said so, because Eugène Atget demonstrates it, particularly with his shots of Paris empty of people that were celebrated by the surrealists for their powerful conveying of both the everyday and also something else, a suspense, a foreboding.[15]

Each of the themes integral to this topos is embedded in a cluster of associated themes and tropes. The art of photography, entwined with the fine arts, is structural to the scene, as is the photographer, a *flâneur* through the streets of Paris in Vilar's novels, as were Atget and Benjamin before him; the city, especially Paris, an imaginary object in literature and image, site of crime, rich in historical detail and personal memory; and the *noir*, both *roman noir* and *film noir*, inheritor of the rich legacy of the Gothic imagination, of the nineteenth-century literary Paris of Poe, Sue, and Hugo, and of the surrealists. And finally politics, because the crime on the street is so often a state crime, and because the power structures of society are revealed through the fundamental and hierarchical imposition of order on the street and its architecture.

This scene of the photographer in the city is close to Susan Sontag's view of the *flâneur*-photographer: 'The photographer is an armed version of the solitary walker reconnoitering, stalking, cruising the urban inferno'.[16] She cites 'Atget's twilight Paris of shabby streets and decaying trades, the dramas of sex and loneliness depicted in Brassaï's book *Paris de nuit* (1933), the image of the city as a theater of disaster in Weegee's Naked City (1945)', concluding that the *flâneur* 'is not attracted to the city's official realities but to its dark seamy corners, its neglected populations — an unofficial reality behind the façade of bourgeois life that the photographer "apprehends," as a detective apprehends a criminal'.[17] There are, however, significant differences. Sontag argues that the *flâneur* finds the world 'picturesque', whereas Vilar's photographer views the street with a political eye, not the eye of the detective. Moreover, his images are always presented in a relationship with texts. The photograph documents the scene, the *roman noir* develops it. The second part of the introduction to the exhibition sets out more fully this other fundamental aspect of the 'theatre of crime': the image in fiction is also a fictional image:

> Car une photo ne raconte rien. Elle se contente de montrer. Muette, elle suggère une légende. C'est-à-dire toutes les histoires possibles. L'empreinte du réel, cadré sur la pellicule sensible, ne demande qu'à devenir fiction. [...]

> Les planches exposées [...] ne sont que repères pour des récits aléatoires. Elles tendent à s'agencer comme des lames de ce Tarot qu'il faut toujours interpréter. Et comme au Tarot, ce n'est pas tant l'image qui compte que son lien, son rapport à d'autres images.
> Le reste est affaire de flânerie et de goût pour les rues fatales.
> A vous de voir.
>
> [For a photo does not recount anything. It merely shows. Being silent, it suggests a caption. Which is to say, all possible stories. The imprint of reality, framed on the sensitive film, asks only to become fiction. [...] The prints in the exhibition [...] are just cues for random narratives. They tend to be combined like the blades of the Tarot, that always need interpreting. And as with the Tarot, it is not so much the image that counts as its relationship to other images.
> The rest is a matter of *flânerie* and of an inclination for the fatal streets.
> Your turn to see.]

For Vilar, the photograph is an inexhaustible producer of fictions. Fictions proliferate on the terrain of the silent image, or from the multiple connections of their multiple juxtapositions. The pack of tarot cards, each bearing meaning and generating meanings through the new sequences of the shuffled cards, echoes Benjamin's comment that the photographer is the descendant of the augurs and *aruspices* of classical Rome, readers of signs and omens, such as the entrails of freshly slaughtered chickens.[18] If the task of photographers is to reveal guilt, they do so in order to inform future actions. Any crime fiction is a search for answers, and the historical, cultural, and material texture of the city is an intrinsic part of the quest, thematically and structurally, through the trajectory in the 'rues fatales', both topographical, textual, and visual. Games of chance are integral to the narrative development of his novels, since they have the power to reveal otherwise hidden connections and create new pathways; we are on the terrain of Borges, Cortázar, and the surrealists' 'hasard objectif' [objective chance]; Vilar refers to 'la sensibilité des coincidences poétiques' [awareness of poetic coincidences].[19]

Vilar uses the *jeu de l'oie* [goose game] as his preferred mechanism for connecting chance and necessity, contingency and logic, the arbitrary nature of fiction interlocked with its inherent teleology that structures parts of the narrative and articulates the elaborate interaction of sequence and chance through the streets of Paris. It is a popular centuries-old board game of sixty-three squares laid out in a snail pattern that exists in innumerable themed versions. Progression involves not only the chance roll of the dice and the obstacles and traps of particular squares when one lands on them, but also a list of overarching rules that are in play as well. The necessity of the patterns and rules linking the squares, often determined by the chosen narrative theme, is often only revealed as the plot advances, as are the many deviations of chance, traps, obstacles, encounters, or events.

A 'fiction machine' is the term Anne Ducrey applies to Camus's *L'Étranger* in the context of it being read as a crime novel; with their intricate structure of quest and interpretation, combining action in the past with investigation in the present governed by the teleological aim of resolution, all crime novels are constructed in a complex narrative apparatus.[20] If the *jeu de l'oie* organises complicated scenarios of progression, the undecidability of the silent image and the proliferation of narratives thus generated by it ('toutes les histoires possibles') is often conveyed in Vilar's work by the oscillation between original and copy or copies, the play of repetition and difference — in the simulacrum, the model, in *trompe l'œil* — that develops and expands one of the primary conundrums of realism, that it is never the reality it claims to be.

Rosalind Krauss takes Benjamin's notion of the optical unconscious to discuss a number of avant-garde works, including those of the surrealists and Duchamp, to counter the rationalist optics of modernism and construct a counter-history on whose terrain markers would point to 'the way the foundations of modernism were mined by a thousand pockets of darkness, the blind, irrational space of the labyrinth'.[21] Vilar inflects this decisively in the direction of *le noir* and criminality, which is consistent with the heritage of the gothic imaginary in French literature, but which will be combined with the tropes of *film noir* and the murderous violence of a world in crisis in texts that integrate multiple disruptions of surface realism and its false certainties with the polished story-telling of the *roman noir*.

The chapters of this book are organised thematically, taking the novels in very broadly chronological order. Chapter 1, 'Black is Black', sets out the political and cultural contexts that helped shape Vilar's approach to the *roman noir*, starting with his years on the Trotskyist newspaper *Rouge*, writing hundreds of articles and covering a wide range of cultural topics. A consideration of the literary and art magazine *Tango* (1983–85), and his contributions to it, demonstrates how far his work resonated with a certain counter-culture of the 1980s, with its multiple roots in the political art of contestation and the interrogation of literature from the 1960s onwards, and in Parisian working-class culture. The crime fiction genre is another important context, one which Vilar presented in his preface to the French translation of Ernest Mandel's study *Delightful Murder: A Social History of the Crime Story* (1984).[22] Finally this chapter looks at the *figuration narrative*, since another arena exploring the visual and textual dimensions of the *roman noir* was avant-garde art of the 1960s, which with the work of Jacques Monory in particular is an integral part of several of Vilar's novels.

Chapter 2, 'Murder in the Art World', considers the first two novels, *C'est toujours les autres qui meurent* (1982) and *Passage des singes* (1984), both of which revolve around art, its ideological and political tensions and contradictions. The former introduces Duchamp, contemporary political art, and the modern art museum, with a complex referentiality and 'double *détournement*' operated upon the master of *détournement*; the second tackles the tensions between political art and the market, and multiple layers of fraud and forgery. The chapter seeks to establish the broader political importance of the ludic deployment of reference, illusion, and art.

The texts centred particularly on Paris are discussed in Chapters 3 and 4, the first considering early texts devoted to Paris, the second concentrating on the 1989 novel *Les Exagérés*. Chapter 3, 'Paris Crime Scenes I: The Imaginary City', discusses the photobook *Paris la nuit* (1983), two short stories, and the 1986 novel *Bastille-Tango* that deals with the aftermath of torture and murder in the Argentina of the junta as played out in the lives of Argentinian exiles in Paris, where political crimes and crimes of passion and murder intertwine to the music of the tango and its consummate eroticism of love and death. Chapter 4, 'Paris Crime Scenes II: History and Memory', takes *Les Exagérés*, where the story of a film about the French Revolution is the setting for a multi-facetted presentation across many different modes of the history and memory of political confrontation in Paris, and argues that Vilar's citational narrative offers a distinctive configuration of history, politics, and historiography.

Chapter 5, 'Criminal Art', uses the metaphor of transgressive art inscribed on the surface of the city to elucidate literary and political structures of texts where the city itself is the theatre of crime: Venice in *Etat d'urgence* (1985), which focuses on the issue of left-wing terrorism and the Red Brigades, and Djemila, a classical ruined city in Algeria, in *Djemila* (1988), where the politics of the left and the far right in contemporary Paris in the run-up to the 1988 presidential elections involve violent pasts in the French Resistance and the Algerian War.[23]

Chapter 6, 'All That is Solid Melts into Air', takes a phrase from the *Communist Manifesto* to highlight the melancholic nature of the various literary and political quests in the photobook *Sherlock Holmes et les ombres* (1992) and *Nous cheminons entourés de fantômes aux fronts troués* (1993), two texts that involve London and Prague, and Paris and Prague respectively, and that include a direct narration of the past as part of the plot.[24] With different cities and different moments in time, different stories being narrated as well as the same story being narrated in different ways, these are complex investigations of evidence, knowledge, and reliability in the present and in the past. From show trials and show concentration camps to the upheavals of 1989, it is argued that the only resolution seems to be a fictional one.

The final chapter, 'Memento mori', looks at Vilar's fictional texts that interact with and effectively comment on Monory's complex paintings in two exhibition catalogues of 1990 and 2014.[25] Monory's work has been extensively discussed in art criticism and notably in major texts by the philosopher Jean-François Lyotard. Both Monory and Vilar explore the intricate interrelations of fiction, photography, and painting in the context of death and *le noir* in film and fiction, and this chapter argues that Lyotard's argument about the staging of new modes of rationality in Monory's work is helpful for understanding the tensions in Vilar's fiction between narrative order and the disorder of the fragment.

Notes to the Introduction

1. Jean-François Vilar, *C'est toujours les autres qui meurent* (Paris: Fayard, 1982).
2. Jean-François Vilar, *Passage des singes* (Paris: Presses de la Renaissance, 1984) (winner of the Prix du Festival policier de Reims, 1984); *Etat d'urgence* (Paris: Presses de la Renaissance, 1985); Jean-François Vilar, *Paris la nuit*, photographs by Michel Saloff (Paris: ACE, coll. Le Piéton de Paris, 1982).
3. 'Du côté du polar français', *Apostrophes*, 19 April 1985. *Apostrophes* was a weekly prime-time cultural television programme, hosted by Bernard Pivot, that ran from 1975 to 1990.
4. 'Le Grand Prix Hammett du roman noir attribué pour l'année 1998 à Jean-François Vilar, pour l'ensemble de son œuvre', press release consulted in the Bibliothèque des littératures policières.
5. Jean-Christophe Brochier, *Petits remèdes à la dépression politique* (Paris: Don Quichotte, 2017),

p. 13. Brochier also records Vilar was writing a novel about Theresienstadt called *Le Bazar*, and that he agreed to write expanded versions of the serialised chapters of *Paris d'octobre*. Brochier received thirteen of them, together with illustrations by Miss Tique, the street artist who figures briefly in *Bastille Tango* (*Petits remèdes*, pp. 167, 169, 171, 184).

6. Jean-François Vilar, *Bastille-Tango* (Paris: Presses de la Renaissance, 1986); *Les Exagérés* (Paris: Presses de la Renaissance, 1989).
7. Madeleine Frédéric, *La Stylistique française en mutation?* (Brussels: Académie royale de Belgique, 1997); Jean-Olivier Majastre, *Approche anthropologique de la représentation: entre corps et signe* (Paris: L'Harmattan, 1999).
8. Kristin Ross, *May 68 and its Afterlives* (Chicago & London: University of Chicago Press, 2002); 'Parisian noir', *Literary History*, 41.1 (Winter 2010), 95–109.
9. Annie Collovald and Eric Neveu, '"Le néo-polar": du gauchisme politique au gauchisme littéraire', *Sociétés & Représentations*, 1 (2001), 77–93.
10. Kerstin Schoof, 'Les Photos dans les polars de Jean-François Vilar', trans. by Michel Marx, <http://pagesperso-range.fr/arts.sombres/polar/8_dossiers_article_kertin_schoof_fr.pdf> [accessed 25 April 2010]; Marie-Claire Bancquart, *Paris dans la littérature française après 1945* (Paris: La Différence, 2006), Chapter 7; Margaret Atack, 'Streets and Squares, *quartiers* and *arrondissements*: Paris Crime Scenes and the Poetics of Contestation in the Novels of Jean-François Vilar', in *Crime Fiction in the City: Capital Crimes*, ed. by Lucy Andrew and Catherine Phelps (Cardiff: University of Wales Press, 2012), pp. 85–106.
11. Biographical details in Frédéric Fajardie and others, *Black Exit to 68: 22 nouvelles sur mai* (Montreuil: La Brèche-PEC, 1988), p. 206.
12. The *flâneur* was a noted nineteenth-century type, an observer of city life who was also on show as he strolled through the streets and arcades.
13. *Catalogue du 7e Festival du roman et du film policier* (Reims, 1985) (consulted in the Bibliothèque des littératures policières, Paris).
14. For the translation of the quotation from Walter Benjamin's 'Kleine Geschichte der Photographie' (1931), see: 'Little History of Photography', trans. by Edmund Jephcott and Kingsley Shorter, in *Selected Writings*, ed. by Michael W. Jennings and others, 4 vols (Cambridge, MA, & London: Belknap Press, 1996–2003), II (1927–34), 527.
15. See Alain Buisine, *Atget ou la mélancolie en photographie* (Nîmes: Jacqueline Chambon, 1994), pp. 67–81 & 123–27.
16. Susan Sontag, *On Photography* (London: Penguin Books, 1979), pp. 55–56. Vilar reviewed *On Photography* in *Rouge*: 'Juste des images: "La Photographie" essai de Susan Sontag', *Rouge*, 896 (28 September to 4 October 1979), 24.
17. Sontag, *On Photography*, p. 42.
18. Vilar omitted the phrase from his quotation above.
19. Alexis Violet [Jean-Michel Mension], 'Série rouge', interview with Jean-François Vilar, *Rouge*, 1170 (25 July to 22 August 1985), 27.
20. Anne Ducrey, 'Le Crime de Meursault: une machine à fictions', in *Romans du crime: littérature générale et comparée*, ed. by Karen Haddad-Wotling (Paris: Ellipses, 1998), pp. 61–85.
21. Rosalind E. Krauss, *The Optical Unconscious* (Cambridge, MA, & London: MIT Press, 1993), p. 21.
22. Jean-François Vilar, 'Noir c'est noir', in Ernest Mandel, *Meurtres exquis: une histoire sociale du roman policier*, trans. by Marie Acampo, preface by Jean-François Vilar (Montreuil: PEC, 1987), pp. 8–12; first published as *Delightful Murder: A Social History of the Crime Story* (London: Pluto Press, 1984).
23. Jean-François Vilar, *Djemila* (Paris: Calmann-Levy, 1988).
24. Jean-François Vilar, *Sherlock Holmes et les ombres*, photographs by Christian Louis (Paris: Le Collectionneur, 1992); Jean-François Vilar, *Nous cheminons entourés de fantômes aux fronts troués* (Paris: Seuil, 1993). *Nous cheminons* was adapted into a radio play for *France Culture*, and into a film, *Les Disparus*, directed by Gilles Bourdos. The first episode of the play is available at <https://www.franceculture.fr/emissions/fictions-samedi-noir/fictions-samedi-noir-samedi-6-janvier-2018> and on YouTube <https://www.youtube.com/watch?v=4JIFg-AD27w>, as

are the two subsequent episodes: <https://www.youtube.com/watch?v=csOmg4Qj-Tc and https://www.youtube.com/watch?v=TdQG1u4Hdbk>. The trailer for Les Disparus (1998) is available at <http://www.allocine.fr/video/player_gen_cmedia=17576030&cfilm=17576.html> [all accessed 21 August 2018].

25. Jean-François Vilar, 'Poses', in Jacques Monory, *Come-back*, exhibition catalogue (Geneva: Galerie Sonia Zannettacci, 1990); 'Memento mori', in Jacques Monory, *Memento mori*, exhibition catalogue (Geneva: Galerie Sonia Zannettacci, 2014).

CHAPTER 1

Black is Black

Reading Vilar pulls the cultural map of the 1960s and 70s into a different shape, connecting movements and intellectual debates that are often approached separately. Vilar's novels embrace political contestation in the visual arts, in history and politics from the French Revolution to the Algerian war, and in the everyday in a politicised map of France. *Le noir* in his work is as much visual as textual, and drawing not primarily on the classic channels of the hard-boiled American fiction and American *film noir* that produces the Franco-American phenomenon that was the Série noire, but on the French history of *le noir* from Sade, the 'roman noir anglais' as the gothic novel was often termed, nineteenth-century century literature of mystery, modernity, and the city, to surrealism and its literary and visual pantheon. In order to contextualise and develop these connections, this chapter examines his writing before and alongside his novels for the Trotskyist newspaper *Rouge* and the cultural magazine *Tango,* as well as the relation of his work to post-1968 French crime fiction.

Les Années *Rouge*

'Vilar' was the pseudonym he had used for his political activism, and he gave very little information about his early life. He was born in 1947, to a Jewish family originally from Odessa,[1] became involved in politics around the mid-sixties in the Trotskyist Jeunesse communiste révolutionnaire (JCR), studied philosophy at Nanterre, and was fully engaged in May 68 when he was working as a special needs teacher (*éducateur spécialisé*), a student, and a Trotskyist militant. He described his experience variously as a classic Quartier Latin one — a May of barricades, demonstrations, and arrests — and one spent between barricades and the maternity wing.[2] He had married young and had a son, of whom he soon had sole charge after a divorce. His military service was therefore deferred for some time, and completed in 1973–74.[3] During and after his military service he was involved in the *comités de soldats,* which were set up to organise conscripted soldiers and defend them where necessary. This was a major issue at the time; he wrote extensively about repression in the army in 1976.[4] Vilar became a full-time activist with the Ligue communiste, and then a full-time journalist from 1976 on the Ligue's newspaper *Rouge* until 1981.[5]

The first issue of *Rouge* was published in September 1968. A fortnightly newspaper at the outset (though from March 1976 to January 1979 it was published as a daily paper), it included significant coverage of international politics, from anti-colonial struggles to the miners' strike in the UK, as well as of internal French politics and the work of the Ligue, supporting strikes, confronting the extreme right, and offering detailed critiques of the government. The 1972 manifesto of the Ligue set out a detailed programme for revolutionary struggle against exploitation and the building of a new socialist economics and a new socialist politics. It drew up the battle lines against the imperialist bourgeoisie of the 'Old World', hailing the struggles taking place across the world: 'This great mass of humanity of millions of hungry, oppressed and exploited people has said: enough!'.[6] May 68 is presented in this document as a building block, the 'starting line' that had mobilised youth and workers; now it was a case of building the political organisation and movement to transform a mass revolt into the revolution.[7] The social programme — for schools, for health, for housing, for transport — was detailed, and the revolutionary importance of the young was given great prominence. The demands included: freedom from the family as a unit of bourgeois oppression, freedom from the army and military service as a means of imposing bourgeois order, and freedom from discrimination, focused on the vote at sixteen, and an end to the repression of homosexuality. The demand for women's liberation was translated into a series of specific points: the social recognition of domestic work, an end to discrimination, equal pay, and the freeing of women's sexuality from reproduction with access to contraception and abortion, for minors as well. The fight against colonialism was aligned with a commitment on immigration: 'French workers, immigrant workers: same boss, same struggle'.[8] From the state to twenty-four-hour crèches, it is a comprehensive analysis of the revolutionary change, in relation to politics, economics, and society, for which the Ligue was fighting. Within that policy framework, *Rouge* brought evidence of oppression and resistance, nationally and internationally, on all these fronts.

The 1970s were turbulent times, politically, and the pages of *Rouge* were full of drama: campaigns being waged, reports of police violence, of the dissolution of the Ligue after violent clashes with the extreme-right Ordre nouveau in 1973 and the imprisonment of leading militants Pierre Rousset and Alain Krivine, who stood as presidential candidate for the Ligue in 1969 and 1974, of campaigns for imprisoned soldiers, and of the bitter struggles for freedom and independence, from Vietnam to East Timor. The Bobigny trial of three women for an illegal abortion had extensive coverage, as did the events at the Lip factory that was occupied and then run by the workers from 1973. The policy commitment in favour of homosexuality was translated into good coverage of the campaigns, but unfortunately in a manner that drew strong rebukes from the Front homosexuel d'action révolutionnaire (FHAR) and a formal, if limited, apology from the paper. A FHAR demonstration was welcomed, but the fact the demonstrators dressed up and paraded in all sorts of drag costumes was roundly criticised as 'not serious' and detrimental to the cause.[9] The political focus was to organise *l'avant-garde ouvrière*, the political touchstone was the working class and the class struggle. Every opportunity was taken to show the Communist Party in a poor light: hostility to 'les Staliniens' ran very deep.

Brochier notes, as many others have done, that Vilar had editorial responsibility for the cultural pages of *Rouge,* although he is not mentioned in that capacity in Jean-Paul Salles's comprehensive study of the Ligue.[10] Nonetheless, Salles stresses the importance of the commitment to the coverage of culture in *Rouge,* and its eclecticism, which Vilar's articles certainly confirm.[11] Jean-Michel Mension, a former situationist and communist who was involved in the Ligue from the late 1960s and wrote extensively for *Rouge* under the name 'Alexis Violet', started writing for the 'Culture' column after Vilar left.[12] His goals certainly applied to Vilar's work: 'to help the worker readers of our newspaper understand what was happening on the cultural front, and develop their critical sense. [...] To reveal the function and place of culture in the political struggle, and introduce little known work'.[13] The range of Vilar's writings, particularly in the later years of his involvement, was impressive. His early articles were dominated by a few key topics: the military, controversies in Catholic circles, the case of Roland Agret, unjustly sent to prison in 1973 for the murder of a garage owner who would turn out to have been a member of the Gaullist 'parallel police', the Service d'action civique. Vilar reported on the ramifications of his appeal and his hunger strike with indefatigable support.[14] He wrote regularly on new *bande dessinée* publications, and demonstrated his flair for story-telling with many articles on the social fabric of life in France, such as on the annual Braderie de Lille, or the Fête de l'humanité, that gave a sense of the social occasion with titles such as 'En attendant l'omelette campagnarde' [Waiting for the Rustic Omelette], 'Entre frites et affiches' [Between Chips and Posters],[15] or that enlarged the socio-political compass to invite reflection on the quirky everyday. '56 sardines, 30 puces, 50 pieds de vignes et 893 boîtes de foie gras' [56 sardines, 30 fleas, 50 vines and 893 bottles of foie gras] is a delightful stroll through the poisoned dogs or the La Rochelle sardine-eating competition of the *fait divers* columns of the mainstream press, that still ends seriously enough: 'Voilà, un petit week-end de chiens écrasés qui vous évitera de lire *France Soir* par-dessus la tête de votre voisin. Vous n'en aviez rien à foutre? C'est pourtant ça *aussi* l'actualité' [There you have a little weekend of minor news items that means you don't have to read *France-Soir* over your neighbour's shoulder. You don't give a toss? But this is *also* the news].[16]

While continuing to write on a range of social and political issues, for example Chirac and the Right in 1981, the 'sans-papiers', and immigration, Vilar's writings on culture became increasingly important in number. His full-page review of *Poésie sonore internationale* by the experimental sound poet Henri Chopin exemplifies the engaged approach to conveying the significance of avant-garde art, situating the work within an understanding of the political nature of language, knowledge, and power structures, and offering a detailed exposition of its content, and its relation with Futurism and Dadaism, presented as freeing words and meaning from the terrorism of written language. Exploring the difference between contestation and subversion, and the use of tape recorders in creatively distorting the human voice and other sounds in multiple ways, it concludes that this book is 'non pas un instrument d'esthète, mais un apport à la vie quotidienne en ce qu'elle se veut un peu libre' [not the instrument of an esthete, but a contribution to living daily life with some freedom].[17] With Mension he interviewed world musicians who would be involved in the Fête de Rouge in March 1981, including Henri Guédon, Pierre Ackendengué, and Sugar Blue. His reviews of works by writers such as Alfred Döblin, Günther Grass, Boris Vian, William Burroughs, Alain Robbe-Grillet, or exhibitions of artists and photographers — Edward Kienholz, Diane Arbus, Arthur Tress, Duane Michals among many others — underlined their attention to the themes of crisis and anxiety, of a world beginning to crack apart, as well as their ability to bring a critical view on social pieties and conventions of all kinds. Vilar's review of a Monory exhibition in 1980 stressed the political urgency of art that connects the violence and sense of catastrophe which inform the everyday. It is:

> Une chronique de l'époque. Chronique dure, qui s'immerge dans nos images les plus familières, les plus quotidiennes. Celles de la télé, des journaux. Images sur lesquelles se détachent nos vies, nos silhouettes, nos visages. [...] Brouillage intense où tout se superpose, mais où tout reste, imprimé dans la rétine: accoutumance à l'hyperviolence du monde et de ce monde-là, en crise. La nôtre.[18]

> [A chronicle of our times. A harsh chronicle that sinks into our most familiar, most frequent images of daily life. Those of the TV, of the newspapers. Images against which our lives, our silhouettes, our faces stand out. [...] An intense scrambled mixture where everything piles up, but where everything remains, imprinted on our retinas: it is a habituation to the hyperviolence of the world and to that particular world, in crisis. Our own.]

Two elements merit particular comment in the light of the importance of history and memory, and of the experience of the Holocaust, in Vilar's novels. Firstly, the extent to which the political past is part of the living political present in their pages, and to which events that were barely mentioned in mainstream French culture are vividly recalled. The Commune, for example, is commemorated frequently, as are the key dates and actions of Trotsky's life. In 1978, *Rouge* published an interview with Jean van Heijenoort, who worked for a time as Trotsky's secretary, illustrated by a photograph of Trotsky in Royan in a group which also included van Heijenoort and Rudolf Klement, both of whom feature in his novel *Nous cheminons entourés de fantômes aux fronts troués*.[19] Retrieving the events of the Algerian war and the German Occupation would be dominant features of French social and cultural history in the 1980s, but in the pages of *Rouge* the Algerian War is part of a living memory, as are the police killings of Algerians in Paris in October 1961 and the deaths at the Charonne metro station the following February, the latter caused by a police charge at the end of a massive demonstration against the underground, extreme right-wing, paramilitary Organisation armée secrète (OAS). Demonstrators rushed down the steps to the metro to escape the charge, only to find the metal gates closed. Nine died, and Daeninckx, Fajardie, and Thierry Jonquet have all recalled the impact of the events on them as children, as they attended the demonstration or the huge funeral for those killed. It has been generally acknowledged that the Charonne deaths overlaid and displaced the events of 17 October 1961 for the left in

France, but this was not true of the Ligue.[20] In March 1972, a scathing article on the response to the kidnapping and release of the Renault executive Robert Nogrette began a long list of police and state killings by referring first to the killings of 17 October 1961, and secondly to the deaths of 8 February 1962:

> La police ratonne, des Algériens sont jetés dans la Seine, la gangrène algéroise gagne les flics français. La France n'en reste pas moins un pays civilisé. Neuf manifestants contre la guerre d'Algérie sont proprement assassinés au métro Charonne. La France n'en reste pas moins un pays civilisé.[21]

> [The police go on the attack against Algerians, Algerians are thrown into the Seine, the gangrene of Algiers has reached the French cops. France is nonetheless a civilised country. Nine demonstrators against the Algerian war are assassinated at the Charonne metro station. France is nonetheless a civilised country.]

In July 1972, a group of articles on Algeria, including by Edwy Plenel (writing under the name of 'Joseph Krasny'), carried two of the Elie Kagan photographs of the 17 October killings, the second captioned: '17 oct 1961 rue des Paquerettes à Nanterre, un Algérien sauvagement assassiné par la police' [17 Oct 1961 rue de Paquerettes in Nanterre, an Algerian savagely murdered by the police], as well as a photograph of a demonstration 'against French colonial policy' of 18 November 1961. Plenel makes the point, mentioning specifically Alain Krivine, that 'the generation of revolutionary activists that produced many of the extreme-left in France was born as a result of the impact of the Algerian war. [...] This is not the least of the victories of the martyrs of the Algerian people'.[22] This was the history of those working at *Rouge*, the 'anti-colonial generation', and whose importance in May 68 was flagged up very early.[23] The philosopher and Trotskyist militant Daniel Bensaïd recorded that the events of 17 October passed him by, but Charonne was a huge shock and spurred him into political action. He was fourteen years old.[24] Mension was responsible for the well-known slogan painted by the River Seine: 'Here Algerians are being drowned'; Elie Kagan, who took the only photographs on 17 October of the bodies of Algerians, of demonstrators with bloody faces, of demonstrators being rounded up in the metro, published news photos in *Rouge* throughout the 1970s.[25] These events were part of their political identities.

Maurice Papon became notorious in the 1980s for his involvement, as Préfet de Police in Paris, in the events of 17 October 1961 and February 1962, and, as a Vichy official, in deportations of Jews from France. In May 1981, *Le Canard enchaîné* carried a major article detailing Papon's responsibilities in both these atrocious events.[26] *Rouge* also reminded readers of his 'dirty hands', particularly for Charonne, but also for the Algerian deaths in 1961, on his appointment as Budget minister in 1978, describing him as 'Papon des assassinés de Charonne, des cadavres algériens retrouvés dans la Seine [...]. Un homme de la continuité. Une insulte vivante' [Papon of those assassinated at Charonne, of the Algerian corpses retrieved from the Seine [...]. The continuity man. A living insult].[27] In his review of *Les Porteurs de valises* (1979), the ground-breaking study of the networks distributing cash to the Algerian militants in France, Vilar highlighted the role of Papon, still a government minister, in a detailed account of 17 October.[28] Both Vilar and Bensaïd endorsed Walter Benjamin's view of the past as animated by the concerns of the present, often quoting the injunction to: 'historiciser le présent pour actualiser le passé' [historicise the present in order to update the past].[29] Vilar's review of the play *Vichy Fictions*, which intertwines past and present to inform today's political stances, is a case in point. This is the message throughout the 1970s, these battles are our battles:

> 1980: Pour comprendre l'actualité brûlante de Vichy Fictions, et le peu d'innocence dont nous pouvons nous prévaloir, un exemple, un seul. En ces jours où le racisme est vilipendé dans les colonnes de la presse Hersant — qui a le passé qu'on sait — un anniversaire est passé presque inaperçu (à l'exception du journal *Libération* le 19 octobre 1980); plusieurs dizaines d'Algériens qui manifestaient pacifiquement pour protester contre une loi raciste de couvre-feu étaient massacrés en plein Paris. On n'était pas sous Vichy, mais sous la Ve République. Les responsables de cette tuerie sont encore en poste. Les partis et syndicats ouvriers n'ont pas lancé le moindre mouvement de grève. L'oubli, comme la mémoire, sont des enjeux politiques. Vichy Fictions, spectacle parfait, ne montre pas autre chose; il faut être aveugle pour ne pas voir à que point le passé taraude notre présent.[30]

> [1980: to understand the burning importance of Vichy Fictions today, and how little we can pride ourselves on our own innocence, I have one example. In these days when racism is vilified in the columns of the Hersant press — whose past we all know about — an anniversary has passed almost unnoticed (except for the newspaper *Libération* of 19 October 1980): dozens of Algerians who were demonstrating peacefully to protest again a racist curfew law were massacred in the centre of Paris. We were not under Vichy, but under the Fifth Republic. Those responsible for this mass killing are still in post. The working-class parties and unions did not call a single strike. Forgetting, like remembering, is political. This is precisely what Vichy Fictions, a brilliant spectacle, is showing us; you have to be blind not to see how far the past torments our present.]

Another striking feature shared by the intellectuals in the Ligue was that a large number of them were Jewish. The knowledge of the deportations during the Occupation, and of the round-up of the Vélodrome d'hiver, was part of family history for many of them, which may explain the regular references to it from the early 1970s. The issue of 19 February 1972, for example, quoted at length from a virulently anti-semitic book, *La Condition publique et privée du juif en France* published in 1942 and co-authored by Joannès Ambre, not as a history lesson but as a lesson in continuity, since Ambre was prominent in Lyon politics at the time.[31] In *C'est toujours les autres qui meurent*, Villon asks Victor whether he is Jewish: 'Non. Mais... il y a une empreinte très forte de tout ça qui a pesé sur les organisations révolutionnaires. C'est connu' [No, but... there's a strong imprint of all that and it has left its mark on the revolutionary organisations. It's well known], going on to reflect that 'il m'appartient, et à moi seul, de savoir comment les Blumfeld sont devenus Blainville, au milieu des années 40' [it is for me, and for me alone, to know how the Blumfelds became the Blainvilles, in the middle of the 1940s] (*CTA*, p. 32). Salles considers that this personal experience of the activists underpins the very strong stand on anti-racism as well as anti-semitism in the Ligue.[32] Like Alain Krivine,

Mension was born into an eastern European Jewish family, whose communist father would have major responsibilities in the Resistance: 'the Jewish question was quickly settled in my family: all those who accepted wearing the yellow star died in deportation, the others joined the Resistance and survived'.[33] A Resister cousin died in Buchenwald; three of his aunts were deported and killed; Maitron records him losing nineteen family members in the camps.[34] The grandparents of Michel Recanati were deported and died in the camps.[35] Daniel Bensaïd's family included Communards on his mother's side, and political activists too on his Jewish father's side. He records the deportation and deaths of his father's two brothers. His father was arrested but remained in Drancy for the duration of the Occupation (Bensaïd credits his formidable mother for this).[36]

The Holocaust becomes increasingly important in Vilar's novels and he also wrote lengthy reviews related to it, including one of *Vichy et les juifs* by Michael Marrus and Robert Paxton (1981), prominently highlighting Papon's role, and a severe critique of *L'Idéologie française* (1981) by Bernard-Henri Lévy, whom he describes as a 'bricoleur d'idées et jongleur mondain' [a society entertainer who cobbles together ideas].[37] Vilar's article 'Nouveaux juifs' is an acerbic examination of the anti-semitic traps of 'assimilation' in Alfred Fabre-Luce's book *Pour en finir avec l'antisémitisme* (1979) which asserts that Jews cause anti-semitism: give up being Jewish, and the Jewish problem will go away.[38]

Plenel argues that the internationalism of the Ligue saved it from the narrow sectarianism of other *gauchiste* organisations, and it is certain that its commitment to independence and anti-colonial struggles was a central one in virtually every issue of *Rouge*. He underlines the vicarious identification with the historic heroes of Trotksyism for those involved in the international or security sides of the Ligue's work, both of which integrated illegal, forbidden activities. In *C'est toujours les autres qui meurent*, Vilar ironises the belief in the imminent revolutionary overthrow of world order, which Plenel sees as inevitably part of the Trotskyist heritage, but the tragic lucidity of that heritage is more than pertinent for these novels that pay increasing attention to those crushed by history. Remembering the suicides of Trotsky's daughter Zina in 1934 and of his supporter Adolph Joffé in 1927, Plenel presents them as moments when the heroic story of Trotskyism entered into collective tragedy, between the gulags and the Shoah:

> For our political education was based not on victory but on defeat. Our heroes had died defeated, and, far from lamenting the fact, we thought their sacrifice was valuable for its promise. What we took from tragedy was not a morbid inclination for it, but what it meant: clarity of vision (la lucidité)'.[39]

Tango, 1983–85

Tango was a cultural magazine created by Jean-Louis Ducournau, published by the Association Les Passagers de la nuit.[40] There were four issues, and it quickly took on a cult status. With a huge variety of articles, short stories, drawings, illustrations, and photographs, and page layouts that never repeated themselves once from the first page to the last across all four issues, it was an artistic and thematic triumph:

> *Tango* est une revue que chacun de nous aurait aimé faire. *Tango* est le havre des gens aimables, des amoureux de la littérature, des sports et des danses chaloupées, la preuve? Dans *Tango*, on retrouve Doisneau, Ricardo Mosner, Cortázar, Jean-François Vilar... *Tango*, c'est l'aventure d'un dingue de Paris, des 'sub-cultures' comme disent les gens sans âme. *Tango*, c'est un petit air d'accordéon, un parfum de Malabar, une couleur de Série Noire, un fumet de café-calva, un froissement de rayonne et de satin, au Balajo.[41]
>
> [*Tango* is a magazine that any of us would have liked to create. *Tango* is the refuge for friendly folk, lovers of literature, of sport and of swaying dances. The proof? In *Tango*, you will find Doisneau, Ricardo , Mosner, Cortázar, and Jean-François Vilar... *Tango* is the adventure of someone who's crazy about Paris, about 'sub-cultures' as the soulless call them. *Tango* is a little tune on an accordion, a perfume from Malabar, a colour of the Série noire, an aroma of coffee and calvados, a rustle of rayon and satin, in the Balajo.]

Tango had a creative exuberance that celebrated music, Paris, Latin American culture, and French working-class and popular culture: the *bal-tango*, the Tour de France, Johnny Hallyday, Gene Vincent, Tom Waits, *roman noir*, Latin American tango songs and music, Carlos Gradel, Luis Borges, Julio Cortázar, with a cornucopia of cartoons, illustrations, drawings, and black-and-white photographs (for example Doisneau's studies of a couple dancing the tango in the second issue, or of Léo Malet in the fourth). Poetry, fiction, photography, and art combine with music and sport to celebrate a sense of creative adventure and travel, quite literally so in the final section of each issue devoted to port towns. Claude Dubois argued that the Right Bank's working-class culture of singers, writers, and *bals-musette* was being restored to its rightful position after years of intellectual and cultural dominance by Saint-Germain des Prés: 'Des noms, des lieux d'une importance extrême pour le populo parisien, mais le populo parisien qui s'en soucie? des noms, des lieux qui n'apparaissent dans aucune littérature, et pour cause! Les Camus, les Sartre étaient tous à Saint-Germain' [Names and places that are extremely important for the people of Paris, but who cares about the people of Paris? Names and places that don't figure in any literature, which is logical. The Camus and the Sartres were all in Saint-Germain].[42]

The third issue, *Les Fous du vélo*, opened with articles on and by Julio Cortázar, including beautiful photographs of Rita Renoir, the actor and former performer in the Crazy Horse nude shows, performing her one-woman show, 'Pour Julio mon corps sans hasard', together with the Cortázar text that had inspired the show.[43] It closed on a series of articles and inserts celebrating the Tour de France; it even included a free board game, *Le Jeu de la Tour de France*. Vilar's short story in this issue, appropriately called 'Tandem', entwines Cortázar's famous novel *Hopscotch* and the news of his recent death in its story and is illustrated by Vilar, including a full-page drawing of two figures in front of the bridge over the canal de l'Ourcq, a naked woman on a bicycle looking impassively out of the picture, and a rather morose self-portrait of the author holding a cat.

The fourth issue, where Vilar is acknowledged in the list of photographers and in the list of those who worked on its conception and production, is presented as 'Chronicles of nights of Paris, a great film, in black-and-white' (no colour at all in this issue), with sections on Alexandre Trauner, the legendary producer responsible for *L'Hotel du nord* (interviewed by Vilar and Ducournau), on Johnny Hallyday and Vince Taylor, on boxing, on inhabiting the night of Paris, on the tango, and on Léo Malet's 'Le Dernier Piéton de Paris'. 'La ville, la nuit, l'amour, la mort', the title of an interview with the actor Richard Borhinger, is a neat summary of their thematic agenda. In the final words of this final issue, Ducournau offers a condensed poetics of *Tango*, with its maelstrom of strong emotions, powerful music, and passionately erotic dances of love and death, in the lonely night-time cabarets:

> TANGO lève l'ancre. [...] — tango buissonnier sur les routes de France, tango des Portes de la Nuit, des bars tristes et des assassins, des terrains vagues et des quais sous la lune... [...]
> Les lumières de la ville se sont éteintes.
> TANGO, une caresse nocturne qui se retire...[44]

> [TANGO is raising the anchor. [...] A truant tango on the roads of France, a tango of the Gates of the Night, of the sad bars and of the assassins, of the wastelands and river banks beneath the moon... [...]
> The lights of the city have gone out.
> TANGO, a nocturnal caress that is drawing away...]

Vilar's contributions are both visual and textual: a short presentation of the portfolio *Tango y Milonga* by the Argentinian artist Munoz and the writer Sampayo with two striking plates from the book; a very detailed art work, 'Repérages pour un Paris des surréalistes et de quelques autres flâneurs': a collage of maps, photographs, and notes of the events, people, and places of surrealist Paris over several pages; 'Bastille-Opéra': three photographs of the demolition of the Paramount cinema that would be replaced by the new opera house, with hand-written and typed notes and very unsettling fragments of film negatives, dramatic images seemingly of extreme pain rendered more intense by the reversal of black and white on the grimacing face — all material that will be drawn on in *Bastille-Tango*. A letter to Malet's detective from Vilar's photographer Victor Blainville, 'Cher Nestor Burma', sets out their common agenda as detectives of the night in Paris. He also interviews Malet with Ducournau.[45]

Léo Malet was an iconic figure in the history of the *roman noir* and the literature of Paris. His post-war series of fifteen crime novels, whose umbrella title of *Nouveaux mystères de Paris* evoked Eugène Sue, has been described as a *jeu de l'oie*, since he set each one in a separate *arrondissement*.[46] His involvement in the surrealist movement in the 1930s is echoed in the photographs illustrating the interview, of Malet at a desk in a room overflowing with books and objects, with rather statuesque naked young women standing nearby. In his introduction to his maps of surrealist Paris, flanked on the facing page by a Doisneau photograph of a young woman with twin brightly illuminated little Arc de Triomphes mirrored in her dark glasses, Vilar quotes André Breton: 'La grande inconnue est la pensée de Paris actuel. Paris, ses rues, ses places, aux derniers documents produits, sont une énigme' [The great unknown is the thought of Paris now. Paris, its streets, its squares, to the most recent documents produced, are an enigma].[47] Thus setting one theme for the trajectory through the maps, tracing puzzling affinities, from the passage de la Fidélité to the passage du Désir, from the rue Niepce to the rue Daguerre, each a springboard resetting the *jeu de l'oie*.[48]

Bastille-Tango is the novel that is the closest, thematically and textually, to the *Tango* project; the iconography of night, *le noir* and black-and-white photography irradiates through Paris, its people in cabarets, on streets, and the writers, artists, and photographers who have worked within that literary and visual sensibility. But there are echoes of it in all Vilar's works.

La Littérature délinquante

'Je n'ai jamais aimé la littérature policière, ce qui m'intéresse, c'est la littérature délinquante' [I've never liked detective literature, what interests me is delinquent literature].[49] 'Delinquent literature' is an appropriate term for a genre that already has multiple designations. Vilar lists several in 'Noir c'est noir': 'Les étiquettes varient. On parle de roman *policier* ou *criminel* ou *à énigme*, de *polar*, de *thriller*, de *roman noir*' [There are various labels. One talks of the *detective* novel, or *crime* novel, or *mystery* novel, or *polar*, *thriller*, or *roman noir*].[50] His first novel came out just after what has been called the 'explosion of 1979',[51] the proliferation of crime fiction novels coming in the wake of the work of Jean-Patrick Manchette — 'notre père à tous' [father to us all] — who brought contemporary politics into *le polar*, the kidnapping of the Moroccan politician Ben Barka (*L'Affaire N'gustro*, 1971) and left-wing terrorism (*Nada*, 1973).[52] That many authors of political crime fiction emerged from active participation in left and extreme left politics has long been noted;[53] and the whole phenomenon of the renewal of crime fiction in the post-68 decades and its importance as a genre in post-war French cultural history has received extensive critical attention that has highlighted its role in working through complex questions of national identity, has tackled some of the major historical issues still reverberating through French society, such as the German Occupation and the Holocaust, and has given new imaginative and critical energy to the whole notion of committed literature.[54]

There is, then, a recognised genealogy of crime fiction since the racier *polar* tended to supplant the *roman policier*, with a formal detective investigating the individual aberration of the crime and restoring law and order with his successful resolution of the enigma.[55] Schweighaeuser also stresses the importance of literary originality as one of the components of this renewal. Across its multiple forms it is a genre that has traditionally deployed linguistic virtuosity and cultural reference, as any fan of Frédéric Dard's *San Antonio* series will know. Manchette's *Nada* references Roger Vailland's story of a resistance group in *Drôle de jeu*, with a copy of his *Ecrits intimes* on the farmhouse table to point the reader in the right direction:

> La qualité commune des adeptes du néo-polar est le refus de croire que le genre est un moule dans lequel il serait suffisant de placer un certain nombre

d'ingrédients. Chaque œuvre nouvelle doit être une remise en question et de l'écriture et de l'auteur lui-même.[56]

[Common to the practitioners of the *néo-polar* is the refusal to believe that the genre is a mould into which it is enough to pour the basic ingredients. Each new work must be a questioning both of writing and of the author.]

Although the styles went from the hard-hitting and the hard-boiled to the fantastic, and although there were many common features around the city, transgression, and an understanding of socio-political criminality that would often focus on the state, literary quality and stylistic virtuosity counted too. As Demure points out, the writing of this inherently irreverent genre often espouses extreme rage and derision, given that it has left the cosy world of the innocent and the guilty, where the latter are always found out and punished.[57] Vilar agreed: 'Le roman noir est une littérature du temps de crise. C'est ce qui fait la modernité de ses récits crépusculaires et c'est en cela qu'il participe d'un désordre qui ne se résorbe pas au dernier chapitre' [The *roman noir* is a literature of crisis. That is what makes the modernity of its gloomy tales and that is why it partakes of a disorder that is not cleared up in the last chapter].[58] He cites Breton, Kafka, and Poe, as well as Dashiell Hammett, who, biographically and narratively, embodies the cruel contradictions and ethical dead ends of the age. Vilar recalls Hammett's closeness to the American Communist Party:

'Raconteur d'histoires, Dash se veut aussi sujet historique. [...] Hammett, briseur de grève et stalinien: une figure de crapule? Non. Une figure tragique, disloquée et, d'un certain point de vue *morale* en ce siècle sans morale *possible*. [...] Les romans de Hammett [...] manifestent cette crise radicale dont nous sommes loin d'être sortis. Ils en fouillent les recoins, exhibent les lambeaux sanglants de nos pauvres rêves.[59]

[Dash is a storyteller who saw himself as an historical subject. [...] Is Hammett, strike breaker and Stalinist, a despicable figure? No. A tragic figure, dislocated, and, from a certain point of view, *moral* in this century without any *possible* morality. [...] His novels [...] reveal the radical crisis that still enfolds us. They search through its darkest corners, they brandish the bloody rags of our poor dreams.]

Vilar places his own work in this lineage in 'Noir c'est noir', making it clear that he finds the political contradictions more interesting than locked room puzzles; the term he finds most satisfying is *roman noir* in its original sense of 'gothic novel': 'Le roman noir n'évoque pas seulement le crime. Il renvoie à un mystère, à une opacité sociale plus lourde, plus oppressante, qui implique la violence' [The *roman noir* evokes more than crime. It refers to a mystery, to a heavier, more oppressive social opaqueness, which implies violence].[60] And this emphasis on the cultural lineage of the *roman noir* in post-war France brings a different set of works into focus, as well as the text-image relation that is so central to Vilar's novels. The gothic novel combines a particular topography of ruins, of dark labyrinthine spaces, mysterious castles, convents, horrible crimes, and ghastly cruelty with the sensibility of mystery and horror. Lee Horsley presents in some detail the lasting impact of the gothic on crime fiction, in its exploration of the transgressive, the irrational, the bodily horror, particularly in the contemporary creation of the serial killer, for example.[61] The topography of labyrinth, dungeon, and cellar, of horror and criminality, is reconfigured in the nineteenth century, in the works of Edgar Allen Poe (translated by Baudelaire), Eugène Sue, and Victor Hugo. In the sense of representing that which is beyond the calm ordered surface of the everyday, *le noir* was celebrated by the surrealists, disorder and irrationality offering access to the surreal. As in Breton's *Anthologie de l'humour noir*, this is the sense that prevailed and underlay the forging of the term *film noir* for the murderous, violent, American gangster films of the 1940s that had such success in France when they were screened after the war. As the *bon mot* goes, the Americans made it, and then the French invented it.[62] The visual continuity between the black-and-white French films of the 1930s and 1940s, the poetic realism of Prévert and Carné, the crime films of Henri Clouzot or Jacques Becker's *Goupi mains rouges* (1943), with their dramatically lit faces and scenes, means they connected very directly with the established meaning of *noir* and overdetermined the choice of *film noir* for the Hollywood B movies.[63] In his preface to the famous *Panorama du film noir américain*, Marcel Duhamel, who worked on films with the Prévert brothers in the 1930s and later founded the Série noire crime fiction imprint for Gallimard, quietly contradicted the authors' view that a new kind of American film reached France in 1946. *Film noir* went back to the origins of cinema, he argued, pointing to silent French films of the first decade of the century such as Louis Feuillade's *Les Vampires*, American gangster films of the 1920s and 1930s, and German expressionist films of the 1930s.[64] The connections between American films and the expressionist aesthetic of the 1930s that directors like Fritz Lang took to Hollywood as they escaped from Nazi Germany are also well known (the stills illustrating the *Panorama du film noir américain* include American films by Lang and fellow German exile Robert Siodmark). For a generation too young to have seen these American films in the 1940s themselves, the Nouvelle Vague brought it to them, as Godard, Truffaut, and Chabrol celebrated the American *film noir* and brought it to life in their films — Belmondo's Bogart imitation and the homage to *The Harder They Fall* in *A bout de souffle*, Truffaut's filming of David Goodis's *Tirez sur le pianiste*, Chabrol's celebration of Hitchcock and crime, closing the loop with his film of Manchette's *Nada*. More than once Vilar's novels salute the memory of Michel Poiccard (of *A bout de souffle*), who died in the rue Campagne-Première.

There is a constellation of works and references, then, that the contemporary *roman noir* brings into focus, for they are part of the culture of the young crime writers of the 1970s and 1980s. Vilar's novels and other collective works he contributed to demonstrate the symbiotic relationship between *film noir* and *roman noir*. The cinematic style of writing of the *néo-polar* is often commented on; what is more important here is that both *film noir* and *roman noir* prove to be excellent forms through which to channel contemporary socio-political criticism. For the group who collectively produced *Tango*, and more broadly for the whole contestatory counter-culture from the 1960s onwards, *le noir* was as much visual as it was textual.

The *Apostrophes* edition of July 1979 would suggest this was true more generally. This particular programme was devoted to 'Le Polar', with Jean-Patrick Manchette, A.D.G., Serge Montigny, and Catherine Arley joined by Pierre Boileau, Thomas Narcejac, and Léo Malet of the previous generation. But the credits show, not the usual series of covers of the authors' works, but a parade of stills of famous *noir* films, including Peter Lorre and Humphrey Bogart in *The Maltese Falcon*, Gene Tierney in *Laura*, and Bogart and Lauren Bacall in *Key Largo*.[65] The filmic and the fictional are part of the same imaginary, as is evident too in some of the collective publications to which Vilar contributed. *Agenda Polar 1986* was a diary: ten crime writers wrote a short chapter each spread over a sequence of days.[66] As well as the story, the diary is an Aladdin's cave of many dozens of images of *film noir* from the 1930s to the 1980s. *La Ville est un roman* is another collective publication, edited by Hervé Delouche for an exhibition celebrating the 150th anniversary of the publication of Poe's 'Murders in the rue Morgue'.[67] *La Ville est un roman* consists of three documents in a folder. The first is *La Cité*, a newspaper dated 9 December 1841 that includes the full story as if it were a news report. The second is *Le Chroniqueur du cent-cinquantenaire* [The Chronicler of the 150th Anniversary], a newspaper highlighting a key event for each of the fifteen decades, using Perec's novel *La Vie mode d'emploi* as a model, with its multiple stories for each flat in a large building, for example: 1861 Karl Marx on crime, 1891 the police killing of workers on a 1 May demonstration for an eight-hour working day, 1931 the Dusseldorf Vampire who killed little girls and inspired Fritz Lang's film *M*, 1941 Drancy, 1951 Hammett and McCarthyism, 1961 the Paris killings.[68] These are accompanied by reports of events, lists of dates, and images, from *roman noir* publications and *film noir* pictures (such as Clyde Barrow and Bonnie Parker) to the wars, crimes, scandals, killings, and murders, historical and fictional, that are their primary material. The third newspaper-type document, *Métropolis*, contains sixteen short stories by crime writers, each set in a different city. Vilar's 'Le Réveil du Golem' is a story of Prague. All the documents are visually rich with black-and-white photographs and striking drawings by well-known cartoonists and graphic novel artists: Guido Crepax, Dragan, Siné, and Tardi. It is a comprehensive celebration, historical and contemporary, of the complex network of images, spaces, and stories that constitute the *noir* city.

Vilar's cities include the subterranean passages, the shadows and shades of the gothic crossed with the strange, artificial, and perverse iconography of surrealism. Mannequins, so prized by the surrealists as being on the uncanny borderline of living and dead, damaged and murdered, appear in novel after novel. Characters roam in dark underground passages and subterranean canals, where violence, present and past, lurks (for example, the bones of those who died in the 1830 and 1848 Revolutions lie under the column of the Génie of the Bastille). In addition to this cultural lineage of gothic and surrealist scenography of horror, the imbrication of visual and textual *noir* in the culture of 1960s and 1970s France means that *film noir* is as much reactivated by French culture of the 1960s as it is looking back to the foundational moment of the post-war 1940s.

La Figuration narrative

If *roman noir* and *film noir* are mutually present in the cultural imaginary of the *noir*, the latter is also a major strand in the art and culture of contestation that is integral to the plot of Vilar's first two novels, and an important context given his direct engagement with the work of Jacques Monory, who also wrote *romans noirs*.[69] Monory's work was a significant thread in this rich dissection and critique of the society of the image, of representation and politics in the works of artists associated with the *figuration narrative* and *nouveau réalisme* movements, contemporary with the *nouveau roman* and the *nouvelle vague* from the late 1950s, and massively engaged in the Atelier des Beaux-Arts in 1968 and beyond.[70] 'La Peinture est un roman noir' is the title of a section which grouped paintings by Monory, Peter Klasen, Valerio Adami, Peter Stämpfli, and Antonio Recalcati in the large 2008 retrospective held at the Grand Palais in Paris.[71]

The *figuration narrative* group was brought together by Gérald Gassiot-Talabot for what has been seen as an inaugural exhibition in 1964, *Mythologies quotidiennes*, held at the Musée d'Art moderne de la Ville de Paris. This period was an extremely productive one for French artists as they responded to the work of the abstract expressionists and Pop Art, accompanied by manifestos, wide-ranging debates, and theorisations in important catalogues and periodicals such as *Art Vivant* and *Opus international*. *Figuration narrative* was defined firstly against Pop Art, which Gassiot-Talabot argued did not engage with a political critique of the images of contemporary society, advertising, and the media that it took as its subject, but rather celebrated them. In 1964, he wrote that Warhol and other Pop artists were focused on the 'brute fact of the object, without plastic interpretation, without subjective emotions, usually mechanically reproduced'.[72] Secondly the *figuration narrative* stances were defined against the *nouveau réalisme* group. Associated with the art critic Pierre Restany, it included Niki de St Phalle, Martial Raysse, Yves Klein, and the *affichistes* François Dufrêne, Raymond Hains and Jacques Villeglé (who worked with torn posters from the streets). With the work of Arman and Daniel Spoerri in particular, they were also exploring the object, image, and representation in a social context, and the artists in both groups were dismantling the art historical tenets of representational realism, using photographs, commercial images, adverts, graphic novels, and cartoons. The films of Jean-Luc Godard are close to the work of these very diverse creative artists, where the cultural codes of representation in an image-saturated society, the social clichés and received ideas of everyday life, are as much the focus of acerbic visual wit and processes of dismantling as are the politics of the Fifth Republic, consumer society, and the Vietnam War. Godard commented that the subject of his early films was cinema, nothing but cinema,[73] but the practice of contestation was generally freighted with a strong political content, and the differences were marked and real, as one can see in Jean-Louis Pradel's argument in the catalogue for *Mythologies Quotidiennes 2*, that the *nouveaux réalistes* made a fetish of the object, whereas the *figuration narrative* group preferred the critical techniques of estrangement ('distanciation') to techniques of appropriation.[74] The engagement with the political was unmistakable, in the images of the Vietnam War invading domestic interiors in Erró, Bernard Rancillac's interrogations of racism, Hervé Télémaque's work on colonialism and power in the Caribbean, and the disquieting red silhouettes on the streets of Paris in Gérard Fromanger's series 'Boulevard des Italiens'. The very title of their first exhibition, *Mythologies quotidiennes*, with its deliberate references to Roland Barthes's critique of the ideological discourses of contemporary culture in *Mythologies*, points to the theoretical engagement of this group of artists with contemporary society and with the artefacts and practices of everyday life in all its guises. The explosion in importance of material objects to the consumer economy and the complex connotations of possessing and branding are highlighted in literature and film. Michael Sheringham traces the complicated debates around the everyday in the cultural analyses of Lefebvre, Blanchot, Barthes, and others, including Perec and Godard; these were debates that were also raging in relation to art.[75] In the *Mythologies quotidiennes* exhibition, everyday objects were placed in exhibition cases, to make the point about the invasion of images in everyday life.[76] The everyday ranges, then, from 'the scrapings from dustbins or from Prisunic', to use Dominique Noguez's phrase,[77] to received ideas in the case of Jacques Monory, as Sarah Wilson points out: 'The "everyday", not as in Henri Lefebvre's Marxist material world but as an imaginary repertory of clichés', alongside an interrogation of image, representation and painting — it is no accident that these are the years of the rediscovery of Marcel Duchamp.[78]

'Roman de crise donc roman critique'[79]

The political noir of the 1970s onwards has certainly incorporated the lessons of Hammett and Chandler in relation to the representation of the city and the wider social and political contexts of criminality, but often without either detective or private investigator, and widening even further the definition of guilt to encompass state crimes, class crimes, and the unearthing of historical crimes. Vilar's model is not crime and investigation, and its ramifications, it is the puzzle, the jigsaw, the maze, the labyrinth; his characters are not the marginalised of the urban wastelands: his misfits are intellectual misfits, social misfits in Victor's case because of intellectual and political allegiance to extreme left militancy, negotiating the cultural milieu of film-making, television, and journalism. The crimes are crimes of political violence, state violence, colonial violence, in the service of oppressive regimes, in the service of the imposition of order which is the order of the state and the bourgeoisie, although full attention is paid to the negotiation of the political choices of the past, between the gulags and the Holocaust. And to the betrayals and compromises and devious accommodations that accumulate once there is no *possible* morality:

> Se prétendre 'innocent' au XXe siècle, c'est être un peu demeuré, voire crétin, ou alors carrément salaud. Le siècle des guerres et des révolutions, donc des utopies à portée de main, est forcément celui des trahisons et des procès. On est toujours coupable vis-à-vis d'une utopie frôlée, simplement entrevue, latente. Le roman noir, en ce qu'il a de meilleur, enquête sur une crise sans solution apparente, rabote quelques illusions sans espérer une issue proche. Il fait de nous des passagers de la nuit.[80]

[To claim 'innocence' in the 20th century is to be a bit slow, or frankly stupid, or an out and out bastard. The century of wars and revolutions, therefore of utopias just within reach, is necessarily a century of betrayals and trials. One is always guilty in relation to any utopia that has been almost touched, simply glimpsed, or latent. The *roman noir*, at its best, investigates a crisis that has no obvious solution, scrapes the surface off a few illusions without counting on finding a way out any time soon. It turns us into passengers of the night.]

Sheringham wrote of Georges Perec that he once surprised an audience by:

> Insisting on a ludic, citational and rhetorical approach to writing. Rejecting both Sartrean 'littérature engagée' and the sterility of the 1950s *Nouveau Roman*, Perec positioned himself as a realist writer, but one for whom the relation between language and the world was far from straightforward.[81]

There are many Perecian echoes in Vilar, who also wrote ludic, citational novels within a realist frame, but ones that were certainly politically committed to the Trotskyist politics of class and internationalism, and that also drew on the exuberance of Duchamp and the spirit of *Tango*, or more bitter ironies of *trompe l'œil* and fakery, to question language, meaning, representation, and the possibility of interpretation in fundamental ways. These are explored across the following chapters.[82]

Notes to Chapter 1

1. Edwy Plenel, 'Jean-François Vilar: étoile filante du roman noir', *Mediapart* <https://blogs.mediapart.fr/edwy-plenel/blog/221214/jean-francois-vilar-etoile-filante-du-roman-noir> [accessed 23 December 2014].
2. Chrystine Brouillet, 'J.-F. Vilar de la nuit', *Nuit Blanche*, 26 (1986–87), 56 <http://id.erudit.org/iderudit/20641ac> [accessed 18 May 2020]; Fajardie and others, *Black Exit to 68*, p. 206.
3. Interview with Eric Bentolila, one of twelve interviews carried out in 1990–91 and reprinted in *Temps noir, la revue des littératures policières*, 14 (2011), 41. Different dates are given in other pieces, suggesting he returned from military service in 1972. He refers to nine years of having been a professional militant on leaving *Rouge* in 1981. I have not drawn on his email exchanges with me at all, since he would obviously have wished to authorise what was used, and unfortunately this was not possible.
4. For an overview of the importance of the 'travail armée' for the LCR, see Jean-Paul Salles, *La Ligue communiste révolutionnaire (1968–1981): instrument du Grand Soir ou lieu d'apprentissage?* (Rennes: Presses universitaires de Rennes, 2005), pp. 189–96. See the sections on young people in the manifesto of the Ligue: *Ce que veut la ligue communiste: manifeste du Comité Central du 29 et 30 janvier 1972* (Paris: François Maspero, 1972). *Le Procès de Draguignan*, ed. by Denis Richard and Elisabeth Carrière, illus. by Cabu (Monaco: Le Rocher, 1975), brings together many documents of the trial of three soldiers for subversion. Their liberation was front page news for *Rouge* in January 1975. Two of them, Robert Pelletier and Serge Ravet, later wrote *Le Mouvement de soldats: les comités de soldats et l'antimilitarisme révolutionnaire* (Paris: Petite collection Maspero, 1976).
5. The Ligue communiste was dissolved on government order in 1973, after an attack on a meeting of the extreme right Ordre nouveau. The Ligue communiste révolutionnaire was formed in 1974. In 2009 it dissolved itself, joining with others to found the Nouveau parti anticapitaliste.
6. *Ce que veut la ligue communiste*, p. 13
7. Ibid., p. 73.
8. Ibid., p. 159.

9. [Anon.], 'A propos du FHAR' (*Rouge*, 156 (6 May 1972), 4) complains about the 'lamentables et les grotesques exhibitions du FHAR [...] Défiler en travesti, ce n'est pas lutter contre la morale bourgeoise'[the lamentable and grotesque displays of the FHAR. [...] To parade in drag is not the way to struggle again bourgeois morality] but is playing into the bourgeoisie's hands 'assumant le rôle, l'image, le statut dérisoire qu'elle assigne aux homosexuels' [taking on the role, the image and the derisory status it accords to homosexuals]. The stinging reply ([Anon.], 'Lettre du FHAR', *Rouge*, 159 (27 May 1972), 6) pointed out FHAR did not need their approval and explained their ideological agenda. It was accompanied by a party line statement of equal length complaining of their arrogant flippancy ('désinvolture') and that they took no account of how the working class perceived them.
10. Brochier, *Petits remèdes à la dépression politique*, p. 172; Salles, *La Ligue communiste révolutionnaire (1968–1981)*, p. 282. One article by Vilar on Sade is noted.
11. Salles, *La Ligue communiste révolutionnaire (1968–1981)*, pp. 271–89.
12. Jean-Michel Mension (Alexis Violet), *Le Temps gage: aventures politiques et artistiques d'un irrégulier à Paris* (Paris: Noésis, 2001), pp. 334, 366.
13. Ibid., pp. 366–67.
14. See Vilar's signed articles in *Rouge* in October 1976 and Roland Agret, *Coupable d'innocence* (Paris: Ramsay, 1984). Agret was released in 1977.
15. Jean-François Vilar, 'En attendant l'omelette campagnarde', *Rouge*, 150 (11–12 September 1976), 7 ; 'Entre frites et affiches', *Rouge*, 151 (13 September 1976), 8.
16. Jean-François Vilar, '56 sardines, 30 puces, 50 pieds de vignes et 893 boîtes de foie gras', *Rouge*, 145 (6 September 1976), 9.
17. Jean-François Vilar, 'Poésie sonore internationale', *Rouge*, 890 (4–10 January 1980), 25.
18. Jean-François Vilar, 'Le Catalogue mondial des images incurables de Monory', *Rouge*, 904 (1–6 February 1980), 22.
19. [Anon.], 'De Prinkipo à Cayoacan', interview with Jean van Heijenoort, *Rouge*, 616 (3 April 1978),11–12. Klement (and his subsequent murder) figures in Alfred Katz's diary, and van Heijenoort (whose biography is used for the character of Levine) features in the 1989 narrative.
20. Jim House and Neil MacMaster, *Paris 1961: Algerians, State Terror, and Memory* (Oxford: Oxford University Press, 2006), pp. 17, 185.
21. [Anon.], 'Les Mains sales', *Rouge*, 149 (18 March 1972), 5. *Ratonner* is a racist term for attacks on Algerians. The use of *la gangrène* often refers to police torture of Algerians in Paris during the war (after a book with this title), but here is clearly referring to torture in Algiers.
22. Joseph Krasny [Edwy Plenel], 'Algérie', *Rouge*, 166 (15 July 1972), 7. The importance of the internationalist politics of the Ligue is strongly stressed in Hélène Adam and François Coustal, *C'était la Ligue* (Tarbes & Paris: Arcane 17 & Syllepse, 2019).
23. Edwy Plenel, *Secrets de jeunesse* (Paris: Stock, 2001), p. 165; Margaret Atack, *May 68 in French Fiction and Film: Rethinking Society, Rethinking Representation* (Oxford: Oxford University Press, 1999), p. 112.
24. Daniel Bensaïd, *Une lente impatience* (Paris : Stock, 2004), p. 48.
25. Mension, *Le Temps gage*, pp. 208–09. See House and MacMaster, *Paris 1961*, p. 232.
26. Nicolas Brimo, 'Papon: aide de camps', *Le Canard enchaîné*, 6 May 1981, p. 4.
27. Jean-François Vilar, 'Papon-Charonne', *Rouge*, 616 (6 April 1978), 3.
28. Jean-François Vilar, 'Les Porteurs de valise' [review], *Rouge*, 893 (16 November 1979), 16.
29. Violet, 'Série rouge'.
30. Jean-François Vilar, 'Vichy Fictions' [review], *Rouge*, 941 (24–30 October 1980), 21–22.
31. Fernand Lœilleton, 'La Mémoire courte ou les dents longues?', *Rouge*, 145 (19 February 1972), 16. The book gave a comprehensive list of all the statutes concerning Jews passed in France; the article quotes from its conclusion, hoping that once the French nation is no longer mortgaged to Jews, it will be able to find a French solution to its current tragic situation. The conclusion and annex to the book have been uploaded to <https://germanpropaganda.org/la-condition-publique-et-privee-du-juif-en-france/> [accessed 13 April 2020].
32. Salles, *La Ligue communiste révolutionnaire (1968–1981)*, pp. 308–09; and see Yaïr Auron, *Les Juifs d'extrême gauche en mai 68* (Paris: Albin Michel, 1998).
33. Mension, *Le Temps gage*, p. 22.

34. The famous Maitron biography is available online at <Maitron.fr> [accessed 18 May 2020].
35. <Maitron.fr>. Recanati was active in 68 and the Ligue communiste. He committed suicide in 1973 and is commemorated in the film *Mourir à 30 ans* directed by Romain Goupil.
36. Bensaïd, *Une lente impatience*, pp. 33, 48.
37. Jean-François Vilar, 'A propos de "Vichy et les juifs" de Marrus et Paxton: la continuité du racisme d'état', *Rouge*, 970 (22–28 May 1981), 23; 'L'Idéologie française selon B.-H. Lévy', *Rouge*, 955 (6–12 February 1981), 23.
38. Jean-François Vilar, 'Nouveaux juifs', *Rouge*, 885 (21–27 September 1979), 17.
39. Plenel, *Secrets de jeunesse*, p. 134.
40. This was the French title of *Dark Passage*, a 1947 film starring Humphrey Bogart and Lauren Bacall.
41. Extract from *Vertiges* (1 July 1984), quoted in *Tango*, 2nd ser., 1 (2010), inside back cover. (From the second issue onwards of the original series, a page of extracts of press reviews was a regular item, including the information that the 30,000 copies of the first issue sold out in a fortnight.)
42. Claude Dubois, 'Requiem pour le musette', *Tango*, 1 (1983), 44. Dubois also wrote a history of the popular culture of the Bastille area, *La Bastoche*.
43. Rita Renoir, 'Pour Julio mon corps sans hazard', *Tango*, 3 (1984), 15; Julio Cortázar, 'Hommage à une jeune sorcière', trans. by Isabelle Dessommes, with photographs of Rita Renoir, *Tango*, 3 (1984) pp. 16–22.
44. Jean-Louis Ducournau, 'Post scriptum', *Tango*, 4–5 (Spring-Summer 1985), 160.
45. Jean-François Vilar, 'Entretien avec Alexandre Trauner', *Tango*, 4–5 (Spring-Summer 1985), 10–17; '"Tango y Milonga": Munoz et Sampayo', pp. 98–99; 'Repérages pour un Paris des surréalistes et de quelques autres flâneurs', pp. 65–73; 'Bastille-Opera', pp. 131–32; 'Cher Nestor Burma', pp. 118–20; 'Entretien avec Léo Malet', pp. 121–25.
46. François Rivière, 'Leo Malet: un noir jeu de l'oie', *Magazine Littéraire, Le Paris des écrivains*, 332 (May 1995), 61–63; Peter Schulman, 'Paris en jeu de l'oie: les fantômes de Nestor Burma', *The French Review*, 73.6 (May 2000), 1155–64.
47. Vilar, 'Repérages pour un Paris des surréalistes et de quelques autres flâneurs', p. 65.
48. Ibid., p. 65.
49. Jean-François Vilar, in *Jean-François Vilar: 95% de réel*, dir. by Sauvageot.
50. Vilar, Noir c'est noir', p. 7. *Meurtres exquis* contains a final chapter on the French *polar* that is not in the English original, *Delightful Murders*. 'Noir c'est noir' is the title of a very famous 1966 Johnny Hallyday hit, one that is still well known in France; one has, no doubt, to be of a certain age to remember now the original hit in English, 'Black is Black', by Los Bravos.
51. Jean-Paul Schweighaeuser, *Le Roman noir français* (Paris: Presses universitaires de France, coll. Que sais-je?, 1984), p. 71.
52. Violet, 'Série rouge', p. 27.
53. See for example Elfriede Müller and Alexandre Ruoff, *Le Polar français: crime et histoire*, trans. by Jean-François Poirier, preface by Frédéric H. Fajardie (Paris: La Fabrique, 2002); Annie Collovald, 'L'Enchantement dans la désillusion politique', *Le Polar entre critique sociale et désenchantement*, special issue of *Mouvements*, 15–16 (May-August 2001), 16–21. The crime writer A.D.G. who came to prominence at the same time as Manchette, was associated with the extreme-right.
54. In addition to the works already quoted, see: *Roman noir: pas d'orchidées pour les T. M.*, special issue of *Les Temps modernes*, 595 (August-October 1997); Yves Reuter, *Le Roman policier* (Paris: Nathan, 1997); Atack, *May 68 in French Fiction and Film*, Chapter 7; *Crime Fictions*, ed. by Andrea Goulet and Suzanna Lee, special issue of *Yale French Studies*, 108 (October 2005); Claire Gorrara, *The Roman Noir in French Post-war Culture* (Oxford: Oxford University Press, 2003), and *French Crime Fiction and the Second World War: Past Crimes, Present Memories* (Manchester: Manchester University Press, 2012); *Crime and Punishment: Narratives of Order and Disorder*, ed. by Margaret Atack, special issue of *French Cultural Studies*, 12.36 (October 2001); David Platten, *The Pleasures of Crime: Reading Modern French Crime Fiction* (Amsterdam & New York, Rodopi, 2011); *Formes policières du roman contemporain*, ed. by Denis Mellier and Gilles Menegaldo (Poitiers: La Licorne, 1998); *French Crime Fiction*, ed. by Claire Gorrara (Cardiff: University of Wales Press, 2009);

Marc Lits, *Le Roman policier*, 2nd edn (Liège: Le Céfal, 1998); Margaret-Anne Hutton, *French Crime Fiction 1945–2005: Investigating World War II* (Farnham: Ashgate, 2013).
55. See Siegfried Kracauer, *Le Roman policier*, trans. by Geneviève and Rainer Rochlitz (Paris: Payot & Rivages, 2001).
56. Schweighaeuser, *Le Roman noir français*, p. 82.
57. Jean-Paul Demure, 'Écriture et dérision', in *Roman noir: pas d'orchidées pour les T. M.*, pp. 157–63.
58. Vilar, 'Noir c'est noir', p. 9.
59. Ibid., pp. 9–10.
60. Ibid., p. 8.
61. Lee Horsley, *Twentieth-century Crime Fiction* (Oxford: Oxford University Press, 2005), especially Chapter 3.
62. Marc Vernet, 'Film noir on the Edge of Doom', in *Shades of Noir*, ed. by Joan Copjec (London: Verso, 1993), pp. 1–32 (p. 1).
63. David Platten points out that the term *film noir* was indeed being used in France in the 1930s. For his discussion of the development of the *noir* in France, see *The Pleasures of Crime*, pp. 70–72.
64. Marcel Duhamel, 'Préface', in Raymond Borde and Étienne Chaumeton, *Panorama du film noir américain 1941–1953* [1955] (Paris: Flammarion, 1988), p. 9.
65. The website <ina.fr> hosted some extracts of the programme, including the credits and an extract of the discussion where it is amusing to watch Manchette firmly correct Bernard Pivot and insist on the term *néo-polar*, not *polar* for his work <ina.fr> [accessed 11 February 2020, no longer available]. *Apostrophes* programmes are available on this site to subscribers.
66. *Agenda Polar 1986* (Paris: Eden, 1986), to which Vilar contributed Chapter 7.
67. *La Ville est un roman 1841–1991*, ed. by Hervé Delouche (Paris: Conseil Général Seine Saint-Denis & Denoël, 1991). Didier Daeninckx was the literary advisor to the exhibition, and Robert Deleuse its artistic advisor.
68. Didier Daeninckx, 'Archéologie du "un"', *Le Chroniqueur du cent-cinquantenaire*, p. 1, in *La Ville est un roman*, ed. by Delouche.
69. Featuring briefly in Jean-Bernard Pouy, with Stéfanie Delestré, *Une brève histoire du roman noir* (Paris: Seuil, coll. Points, 2016), p. 85.
70. See '68–78', *Opus International*, 66–67 (May-June 1978).
71. *Figuration narrative: Paris 1960–1972*, ed. by Jean-Paul Ameline and Bénédicte Ajac (Paris: Réunion des musées nationaux/Centre Pompidou, 2008), pp. 238–53. The large retrospective devoted to Monory's work in 2014 included the section 'Cinéma et roman noir'. See also Fernando Stefanich, 'Crime and the *Figuration narrative* Movement: The Case of Jacques Monory', in *New Approaches to Crime in French Literature, Culture and Film*, ed. by Louise Hardwick (Oxford: Peter Lang, 2009).
72. Quoted in *La Figuration narrative*, ed. by Ameline & Ajac, p. 21.
73. Jean-Luc Godard, *Godard par Godard: les années Cahiers*, ed. by Alain Bergala (Paris: Flammarion, 1989), pp. 13–14.
74. Jean-Louis Pradel, 'Instrument critique d'un système global du visible', in Gérald Gassiot-Talabot and others, *Mythologies quotidiennes 2*, exhibition catalogue (Paris: Musée d'art moderne de la Ville de Paris, 1977), [n.p.].
75. Michael Sheringham, *Everyday Life: Theories and Practices from Surrealism to the Present* (Oxford: Oxford University Press, 2006).
76. *La Figuration narrative*, ed. by Ameline & Ajac, p. 21.
77. Dominique Noguez, 'Sur le réalisme', *Art vivant*, 36 (February 1973), 32.
78. Sarah Wilson, *The Visual World of French Theory: Figurations* (New Haven, CT, & London: Yale University Press, 2010), p. 88.
79. Vilar describes the *roman noir* as 'novel of crisis, therefore a critical novel' ('Noir c'est noir', p. 10).
80. Ibid.
81. Sheringham, *Everyday Life*, p. 252.
82. I am very grateful to David Platten for his extremely careful reading of this and the following three chapters.

CHAPTER 2

Murder in the Art World

C'est toujours les autres qui meurent (1982) and *Passage des singes* (1984), the two novels discussed in this chapter, won prizes for their assured handling of murder, artifice, and politics.[1] Marcel Duchamp presides over the first one, Walter Benjamin, Eugène Atget, and Andy Warhol over the second. In both, the use of art and artworks at the level of theme and plot connects the political conceptualisation of a world in crisis to its expression in fictional form. These first two novels introduce us to Victor, the key protagonist of Vilar's novels, and to an aesthetic of allusion that keeps the problematic nature of realism and representation at the centre of the story-telling. Vilar explained what led him to this fictional *trompe l'œil*:

> Chez Marcel Duchamp, tout est jeu avec le hasard, le trompe l'œil. Alors je me suis dit qu'écrire un policier avec comme contrainte, d'y introduire un catalogue de Duchamp, d'en faire comme lui un trompe-l'œil, ce serait un joli pari.[2]
>
> [In Marcel Duchamp's work, everything plays with chance, with *trompe l'œil*. So I said to myself that to write a detective novel with the constraint of including a Duchamp catalogue, to turn it, as he does, into a *trompe l'œil*, would be a nice challenge.]

In *C'est toujours les autres qui meurent* — the phrase Duchamp composed for his own tombstone — this has the effect of accentuating the novel as puzzle, as a maze of signs for the reader to decipher.[3] In both novels the multiple citations and allusions, which are at times explicit and more often unacknowledged, highlight the ideological and political tensions and contradictions of avant-garde art in contemporary society.

Victor

Victor Blainville, photographer and former Trotskyist militant, is the main protagonist in the majority of Vilar's novels. His name, like the title of the novel and so much else besides, is generated by the Duchamp catalogue: 'Victor' is the title of the (unfinished) novel that Henri-Pierre Roché wrote about Duchamp; 'Blainville' is the town in Normandy where Duchamp was born. Victor lives alone with three cats, Radek, Kamenev, and Zinoviev, named after prominent revolutionaries tried in the Moscow show trials of the 1930s. Photography is how he makes a living, from portraits and from commissions received from Marc, another former militant who is now editor of the left-wing *Le Soir* (previously *Le Grand Soir*).[4] Victor's passions are Paris, about which he is a living encyclopedia, Duchamp, and surrealism — the haunts, habits, and writings of surrealists and their heroes and *compagnons* such as Lautréamont, Nerval, Duchamp, Atget, Man Ray, and Kiki de Montparnasse. In *Jean-François Vilar: 95% de réel*, Sauvageot's 1997 documentary on his work, Vilar explains: 'Victor n'est pas un enquêteur du tout, ce qui ne veut pas dire qu'il n'est pas en quête de quelque chose' [Victor is not an investigator, which does not mean he is not searching for something].

Victor may not be an investigator, but he is directly involved in the aftermath of multiple unexplained deaths, mainly murders, across the corpus. He is told in the first novel that his role is that of the 'témoin oculiste', the eye-doctor witness, one of the figures in Duchamp's *Large Glass*, and certainly his work as photographer, who looks and watches, records and creates, is also integral to the plots.[5] Vilar judged a photographer to be rich material for a novel, because the photograph also reveals the photographer: he is both inside and outside the picture, a figure Victor repeats in the 'eye-witness doctor' inside and outside the *Large Glass*, and, towards the end of *C'est toujours les autres*, as spectator reflected back to himself in the mirror of a Monory painting.[6] He is a double figure too in the narrative structures of investigation: subject of narration, but often object of investigation, object of study to be followed and photographed, not just by the police, and potential victim, quarry to be hunted and attacked. His political past is also pertinent to these novels which all involve explicitly political themes: the presidential and general elections of 1981 (*C'est toujours les autres*) and of 1986 (*Djemila*), the politics and economics of the commercial art market (*Passage des singes*), the Argentinian junta and Argentinian exiles in Paris (*Bastille-Tango*), the French Revolution and its legacies (*Les Exagérés*), and, in *Nous cheminons entourés de fantômes aux fronts troués*, the fall of the Berlin Wall and the Velvet Revolution in Czechoslovakia in 1989, the 1968 Soviet invasion of Czechoslovakia, and the catastrophic events of 1938, including Munich, the *Anschluss*, Kristallnacht, and the internecine warfare between Trotskyists and Stalinists.

It escaped no interviewer that Victor and Vilar share many features: Trotskyist activism in the past, photography, cats ('Moi, c'est connu, j'aime les chats' [It's well known I like cats], wrote Vilar in *Rouge*), and Vilar enjoyed blurring the boundaries.[7] It is 'Victor' who signs a letter to Nestor Burma,[8] and Vilar's drawing illustrating 'Tandem', the short story of Sybille and Victor, includes a self-portrait.[9] Vilar would reply to interviewers that he could not be Victor since he lived on the boulevard des Filles-du-calvaire, not the quai de Jemmapes; he also more seriously distinguished between himself and his characters in relation to May 68: they, including Victor, may be disenchanted but he, as a committed Trotskyist still contributing to its political aims, though differently, certainly was not. 'Dans mes bouquins, j'ai tendance à raconter ces choses, ce que j'ai cru devoir observer: les désillusions transformées en cynisme. Mais j'insiste, ce cynisme qu'il y a chez certains de mes personnages n'est pas le mien' [In my books, I tend to narrate what I felt I should note: disappointment transformed into cynicism. But I insist, the cynicism of some of my characters is not mine].[10] The lesson of May 68 was that the revolution was not for tomorrow: 'Ça veut dire qu'il faut renoncer? Sûrement pas; ça apprend quelque chose qui est éminemment important en politique: la patience' [Does it mean we should give up? Certainly not. What it teaches is very important in politics: patience],[11] a view echoed by Bensaïd in his autobiography: 'Nous qui étions pressés, nous avons dû nous plier [...] à la rude école de la patience et apprendre la lenteur de l'impatience' [We were in a hurry, but we were obliged to submit ourselves to the harsh school of patience and to learn the slow pace of impatience].[12] But Vilar clearly enjoyed placing elements of his own life in the picture. In 'Volver' (2007), the narrator, who has come to Buenos Aires and is staying in the building where Duchamp stayed in 1918, explains that he uses a pseudonym, his first name taken from the Roché novel, his surname from Duchamp's birthplace, and remarks that this has been his name for so long it no longer feels like a pseudonym any more.[13] A thought one might presume Vilar shared: the patter changes, but the meta-fictional joke remains the same.

Vilar's novels hold in tension a complex reflexivity and the realist conventions of crime fiction; Victor is an important figure in this structure. With his cats, his photography, his taste for white wine, his uninhibited sexual and erotic encounters, and his meetings with his police counterpart and almost friend Villon, he provides the classic coherence of the recurring character who thereby reinforces the conventional referential illusion of a reality outside the text, further cemented by the references back to previous novels, as for example when Ruth in *Passage des singes* picks up a photograph of Rose with a press cutting on the back relating to the ending of *C'est toujours les autres*, or Villon's suffering in *Les Exagérés* is as a direct result of his actions in *Bastille-Tango*. Victor is thus a fictional construct, reinforcing the reality effect, but not the subject of the *énonciation*. Can he know, in *C'est toujours les autres*, that he has a Duchampian name? Rose and her cohort of Bachelors certainly do, their performances of Duchamp are quite deliberate. He observes them, participates in their games, but there is never a suggestion, from himself or the others, that his name, which predates the action, is part of a performance, a surname that moreover was changed from a Jewish one under the Occupation. As narrator, Victor shifts between intra-diegetic and extra-diegetic levels, but is not the (impersonal) subject of the process of self-reflexive narration that is generating the story, notwithstanding Vilar's ludic approach to Victor in interviews.

C'est toujours les autres qui meurent

Victor's erudition, in relation to Paris, its literary, cultural, and political history, and its important figures like Duchamp, is a prominent textual mechanism, starting with the first scene of the first novel. Victor sees a mannequin in a strange pose in the window of a disused shop in one of the covered arcades, the passage du Caire. As anyone who has visited it will know, it is distinguished by its inexpensive clothes shops and fashion mannequins, dressed and undressed, in the windows: 'Il n'y a que cela, passage du Caire. C'est la spécialité du lieu' [That's all there is, in the passage du Caire. It's the local speciality] (*CTA*, pp. 6–7). They can appear unsettling, whole groups of them in serried ranks or in a variety of different poses, staring into the arcade. This one is certainly unsettling: is it a mannequin, is it a corpse? Victor has to scratch at the dirty glass to try and see better; his description as he peers through it and through the hole in the breeze block wall behind it not only confirms the recreation of Duchamp's installation *Etant donnés: 1ᵉ la chute d'eau, 2ᵉ le gaz d'éclairage* [Given: 1 The Waterfall, 2 The Illuminating Gas] — the female mannequin (or corpse) on its back, legs splayed, a light focused on the exposed genitals (sardonically reprising Courbet's *Origine du monde*), a gas light in the left hand, landscape and waterfall images behind — but also places him in the voyeuristic pose that any viewer is compelled to adopt to see the original installation in the Philadelphia Museum of Modern Art, through an aperture in a wooden door.[14]

The use of this installation establishes a vertiginous set of relations between real and imaginary in terms of sex, death, and murder. The three-dimensional staging of the death of the Bride that invokes Dürer's perspective drawing (*Draughtsman Making a Perspective Drawing of a Reclining Woman*), the camera obscura, and Courbet's *Origine du monde*, is also, Jean-Michel Rabaté has convincingly argued, an uncanny repetition of the famous murder in Los Angeles of Elizabeth Short, known as the Black Dahlia.[15] There are many photos online of the appalling death scene, of the naked, dissected, hollowed out body whose left arm is from some angles in a strikingly similar pose to that of Duchamp's model which is also raised, holding the gas light.[16]

Looking, peering, watching, seeing: to place *C'est toujours les autres qui meurent* on the terrain of the intellectual and visual world of Marcel Duchamp is to create multiple perspectives within the problematic of vision and knowledge, interacting with the hermeneutic of the crime story. This is particularly true of Duchamp's *Le Grand Verre: la mariée mise à nu par ses célibataires, même* [The Large Glass: The Bride Stripped Bare by her Bachelors, Even], and *Étant donnés*. The novel opens and closes with these two installations, as at the end Rose — whom Victor first meets in a bookshop called La Broyeuse de Chocolat [The Chocolate Grinder], named after part of *The Large Glass* — crashes through the glass of a fourth floor window opposite the Centre Pompidou in a hail of bullets as Victor, in the final words of the text, leaps for a camera: 'et je photographie Rrose Sélavy dans les noces de son *Grand Verre brisé*' [and I photograph Rrose Sélavy in the marriage of her *Broken Large Glass*] (*CTA*, p. 212).[17] From these two intimately related works is derived a novel where the figures of the 'badaud' [onlooker], the *flâneur*, the *témoin* [witness], the *regardeur* [viewer], the *voyeur* and the spectator proliferate. As these and other major artworks of Duchamp are fragmented through the narrative, we are forcibly reminded that the written is as fundamental as sight to Duchamp's problematic of art.[18] And in both *The Large Glass* and *Given*, the *mise à nu* [stripping bare] is also a *mise à mort* [putting to death]. Each artwork is a *mise en scène* of a murder.

All the names of characters are generated by Duchamp references, as are many of the events and incidental details. Many will recognise *La Roue de bicyclette* in Victor mending his punctured bike and leaving the wheel upright on a stool in his kitchen;

La Belle Hélène, the name of Francis's *café-théâtre* (*La Belle Haleine* [Beautiful Breath]), Duchamp's mock-up of a perfume bottle with a photograph of Rrose Sélavy on the front), *Nu descendant l'escalier* in the photograph of Yvonne walking down a staircase, naked, as does Rose at the end of the novel, or *L.H.O.O.Q*, the Mona Lisa with moustache and goatee beard.[19] Puns and ironic comments abound, such as Duchamp's note 'Retard en verre' [Lateness in Glass] circulating throughout the narrative, from the punning apology for glasses being served late ('des verres en retard') to Victor's understanding after the event that Villon's behaviour pointed to a police massacre: 'Cette histoire n'est qu'une accumulation de retards' [This story is nothing but a piling up of delays] (*CTA*, pp. 201–02). At the sex party Victor attends at Rose's invitation, Victor undresses to play Adam in a *tableau vivant*, where Rose plays Eve and the pose they strike is carefully described. Someone should take a photo, he comments (and of course May Ray did, it is the basis for the episode).[20]

There are many layers to such a playful exploitation of Duchamp's work. French crime fiction has a long tradition of witty wordplay and cultural reference, but this is on a systematic scale that is closer to the rigorous constraints of Oulipo (Ouvroir de littérature potentielle) of which Duchamp was a member. Oulipo recognises the importance of generic and other laws, ensuring literary coherence, while highlighting the gratuitous aspects in producing works governed by intricate and arcane rules and patternings, converging with Duchamp's art work and his approach to art, as he abandoned painting, 'l'art rétinien', and turned to ready-mades and *The Large Glass*. Duchamp's interest in the interplay of chance and necessity certainly embraced narrative. Victor quotes the full entry for *Étant donnés* in *Marchand du sel*:

> Etant donnés: 1e la chute d'eau, 2e le gaz d'éclairage, nous déterminerons les conditions du Repos instantané (ou apparence allégorique) d'une succession (d'un ensemble) de faits divers semblant se déterminer l'un autre par des lois, pour isoler le signe de la concordance entre, d'une part, ce Repos (capable de toutes les excentricités innombrables) et, d'autre part, un choix de Possibilités légitimées par des lois et aussi les occasionnant, etc. (*CTA*, p. 46)
>
> [Given: 1. The waterfall, 2. The illuminating gas, we will determine the conditions of the instantaneous Rest (or allegorical appearance) of a succession (of a group) of *faits divers* seeming to determine each other by laws, in order to isolate the sign of the concordance between, on the one hand, this Rest (capable of all the innumerable eccentricities) and, on the other hand, a choice of Possibilities authorised by laws and also causing them, etc.]

'Peut-on être plus clair?' [Could it be clearer?], he wonders, pointing to this narrative as being just such an 'excentricité', spun out of the centre of *Étant donnés* ('Aucun cadavre en vérité, du moins en vitrine, dans la Galerie Vivienne aujourd'hui. J'échapperai aujourd'hui à cette excentricité-là' [In truth, no corpse in the Galerie Vivienne. I'm spared that particular eccentricity today]). The interaction of laws and infinite possibilities is fundamental to narrative as well as to the games Duchamp and Victor both enjoy. Duchamp was a renowned chess player, and the mannequin in *Étant donnés* is lying on the black and white squares of a game board; Rose plays chess on the squares of the Galerie Vivienne. Rose and Victor invent their laws as they take trajectories through Paris ordered by various thematic links, for example 'waterfall' — Victor checks several fountains unsuccessfully before finding her at the canal sluices near his home.

One could go on, and it is not surprising that this intricate reflexive integration of the work of Duchamp, has attracted critical attention.[21] It creates a labyrinthine surface where the reader is in the position of the perplexed spectator of Duchamp's works, echoed by the perplexity of Victor in the passage du Caire, wondering what is the status of what is being read. The art works become narrative ready-mades, the novel a fictional artefact to match *La Boîte en valise*, the 'portable Duchamp' that he made of all his major works in a suitcase when he left France for America in 1941. The past master of *détournement*, Duchamp is here subjected to it as these 'found objects' are inscribed, as narrative objects and processes, into a second order signification of political contestation.[22]

The novel closes with a great set piece as Rose and her Bachelors, no longer involved in the fraud and extortion that Francis, another former Trotskyist militant, had organised, take the Centre Pompidou and its Museum of Modern Art hostage. Piling all the greats of established contemporary art into heaps, demanding that the Mona Lisa be adorned in perpetuity with moustache and goatee beard, and that urinals signed 'R Mutt' be installed in every museum in France, they no doubt also reminded a contemporary readership that the inaugural exhibition of the newly opened Centre in 1977 was *L'Œuvre de Marcel Duchamp*. The initiative ends badly: surrounded by police from the outset, the Bachelors are killed when the police open fire. This episode is also indexing the contemporary political art of contestation. In 1972, the French President Georges Pompidou was behind the initiative to mount a major exhibition at the Grand Palais, *72: douze ans d'art contemporain*, bringing together many important artists of the *nouveau réalisme* and *figuration narrative* movements.[23] It proved very controversial from the outset, many refusing to be associated with such a celebration in the light of what they saw as the lamentable support for contemporary art in France during these same years. The Front d'artistes plasticiens (FAP) was formed in 1972 — a focal point for dissent and criticism. *Rouge* reported their rejection of the exhibition in February 1972, praising their refusal to be used as instruments of government.[24] At the preview, the FAP organised a demonstration outside the Grand Palais, and the organisers called in the riot police who charged the demonstration. La Collective des Malassis, six artists who espoused a directly politicised role for art, proceeded there and then to remove from the exhibition their major work *Le Grand Méchoui ou douze ans d'histoire*, a set of paintings commenting on contemporary France.[25] 'Les flics de Pompidou à l'assaut des manifestants du FAP!' [Pompidou's cops attacking the FAP demonstrators!] captions one of Elie Kagan's photographs in *Rouge*.[26]

The second narrative thread is equally political, as Victor registers the collapse of beliefs in revolutionary militant action that he, like many others in the novel, has abandoned. The liberal elite of politics and journalism is full of similar 'traitors' who are however doing much better for themselves than Victor. The novel opens on Friday 19 June 1981 and closes on Monday 22 June 1981, which is the weekend of the general election following Mitterrand's historic victory in the presidential election the previous month, electing a left-wing president for the first time since the foundation of the Fifth Republic. Various political positions are in ironic counterpoint to each other. While the clichés of the representation of the socialist victory are mocked — Marc sends Victor out to take photographs of the crowds, edifying images of the joy of the people, 'les prolétaires heureux qui portent des enfants sur leurs larges épaules? Les enfants sont, je suppose, censés lever leur vaillant petit poing?' [happy workers with children on their broad shoulders? Children, I presume, with their valiant little fists raised?] (*CTA*, p. 62) — the politics of regret about May 68 is quite savagely dissected. Rose, who participated in the famous Beaux-Arts workshop in 68 before falling in love with Duchamp's art in Philadelphia in 1969, suggests to Victor that: 'votre gauchisme est devenu pépère, Mai s'est éloigné. [...] je suppose qu'il y a pas mal, de vos copains, qui sont partis comme ça, sur la pointe des pieds' [your leftism has gone old and doddery and May is far away. I suppose quite a few of your pals have tiptoed away]. His response repeats the established Trotskyist line of May 68 as a starting point, but puts it in a broader political context:

> Plus qu'elle ne le pense. Et après? C'était un test, voilà tout. Pas les procès, pas les camps, pas les caves. Rien de bien méchant: rien que l'apprentissage de la durée, de la patience, de la ténacité. [...] On va quand même pas pleurer sur les exaltés déçus qui se sont trompés de hobby. (*CTA*, p. 112)[27]
>
> [More than she knows. And then what? It was a test, that's all. There were no trials, no camps, no cellars. Nothing very nasty: nothing but learning about the long term, about patience, about tenacity. We're not going to cry over the disappointed hotheads who just chose the wrong hobby].

There is however real anger from Victor at the killing of the unarmed Bachelors, anger at Villon, the left-wing cop who he realises afterwards knew exactly where all this was heading, and who insists they were armed. Upon which, Victor rather savagely beats up Villon, a skill he owes to his political past. He concludes by sarcastically suggesting they agree that the Bachelors were armed, and that Villon fell down the stairs. The oppressive powers of the new socialist government in the service of order are thus nailed very precisely, but they are not the only ones working through a logic of coherence at the Bachelors' expense. Rose's only reaction to their deaths is that it is was in the range of possibilities; if her Bachelors are dead she can become a widow, even a 'Fresh Widow'.[28] Victor is not convinced that she did not send them to their deaths for the sake of a pun, but for Rose, the machine took over. Once it was started, there was no stopping it: the place of the Bachelors in the Glass is 'the cemetery of Bachelors'. However, one of the Bachelors has survived to shoot her and she too fulfills her destiny as the Bride meets her death.

The sad end of the Bachelors as victims of the police highlights also the ideological role of the museum as an institution of state. The structural importance of the museum to Duchamp's ready-mades has long been noted — they are only art objects when on display in a museum or gallery. Jean-François Lyotard concluded an essay on *Etant donnés* by drawing attention to its complex theatricality, a staging of vision and voyeurism in an art historical perspective:

> Comment distinguer la narration-représentation humoristique de la crédule, et comment décider de celle que Duchamp nous lègue? Grâce à ceci simplement qu'elle se redouble: le théâtre du nu dans le théâtre du musée, lui-même théâtre d'une autre chose qui sera encore un théâtre.[29]

> [How are we to distinguish humorous from naïve representation-narration, and how are we to decide which one Duchamp is bequeathing to us? Thanks simply to the fact that it operates a doubling: the theatre of the nude in the theatre of the museum, itself a theatre of something else which will be yet another theatre.]

In Vilar's novels, the model on display is a recurring figure. As well as the corpse imitating Duchamp's artwork, Rose is found at one point imitating the pose of the famous Musée Grévin mannequin who appears in Breton's *Nadja*, and in the Centre Pompidou Vilar contemplates models of tramps in exhibition cases, and watches the Bachelors carefully place one of the famous Dolls of Hans Bellmer on the ticket desk. As Lyotard notes, the theatricality of display is one of infinite regress; Vilar deploys the art of citation in a similar fashion to ensure the reader remains within the fictionality of his *trompe l'œil* novel.

Passage des singes

If *C'est toujours les autres qui meurent* ends with a massacre, *Passage des Singes* both starts and finishes with one, the first ordered by, the second carried out by, Dennis Locke, a world-famous artist who is clearly drawn from Andy Warhol. Locke, who is thought to have died in the massacre, was an international celebrity; a description of one of his paintings of a car accident alludes to the crashes in Warhol's 'Death and Destruction' series. Indeed, the image in the first massacre of a woman hanging head down from a balcony as if cut in two by the bullets is strikingly similar to that of one of the bodies hanging from the car in Warhol's *Saturday Disaster: Plebian Way of Death* (1964).

The Prologue, describing the first massacre, is dated September 1981. A video film follows several masked men as they gather and attack a large building in Los Angeles with automatic weapons. The camera tracks the immediate surroundings, including old Vietnam slogans on a wall and broken windows replaced with cardboard. As a carload of killers joins the first two figures, scenes of panic and death unfold; grenades set fire to the house, a child is killed right in front of the camera, corpses are everywhere. This is a famous clip, seen by millions, because, as the final words of the Prologue dramatically inform us, 'Ainsi donc est mort Dennis Locke' [This is how Dennis Locke died] (*PS*, p. 9). The main action starts one year later, as newspapers prepare to focus on the first anniversary of Locke's death, and Victor is sent to Orly to meet his widow Patti Bénédicte, known as 'Kiki'. The Prologue's *fait divers* is thus structurally similar to the opening *fait divers* of *C'est toujours les autres qui meurent* in that, to put it at its most simple, all is not as it seems. The video will be returned to and puzzled over several times in the course of the narrative, particularly when it is finally proven that Dennis Locke was not killed in the massacre.

The plot is complex, driven by a number of shifting enigmas to be solved over four days and four nights, many murders, and a large cast of characters: artists and photographers, journalists, establishment figures, old Nazis, neo-fascist commandos, bodyguards, and hired killers. It is a story of lies and pretence, of imitation and counterfeit, one that charts contemporary inauthenticity in behaviour, politics, art, photography, and spectacle.

If *C'est toujours les autres qui meurent* is pointing to the institutional and ideological power of the state and its cultural institutions, *Passage des singes* is about the market and money, and about the strength of 'recuperation' in its political sense of the appropriation of oppositional and subversive practices diverted from their original aims, neutralised and put to use for the status quo: 'Dennis Locke, figure de proue de la contestation des années 60–70, est devenue une proie pour l'establishment, un gibier à musée, un must pour les collectionneurs' [Dennis Locke, a leading figure of 1960s and 70s contestation, has become a prey for the establishment, museum fodder, a must for collectors] (*PS*, p. 36). Raymonde Moulin highlighted at the time the inherent contradictions of contestatory art, avidly collected and displayed by the rich capitalists it attacks, since the artists have to sell in order to live,[30] a process sardonically related here to other political disengagements:

> Qu'était devenue la base sociale de Dennis Locke, artiste? Des collectionneurs milliardaires? Le nouvel establishment issu des révoltes avortées des années 70? Ceux pour qui le mot 'valeur' se traduit par 'placement' et ceux pour qui il a signifié il y a longtemps, très longtemps, 'engagement'. (*PS*, p. 174)

> [What is now the social base of Dennis Locke, the artist? Billionaire collectors? The new establishment that has emerged from the aborted revolts of the 1970s? Those who translate 'value' by 'investment' and those for whom, a very, very long time ago, it meant 'commitment'.]

Most eloquent, in this market-driven context, is the reference to the 'fin tragique' [tragic end] (*PS*, p. 173) of Dennis Locke, which echoes the controversial series of paintings *Vivre ou laisser mourir: la fin tragique de Marcel Duchamp* [Live or Let Die: The Tragic End of Marcel Duchamp], created by Gilles Aillaud, Eduardo Arroyo, and Antonio Recalcati in 1965, controversially depicting three of Duchamp's iconic works interspersed with paintings of Duchamp being attacked by the artists, then having fallen — or having been thrown — down a staircase, and finally in his coffin, draped with an American flag, with Andy Warhol and five other Pop Art and *nouveau réalisme* artists accompanying it. It was widely interpreted as an attack on the apolitical nature of Duchamp's art, his paradoxical sanctification of the artist who only has to touch an object for it to be a 'ready-made' and therefore art, and his 'tragic end': an American commodity.[31] Such criticisms were also part of the reception of Warhol and the media circus surrounding his activities, as his brutal indictment of the violence and destruction and dehumanisation of the American order is celebrated in museums and in the astronomical prices paid for his work.

The power of the market explains why Locke's missing paintings are such prized commodities, but these are not the only monetarised pieces in the narrative jigsaw. All the characters are driven by money. Victor, Raymond, and Kiki have money problems. Locke's patron and lover Ruth Freytag has inherited a fortune from her late husband Wilhelm. Léni Benway has made a fortune building a press empire. Marc wants Victor to write a profile of Kiki for his special anniversary number to drive up sales and move *Le Soir* into a different league. Victor's motive is his extravagant acquisition of the empty flat above him driven by his artistic ambitions for his photography. Kiki has taken money from Wilhelm's brother Ludwig in exchange for Locke's Paris address, for information is also a valuable commodity here in the drive to solve the various narrative enigmas: why is Kiki in Paris? Where are Locke's paintings? Is Locke alive? What really happened in the Californian massacre, who carried out the shooting and why, and who was filming it? Was Wilhelm Freytag murdered and did Ruth and Locke do it? This network of puzzles explains the carousel of protagonists chasing each other: Ludwig is in Paris to hunt down Ruth and Locke, an American journalist Mike Grable has joined forces with Ludwig to hunt down Locke, Locke is hunting down all those who have betrayed him, Benway wants the pictures, Victor needs information for his article and is also lowering his standards for money:

> — Ce que tu veux, bref, c'est un papier à sensations, une saloperie...
> Marc ne cilla pas.
> Les confrontations de cow-boys solitaires face à la grande aventure, les amitiés viriles et les souvenirs nostalgiques du temps où on était quand même autre chose: ça n'impressionne plus. Reste une question, et moi non plus je ne cille pas:
> — Combien ? (*PS*, p. 27)[32]
>
> ['What you want, in a word, is a sensational article, a piece of trash...'
> Marc did not blink.
> The confrontations between lonely cowboys facing up to the great adventure, to virile friendships and nostalgic memories of the time when, true enough, we were different people: they no longer impress anyone. One question remains, and I don't blink either:
> 'How much?']

As we have seen, Vilar argued that the *roman noir* was admirably suited to exploring the compromises and betrayals in a world in crisis with no obvious solutions, and *Passage des singes* does so from many angles. Victor capitulates to Marc as Marc capitulates to Benway when the latter insists he will no longer fund *Le Soir* if Marc refuses to participate in the televised debate about Locke that Benway is hosting. The only notes of authenticity occur among the Latin American exiles staying with the Chilean artist Maia, though her old friend Roberto has traded revolutionary politics, which are no more, for wreck salvage. Yet he falls for Kiki and tries to run off with her and the missing pictures when Grable and his killers descend, Benway having elicited the address from other left-wing journalists he also financed.

The 'infinite regress' of citation and spectacle that never lands on a stable external reality is also effectively deployed. There are several paintings hanging on the walls of Ruth's flat, as well as an empty bottle-rack. Victor comments that 'Le Derwatt qui est au mur est faux comme tous les Derwatt, mais c'est un beau tableau. Le Locke qui lui fait face me semble authentique, mais qu'est-ce que j'y connais?'

[The Derwatt on the wall is a fake, like all the Derwatts, but it's a fine painting. The Locke opposite it seems genuine to me, but what do I know?] (*PS*, p. 128).[33] The Derwatt is fake on many levels. Firstly he is a fictional character from Patricia Highsmith's *Ripley Under Ground*, a painter who committed suicide and whose later works had been forged by Bernard Tufts, lining the pockets of Ripley, who was not above impersonating him when necessary. The forged Derwatt paves the way for Locke's later paintings having been forged by Raymond, at Locke's instigation. The signatures are genuine, the pictures are not, unless one considers them elevated to authentic art by the sole force of the signature, as Duchamp's ready-mades were. Derwatt's painting is therefore both an indication of the later plot development about the forgeries, which include all the prized missing paintings, and a repetition in miniature of a central process of the narrative itself.

The most telling 'fake' which is not a forgery, but not authentic either, is the opening video of the massacre. Although the fact that Locke was not one of the victims is clear by the third day, only on the final pages is Locke revealed as the cameraman who orchestrated the whole thing as a spectacular 'exit' — 'une sorte de chef d'œuvre qui marquerait mon époque et en rendrait compte. Un beau crime' [a kind of masterpiece that would mark my era and be an account of it. A fine crime] (*PS*, p. 248) — hiring the assassins, including Grable, and eliminating them afterwards, and giving Victor a moment of 'punctum' in the Barthesian sense, when he realises that the child's sudden bewildered look as he is gunned down running towards the camera is because he recognises Locke. Locke is a degraded version of an artist from every point of view: producing poor quality work, putting his signature to forgeries, and using techniques of contestation in his videos with no subtlety whatsoever: 'L'artiste filmant l'artiste se niant comme artiste et mettant en scène les procédés de sa propre roublardise' [The artist filming the artist denying he is an artist and staging the techniques of his own cunning] (p. 187), which is no doubt matched by the artist getting hired killers to kill the artist, in another fake show.

The novel's title, *Passage des singes*, may seem rather tangential to this story of artists and murderers, but it is also pointing to the structural role of the interplay of original and copy. Atget took a well-known photograph of the fountain of the passage des Singes, and Walter Benjamin's remark about Atget's photographs resembling a crime scene is the epitaph to the novel. Atget's distinctive photographs of the city focused on deserted scenes, according to Benjamin, although Victor points out many did include people, and that for him the blurred ghostly shapes of people moving too fast for the early technology were the most moving aspect of these photographs, transcending the documentary record (*PS*, p. 247). Benjamin situates Atget within his own framework of the unique and the multiple, the individual work of art or highly distinctive early photographs contrasted to the infinite reproducibility of the photographic copy, unmistakably marked as an inferior imitation. The political art of contestation of the 1960s and 70s established a critical, often sarcastic approach by deploying the mechanically reproduced images of advertising or television or newsreels to reject the high cultural veneration of the artist and the work of art as masterpiece, and to put the shallow and sinister aspects of the society of spectacle on critical display. Even the world in crisis has become a spectacle in this novel. A video of the Cabaret Voltaire concert where Locke met Kiki shows images of violence, of soldiers and mutilated bodies, on a huge screen behind the band: Vietnam, Nicaragua, El Salvador. 'Très putassier, très efficace' [very whorish, very effective], comments Ruth, while the strong lights from the projectors, 'très concentrationnaires' [very concentrationary], strafe the audience (p. 111).[34]

The emotional charge of the Holocaust is a significant thread running through Vilar's writings. Ruth and the Nazi brothers in part embody that here, though Ludwig's alliance with the extreme-right in Paris maintains past and present in a Benjaminian relation. Ruth's motivation for killing Wilhelm, fuelled by her anger at his complacent pride in her as a young trophy Jewish wife, is complex. She was born the night of the Kristallnacht attacks in 1938, then taken to the United States. Her lengthy, quietly reflective exposition of her life story pauses the action and gives historical depth to it. Her unconsummated marriage to this much older former Nazi was unproblematic for her until she realised he was using her to give himself a good role in his own story: 'Il s'y offrait le luxe d'un destin douloureux. De salaud politique il devenait brave homme' [He gave himself the luxury of having a painful destiny. He turned himself from political bastard into a decent man] (*PS*, p. 142). Victor's silent reaction, as she asks if he understands, is telling: 'Si elle savait!' [If only she knew!] (p. 143). It is one of the several discreet markers of the importance of the Holocaust and anti-semitism to Victor personally. To add to the change of family name during the Occupation, we learn in *Passage des singes* that the cooking of a left-wing Zionist friend, Roger, reminds Victor of that of his grandmother. She is mentioned also in *C'est toujours les autres qui meurent*, in the context of Victor's affection for the Musée Grévin, which will be developed at length in *Les Exagérés*. Furthermore, Victor describes a possible confrontation with Ludwig's neo-fascists as 'une vieille histoire qui remonte à surface' [an old story coming back to the surface]: 'C'est bien ton problème et le mien,' replies Roger, 'On a beau faire, pour nous, c'est toujours une vieille histoire, très vieille. [...] Je marche en pensant à Roger et ses vieilles histoires. Il a raison. Elles nous rattrapent toujours' [This is very much your problem and mine. Whatever we do, for us, it's always an old story, a very old story. [...] I think about Roger and his old stories as I walk along. He's right. They always catch us up] (*PS*, pp. 159–60). The Holocaust and the 1930s will become increasingly central in the later fiction.

In the final episode, Victor tracks Locke down in Atget's studio. Locke has been spending his time in Paris systematically re-taking Atget's images of Paris. Earlier, he bought one of the photographs from an exhibition of Victor's work, choosing Victor's picture of the fountain of the passage des Singes, which again was deliberately reproducing Atget's own shot. Victor wished to document this passage just before the bulldozers, 'les machines de mort' [the death machines], moved in to demolish it to make way for a multi-storey car park (*PS*, p. 196–97), thereby repeating not only Atget's photograph, but also Atget's motivation for many of his pictures, namely recording 'old Paris' in danger of disappearing.[35] This homage in the form of imitation, which has the main criminal and main investigative figure merging on the same spot with a camera and with the ghostly presence of Atget, offers an ironic twist on the reproducibility of the image and the uniqueness of the artist's work.

Conclusion

Duchamp's *Etant donnés* has several functions in *C'est toujours les autres*, functions that are structurally important to Vilar's distinctive combination of *roman noir* and the visual world of art and film. Thematically, it is a *fait divers*. Murder is a classic locus of the *fait divers*, the category of journalism that captures the self-contained event which is both ordinary and extraordinary, the news story that appears in a bland 'other events' list that goes from the minor to the seemingly all-encompassing that dominates headlines. For the surrealists it was the embodiment of 'le hasard objectif', the tear in the fabric of the commonplace that reveals the irrational and the surreal at work. The quality of the *fait divers*, poised between norm and transgression, has provoked extensive intellectual and critical interest, and its importance for crime fiction is well established.[36] Franck Évrard argues that the juxtaposition of the *fait divers* and serialised fiction in the nineteenth-century newspaper facilitated their integration in the crime novel: 'faits divers et roman-feuilleton semblent jouer tous deux de la confusion entre le réel et l'imaginaire au niveau de la fiction mystérieuse et de la réalité de l'enquête' [*fait divers* and serialised fiction seem both to play on the confusion between real and imaginary at the level of the fiction of mystery and the reality of the investigation].[37] The photographs of Elizabeth Short, and the famous Weegee black-and-white images of murders in the city, remind us that the unexpected is also an established trope, and sudden killings another iteration of the brutal, sordid, often sexualised nature of the modern city.

Étant donnés is a work of art, an imaginary object, as indeed are Duchamp's ready-mades. 'C'est le regardeur qui fait le tableau' [It's the viewer who makes the painting], he famously said, a position that sounds close to Sartre's influential concept of 'imagining consciousness' ('la conscience imageante'), although Duchamp is rather stressing conceptual art over 'retinal art', as he called it, that is, the passive consumption of what is visible. Sartre argued that the imaginary object does not exist in the same mode as an ordinary object, we do not 'see' a functional bicycle wheel and Duchamp's *Bicycle Wheel* in the same mode, and Duchamp delighted in situating his work to appear to oscillate between the two. 'C'est le témoin qui fait l'événement' [It's the witness who makes the event] (*CTA*, p. 97), agree Victor and Villon. As Victor scratches at the dirty glass, he does not know what he is looking at: a reconstruction of an art work, an artfully dressed shop window, or an artfully dressed corpse. When he returns to the scene, the window is surrounded by people, by 'des badauds' (p. 18), those who stand around and watch. The *badaud* is the woefully neglected figure who is as just as much a part of the Paris streets as is the *flâneur*.[38] Ludwig's hired killers in *Passage des singes* are slaughtered outside the cafe near Leni Benway's, and are quickly surrounded by a crowd of *badauds*: 'Les badauds en grappe échangent des propos divers sur l'insécurité des villes, le terrorisme international, Chicago-sur-Rotonde et l'incurie de la gauche au pouvoir' [the bunch of *badauds* exchange views on danger in the city, international terrorism, Chicago-on-Rotonde and the negligence of the left-wing government] (*PS*, p. 150).[39] If 'le témoin fait l'événement', it is the *badaud* who produces the *fait divers*, unusual enough to interrupt the flow of everyday life, and simultaneously inscribed on the already written wisdom of common sense, in Barthes's negative sense of ideologically saturated doxa. The same circularity is at work in Victor's commission to photograph the crowds celebrating the Socialist Party victory in the elections. There is a configuration of established signs to be reproduced so that the referent 'victory of the people' is firmly nailed, and Victor duly provides them.

To utter received ideas and clichés is by definition to cite the already said or written. Antoine Compagnon's wide-ranging investigation of citational practices in writing, *La Seconde Main*, takes as its starting point the fact that all writing and reading is always a rewriting, a rereading.[40] All texts are patchworks, worked and reworked; all texts quote, as do all artworks, not only at the level of the *énoncé*, with direct borrowings and references, but at the level of the *énonciation*, across the processes of text production. Vilar's novels invite us to consider how to understand this, across different imaginative modes and across the factual and the imaginary. Photography, painting, and writing are all interwoven in Vilar's writings. Metaphors of layering can be helpful in trying to identify the processes of hybridity, of amalgamating different art forms or different written or visual texts, but capturing the nature of the relationship is difficult. The complex relations of hypotext and hypertext are explored in Genette's *Palimpsestes*, but these are elaborate relations between two texts, or the ludic and intellectually systematic exploitation of multiple connections, as for example in some of Queneau's poems.[41] This does not capture the use of Duchamp's work, with its multiplicity of starting points: machines, mathematics, chess games, language and language games, science of air, water and energy, photographs, images, and models, which in Vilar's novels are combined with many others to generate plot, characters, objects, events, machines (video cameras, cameras, answerphones). Mary Ann Caws uses the metaphor of interference, such as an imperfectly tuned radio transmitting simultaneously more than one station, which again suggests a hybrid merging of entities.[42] But just as Duchamp's work abounds with multiple allusions (one list relating to *Étant donnés* alone runs to three and a half pages), so Vilar's novels are intricate constructions involving a multiplicity of historical, visual, and textual directions in which it points the reader.[43]

The use of *Étant donnés* in the very first scene establishes an important topos, then, one to place beside the street as crime scene because its elements illuminate the citational processes in these fictions, particularly the way they combine surface and space. Victor scratches at the dirty shop window. Scratching at a surface is the key action associated with the palimpsest — scratching with a pen to overwrite what is originally written — and its metaphorical usage in the uncovering of secrets, or the past, scratching to reveal a hidden layer, and is certainly deployed in this way in Vilar's work: 'il suffit de gratter un peu'; 'gratter avec persévérance sur les apparences perverses des choses' [you just need to scratch a little; scratch with perseverance on the perverse appearances of things].[44] But here it reveals, not a hidden layer but a space, an installation, a re-creation. And throughout these novels, spaces are as citational as surfaces. Benway has reconstituted the former brothel *Le Sphinx* in his grand building; inside one room he has reconstituted a famous room from *Le Chabanais*, another legendary brothel. The tacky nightclub in his basement is created in homage to former styles. The buildings of the streets are citational in their constant evocation, in part or in whole, of other buildings, of previous buildings, of people, and of events. For spaces of buildings and streets can be citational in their 'contents' too: Hotel Istria, where Duchamp, Man Ray, Tzara, Aragon, and many others stayed, rue Gît-le-Cœur and the hotel where Burroughs and the beat poets lived, rue Campagne-Première where Michel Poiccard breathed his last. In other words, the reconstitution of *Étant donnés* — and its degraded replica in *Passage des singes*, the peepshow that Victor visits, entering the booth to watch the near naked young woman dancing behind the glass, and photograph her of course — provides a structure: the quest for knowledge involves both surface and three-dimensional space, a structure that will be absolutely central to Vilar's narratives of Paris, Venice, Djemila, and Prague.

Notes to Chapter 2

1. Grand Prix du roman noir Télérama-Fayard and Prix du Roman policier du Festival de Reims, respectively.
2. Jean-François Vilar, in Monique Lefebvre, 'Grand Prix du roman noir Télérama-Fayard: Jean-François Vilar', *Télérama*, 1673 (3 February 1982), 10.
3. The reader is alerted to the importance of Duchamp by Vilar's choice of epigraphs: '"D'ailleurs c'est toujours les autres qui meurent" Epitaphe de Marcel Duchamp (1887–1968) sur sa tombe, à Rouen. Écrit par lui-même' ['Besides, it is always the others who die' Epitaph of Marcel Duchamp (1887–1968) on his tomb, in Rouen. Written by himself], and '"Et Qui libre" Rrose Sélavy' ['And Who Free' Rrose Sélavy]. 'Rrose Sélavy' was the name of Duchamp's female alter ego.
4. This is another in-joke. 'Le Grand Soir' was a nineteenth-century term for the moment of great revolutionary change. Not even the inevitably degraded, devalued political action — from militancy to mainstream journalism — can maintain the revolutionary aspiration, not even as just a sign. Marc has some of the attributes and history of the former Maoist and editor of *Libération*, Serge July.
5. 'Témoin-oculiste' is usually translated as 'oculist witness', but this loses the pun with eye-witness (*témoin oculaire/oculiste*) in English.
6. Interview with Violet, 'Série rouge'; the Monory painting, *Meurtres no 10/2* (1968), also features in the *Memento mori* catalogue discussed in Chapter 7.
7. Jean-François Vilar, 'Bercy-Chirac', *Rouge*, 891 (3–8 November 1979), 19. Collovald and Neveu describe Victor as 'Vilar's double' ('"Le Néo-Polar"', p. 82).
8. Jean-François Vilar, 'Cher Nestor Burma', *Tango*, 4–5 (Spring-Summer 1985), 118–20. Nestor Burma is Léo Malet's detective.
9. Jean-François Vilar, 'Tandem', *Tango*, 3 (July-September 1984), 32.
10. Brouillet, 'J.-F. Vilar de la nuit', p. 57. In *Jean-François Vilar: 95% de réel*, he described Victor as 'assez marqué par 68 et toute la suite, toute les révolutions déçues' [quite marked by 68 and all that followed, all the failed revolutions].

11. Ibid., p. 57.
12. Bensaïd, *Une lente impatience*, p. 12.
13. Jean-François Vilar, 'Volver', in Antonio Seguí, *Seguí*, exhibition catalogue (Geneva: Galerie Sonia Zannettacci, 2009). The text is part fiction, part commentary.
14. As a video uploaded to YouTube shows: <https://www.youtube.com/watch?v=dAlzBx24_vM> [accessed 20 May 2020]. See also Dawn Ades, Neil Cox, and David Hopkins, *Marcel Duchamp* (London: Thames & Hudson, 1999), Chapter 9.
15. Jean-Michel Rabaté, *Étant donnés 1. L'Art, 2. Le Crime: la modernité comme scène du crime* (Dijon: Presses du réel, 2010), pp. 68–80.
16. Rabaté includes facing photographs of the installation and the murder scene, *Étant donnés 1*, pp. 108–09.
17. Duchamp's *Grand Verre* was famously damaged in transit in 1926, and he was pleased with the resulting cracks in it as he explains in this 1956 interview: <https://www.youtube.com/watch?v=DzwADsrOEJk> [accessed 20 May 2020].
18. Having publicly abandoned painting and artworks in 1923 in order to concentrate on chess, it transpired after his death in 1968 that Duchamp had worked on *Étant donnés* from 1946 to 1966, leaving precise instructions for its posthumous installation. See Marcel Duchamp, *The Manual of Instructions for Étant Donnés: 1° la chute d'eau, 2° le gaz d'éclairage* (Philadelphia: Philadelphia Museum of Modern Art, 1987). The title in fact appears among the many notes and diagrams of *La Boîte verte* [The Green Box], Marcel Duchamp, *Duchamp du signe* (Paris: Flammarion, 2013), p. 48, the box of material relating to his major installation *La Mariée mise à nu par ses célibataires, même*, also referred to as '*Le Grand Verre*'. Marcel Duchamp, *La Mariée mise à nu par ses célibataires, même (La Boîte verte)* (Paris: Rrose Sélavy, 1934); the contents are reproduced in *Duchamp du signe*, Chapter 2.
19. The letters of *L.H.O.O.Q.*, when said out loud, give 'Elle a chaud au cul' [Her arse is hot]. 'Avoir le feu au cul' [arse on fire] is to be randy.
20. The photograph, of Duchamp and Bronia Perlmutter, is reproduced in Cécile Debray, *Marcel Duchamp: la peinture, même*, exhibition catalogue (Paris: Centre Pompidou, 2015), p. 14.
21. See especially Frédéric, *La Stylistique française en mutation?*, and Majastre, *Approche anthropologique de la représentation*. See also Nella Arambasin, *Littérature contemporaine et histoires de l'art: récits d'une réévaluation* (Geneva: Droz, 2007)
22. Majastre, *Approche anthropologique de la représentation*, p. 120, Frédéric, *La Stylistique française en mutation?*, p. 114.
23. *72: douze ans d'art contemporain en France*, ed. by François Mathey, exhibition catalogue (Paris: Réunion des musées nationaux, 1972).
24. [Anon.], 'Les Peintres contre l'expo Pompidou', *Rouge*, 146 (26 February 1972), 11.
25. *Rouge* gave extensive coverage to this in May 1972. Michel Lequenne's article 'L'Art du régime et le régime de l'art' (*Rouge*, 158 (20 May 1972), 6) was accompanied by a photograph of the Malassis taken by Elie Kagan. The rather snide caption no doubt explained by the political allegiance: 'Better late than never, the Malassis, a group of artists associated to the CP, pack their bags'. See also [Anon.], 'Les États généraux du FAP', *Rouge*, 157 (13 May 1972), 7, and Michel Lequenne, 'Bide noir pour Pompidou', *Rouge*, 159 (27 May 1972), 7.
26. *Rouge*, 159 (27 May 1972), 7. See also the detailed presentation by Vincent Chambarlhac, 'Traces d'une œuvre: *Le Grand Méchoui* des Malassis en 1972', *Sociétés & Représentations*, 38.2 (2014), 281–94.
27. The reference to cellars is to being tortured.
28. *Fresh Widow* being one of Duchamp's installations, a pun on 'French Window': it's a window but made of dark leather, not glass.
29. Jean-François Lyotard, '*Étant donnés*: inventaire du dernier nu', in *Marcel Duchamp: abécédaire: approches critiques,* ed. by Jean Clair with Ulf Linde (Paris: Musée national d'art moderne, 1977), pp. 86–109 (p. 109).
30. Raymonde Moulin, 'Vivre pour vendre', in Jean Cassou and others, *Art et contestation* (Brussels: La Connaissance, 1968), pp. 121–36.
31. Exhibited in the 1965 *Figuration narrative* exhibition. The artists' explanation and defence of the

work, written in 1966, is reproduced in *Duchamp et après*, *Opus international*, 49 (March 1974), 102. Arguing that Duchamp was a particularly effective defender of bourgeois culture, they proudly acknowledged the destructive nature of the work, which was intended to escape the vicious circle of cultural criticism being culturally appreciated, and sarcastically agreed that only hired killers could have carried out such a monstrous crime, because they did the hiring.
32. The 'cowboys' inevitably recall the ironies of the situationist comic strips where they often featured.
33. And the bottle rack is one of Duchamp's ready-mades.
34. 'Concentrationary' has started to be used to translate 'concentrationnaire', (pertaining to the concentration camps), after the famous *L'Univers concentrationnaire* (1946) by David Rousset (whose son Pierre Rousset was a colleague of Vilar at *Rouge*). See *Concentrationary Imaginaries: Tracing Totalitarian Violence in Popular Culture*, ed. by Griselda Pollock and Max Silverman (London: I. B. Tauris, 2015), and *Concentrationary Memories: Totalitarian Terror and Cultural Resistance*, ed. by Griselda Pollock and Max Silverman (London: I. B. Tauris, 2014). Cabaret Voltaire was a Sheffield band named after the famous Dadaist nightclub in Zurich.
35. In fact in 1981 it was mainly incorporated as a private courtyard into a new upmarket block of flats, as photographs on a contemporary blog make clear, which, as many of the comments below the images point out, is in itself eloquent, in the shift from public to private, of the economic forces at work <http://paris-bise-art.blogspot.com/2014/10/le-passage-des-singes.html> [accessed 28 March 2019].
36. See Roland Barthes, 'Structure du fait divers', in *Essais critiques* (Paris: Seuil, coll. Points, 1964), pp. 188–97; Franck Évrard, *Fait divers et littérature* (Paris: Nathan, 1977); Sheringham, *Everyday Life*; David H. Walker, *Outrage and Insight: Modern French Literature and the 'fait divers'* (Oxford & Washington, DC: Berg, 1995).
37. Evrard, *Faits divers et littérature*, p. 38.
38. Walter Benjamin, 'The Paris of the Second Empire in Baudelaire', in *Selected Writings*, IV, 41.
39. The killings happen outside the Café de la Rotonde.
40. Antoine Compagnon, *La Seconde Main ou le travail de la citation* (Paris: Seuil, 1979).
41. See Gérard Genette, *Palimpsestes: la littérature au second degré* (Paris: Seuil, coll. Points, 1992), pp. 58–68, for his discussion of Queneau, Perec, and Oulipo and their transformational work on a primary text.
42. Mary Ann Caws, *The Art of Inference: Stressed Readings in Verbal and Visual Texts* (Cambridge: Polity & Basil Blackwell, 1989).
43. René Micha, 'Étant donné *Étant donnés*', in *Marcel Duchamp: tradition de la rupture ou rupture de la tradition*, Colloque de Cerisy, ed. by Jean Clair (Paris: Union générale d'éditions, coll. 10/18, 1979), pp. 177–80. Vilar included this volume in recommended reading: 'Le grand Duduche mis en colloque! On aura tout vu' [The great Duduche in a colloquium! Now we've seen everything', in 'Essais', *Rouge*, 897 (14–20 December 1979), 20.
44. Vilar, 'Cher Nestor Burma', p. 119; *NC*, p. 292.

CHAPTER 3

❖

Paris Crime Scenes I: The Imaginary City

It has often been noted that Vilar displays an extensive knowledge in relation to Paris, a city that is both setting and engine for the majority of his novels and short stories. 'Paris is the principal subject of his literary works, the enigma of his numerous novels on the city' reads the rationale for his contribution to *Paris perdu*, a major volume bringing together economic, historical, environmental, architectural, and art historical analyses of the dynamics and the consequences of the extensive changes to the fabric of the buildings and *quartiers* of Paris since the 1950s.[1] Vilar's erudition is part of the way he forges his way through the city, but he is still, knowingly, walking in the footsteps of others on paths he has not invented.[2] He is one of the Paris pedestrians ('piétons de Paris'), in Léon-Paul Fargue's famous phrase, one who walks frequently at night, like the surrealists, and who knows all about Baudelaire's *flâneur*.[3] One important dimension of the Paris that Vilar is charting is the subject of Giovanni Macchia's *Paris en ruines*, examining the trope of Paris about to disappear in French literary work on Paris.[4] 'Le vieux Paris n'est plus' [Old Paris is no more], wrote Baudelaire. Eugène Atget set out to photograph the parts of 'le vieux Paris' spared from Haussmann's sweeping changes, and the photographer Charles Marville had earlier been officially commissioned to do the same. *Paris perdu* addresses the huge changes wrought from the 1960s to the 1980s, and which feature strongly too in Vilar's writings. Paris has often been a narcissistic object of study to itself,[5] compounded by the 'museification' of its centre, and the extremely successful exhibition at Beaubourg in 1981: *Paris-Paris* (a banner for which is seen hanging from the building as the Bachelors take it over) would be a case in point.[6] Paris is at one and the same time a space mediated by language, history, culture, perception, and an imaginary space in the Sartrean sense of an imaginary object, one that exists in the realm of the imagination and is of a different order from its material supports, just as a poem cannot be explained by the quality of ink, paper, and printing process.

'Mon Paris de la nuit est un Paris de l'imaginaire et de l'histoire' [My Paris of the night is a Paris of the imaginary and history], wrote Vilar in *Paris la nuit* (*PN*, p. 11). His neat encapsulation of two of the major dimensions of Paris in his writings structures the approach in this chapter and the next. Like so many critical categories, the separation is a somewhat artificial one: the imaginary and history of

Paris are quite interdependent, together with the conventions of the *roman noir* and tropes of the crime scenes. That said, it is the textual density of the allusive writing on Paris which is the primary focus here, examined in four very different texts: the photobook *Paris la nuit*, 'Paris d'octobre', a story serialised in the newspaper *Le Matin de Paris*, 'Tandem' (1984), a short story in the third issue of *Tango*, and the novel *Bastille-Tango*. The first three deal with a formal challenge: the photobook, serialisation, and, in the case of 'Tandem', the use of the themes of Argentina and the French popular love affair with the bicycle. In all four, political murders, murders of passion, and state massacres are the sombre realities.

'Pour le flâneur, la ville — fût-ce celle où il est né comme Baudelaire — n'est plus le pays natal. Elle représente pour lui une scène de spectacle' [For the *flâneur*, the city — even the one where like Baudelaire he is born — is no longer the land of his birth. It represents for him a stage].[7] The theatrical metaphor is very appropriate for a body of work where the tropes of the 'théâtre du crime' involve the *mise en scène* of photography and art. In the sense of being a staged spectacle for the *flâneur*, it is Paris itself that is the installation. Karlheinz Stierle's magisterial *La Capitale des signes* is a detailed examination of the motif of Paris as city of signs.[8] Starting with the metaphor of Paris as book, it is the hermeneutic city he focuses on, one particularly aligned to crime fiction where the interpretative quest to produce a resolution is central. Roger Caillois's famous comparison of Paris, in his groundbreaking study of the myth of Paris, 'Paris, mythe moderne', to Fenimore Cooper's *Last of the Mohicans*, as a forest of signs to be interpreted by the trackers following these trails of clues, is an early example.[9] Signs need a cryptographer to decode them: Victor fulfills this and other roles in Paris: witness, investigator, and historiographer.

Vilar brings together literature and architecture (writers of 'Paris populaire' such as Eugène Dabit and Henri Calet, the surrealists and mystery writers such as Eugène Sue and Léo Malet, the spaces and buildings of the city), history and film (the events and their actors; Hollywood and the European film from the 1960s: Godard, Wenders, Antonioni) as he walks through a city bristling with signs. The statue of Frédérick Lemaître, famous actor of the 'boulevard du Crime', site of popular *fêtes*, theatre, and crime, reinvented for a new century in Carné's *Les Enfants du paradis* in 1945 (as Victor often points out), stands opposite the statue of the *grisette* (Parisian working girl) by the canal St Martin, where Victor lives. It is one of myriad examples of a spectacle Paris is creating for itself, and of the thematic knots in Vilar's fiction: class, theatre and performance, and crime. As he says, in Paris, everything is connected ('A Paris, tout se tient'). In both his fiction and non-fiction, walking through Paris, particularly at night, is a recurrent theme. Inseparable from his extensive knowledge of the city, it is an intellectual pleasure to be following in the footsteps of writers, particularly the surrealists and the twentieth-century celebrators of working-class Paris. The proliferating links mean the experience of the city is always a multi-dimensional one.

'Paris énigmes' is the title of Vilar's essay for the *Autrement* volume on *Les Vacances* where he sets out the programme of his annual summer holidays.[10] Anticipating aspects of François Maspero's *Les Passagers du Roissy Express* published the same year, he explains that he takes his holidays travelling in Paris, with strict rules: telling everyone he is away, but remaining vague about dates so that chance encounters are not embarrassing; ignoring his mail for the duration, including the postcards he sends home; stocking up on essential supplies (cigarettes, Bourbon, photographic paper, and films for the camera). He sets out on his meticulously planned journey: 'les vacances, c'est le voyage, pas la flânerie' [holidays mean travel, not *flânerie*].[11] He decides on his programme during the long months of *flânerie* the rest of the year, when he maps out possible themes: 'Paris d'Atget ou de Marville? D'Haussmann ou de la Commune? De la révolution, mais laquelle? Paris des voies d'eau? Paris souterrain? Paris d'Hugo, des Goncourt, de Fargue, de Léautaud, de Breton ou Aragon, de Perec?' [The Paris of Atget or Marville? Of Haussmann or the Commune? Of the revolution, but which one? The Paris of waterways? Underground Paris? The Paris of Hugo, the Goncourts, Fargue, Léautaud, Breton, Aragon, Perec?].[12] The photographer-*flâneur* is exploring the range of complex issues that have become familiar in the critical examinations of travel writing: class, difference, otherness and exoticism, gender, stability and instability, past and present, stereotypical views and new imaginings, transgression and criminality. Paris is inexhaustible.

Paris la nuit

A series of large photobooks published from 1981 to 1985, with the title 'Piéton de Paris' in reference to Fargue's classic work, brought together well known photographers and writers; each volume came with a separate guide to the areas mentioned in the text, with maps and information on restaurants and shops.[13] The first volume, *Passages et galeries du 19e siècle*, by Robert Doisneau and the poet Bernard Delvaille, was reviewed by Vilar in *Rouge*.[14] Vilar wrote the text for the fifth volume, *Paris la nuit*, with photographs by Michel Saloff, a young photographer already known for his work on the nightclubs of Paris such as the legendary Le Palace.[15] Several of his photographs, signed 'Michel Saloff-Coste', of the dazzling creatures of the night, including Andy Warhol, can be seen in the section 'Danser sur les décombres' in the *Contre-cultures* exhibition catalogue.[16] A writer of *romans noirs* is hardly a surprising choice either for a text on Paris at night, especially an author of a prize-winning novel where the Paris of the passages is integral to the text, as are the perambulations and arcane knowledge of the photographer-investigator.

Paris la nuit starts with the rue de Nuit, which is logical but misleading; a felicitous, in the circumstances, disappearance, the final letter 's' from the rue de Nuits, introduces a deplorable one: as night falls, Vilar is looking for the rue de Nuit in the Bercy district, a road that was originally named after the côte de Nuits in the Côte d'or region. Bercy was an area of tree-lined streets of wine-cellars named after the wine-producing regions, and the site of the warehouses receiving the wines and liqueurs from France for distribution in Paris. The latter were demolished to build a large sports stadium, some of the former now integrated into a commercial 'Bercy-village'.[17] Vilar was writing in 1982: 'Plus de rue de Nuit, plus la moindre trace. Anéantie la case de départ tellement séduisante de mon Jeu de l'Oie dans le Paris nocturne' [The rue de Nuit is no more, not the slightest trace left. The so very charming square one of my *jeu de l'oie* in nocturnal Paris has been obliterated] (*PN*, p. 8). Night is the theme of this *jeu de l'oie*, one that takes in literature, art, and photography. It starts with Philippe Soupault, organiser of famous Dadaist excursions into the night of Paris: 'Je croyais deviner un but, celui de tous les promeneurs nocturnes de Paris: nous étions partis à la recherche d'un cadavre' [I thought I could guess the goal, the one all night walkers in Paris have: we had set off in search of a corpse] (p. 11). This establishes the final part of the framework of night, death, murder, journey, and game: 'cadavres donc, *cadavres exquis* bien sûr' [corpses then, *exquisite corpses* of course]:

> Le parcours du piéton de la nuit est un jeu dont les règles s'inventent en toute fantaisie, à chaque pas, et où se télescopent souvenirs enfouis et rencontres de hasard, associations d'idées futiles et vraie passion d'amour. Un Jeu de l'Oie en somme, guidé par la seule septième face du dé. (*PN*, p. 11)[18]
>
> [The route of the night-time walker is a game whose rules are invented on a complete whim, with each step, and where buried memories and chance encounters, pointless associations of ideas and genuine passionate love collide. A goose game, basically, guided only by the seventh face of the die.]

And so, as the rue de Nuit leads to the rue du Jour, demolition leads to demolition, for the rue du Jour runs by the demolition site of Les Halles. But the familiar trope of loss and disappearance is here only part of the story. The nocturnal ramble is also a meditation on the politics of space and its illumination in the city, and on the nature and social positioning of the inhabitants of the night.

Vilar's *flânerie* takes him through Montparnasse, Pigalle, and Clichy, the place de la République and the canal Saint-Martin, historic restaurants, high-class brothels, the cemeteries of Père Lachaise and Montparnasse, places in ruins (the passage Colbert), and abandoned places (the gare d'Avron of the Petite Ceinture). The history of the transformation of Paris, and particularly of the introduction of street lighting, gives a political context, that of the reinforcing of order and control in the city, which went together with the introduction of street names and pavements, and the clearing out of the rundown areas of petty criminality known as the 'cours des Miracles'. Policing people and policing space operate in tandem in subtle and unsubtle ways. The Sacré Cœur, built after the Commune, is a glaring example of the defeat of the working class being celebrated by state and Church ('la pâtisserie du Sacré Cœur m'offense' [Sacré-Cœur, the pastry cake church, offends me], *PN*, p. 37). A similar logic operates in the night-time illumination of the great monuments of Paris: 'Lumières — mise en ordre — mise en scène d'une mémoire' [Lights — ordering — staging of a memory] (p. 35). For the victims of the offensive sugary concoction on the hill, the last monument in Paris to turn off its lights at night, there is only darkness:

> Mais, Parisien vivant, et luttant à l'occasion, je constate que s'il y a débauche de lumières pour la première église venue, les édiles n'ont pas trouvé le moindre petit *spot* pour éclairer une fresque de pierre, celle qui rappelle le massacre des

> Communards dans le square escarpé qui longe le Père Lachaise. Rien! Histoire niée! (*PN*, p. 38)
>
> [But, as a living and, on occasion, fighting Parisian, I note that while there is a debauchery of lights for any and every church, the city authorities have not found the smallest *spotlight* to light up a fresco in stone, the one that recalls the massacre of the Communards in the steep square alongside the Père Lachaise cemetery. Nothing! History denied!]

The massacre of thousands of Communards in the 'Semaine sanglante' in May 1871 is not the only crime scene recalled. Vilar remembers a previous walk in the *quartier* where the huge, day-long round-up of Jews took place. On the wall of the Gymnase Japy, not far from Charonne we are told, there is a commemorative plaque:

> Qui rappelle l'horreur: 'A la mémoire des femmes et des hommes rassemblés en ce lieu par milliers le 20 août 1941, ainsi que le 16 juillet 1942 et dont la destination a été le camp d'extermination d'Auschwitz'. La solitude de cette petite plaque me choqua soudain. (*PN*, p. 38).
>
> [Which recalls the horror: 'To the memory of the women and men held in their thousands in this place on 20 August 1941, also on 16 July 1942, and whose destination was the extermination camp in Auschwitz.' The loneliness of this little plaque suddenly shocked me.]

There is no formal record that this was also one of the holding sites where some of the 5,000 Algerians arrested on 17 October 1961 were held, when hundreds were seriously injured or killed in ferocious attacks on a large peaceful demonstration against the imposition of a 5pm curfew: 'Au gymnase Japy, aucune plaque, aucun appel: qui se souvient? C'était pourtant le plus terrible massacre d'ouvriers dans Paris depuis... la Commune. Brouillard sur cette nuit de mémoire' [At the Japy gymnasium, there is no plaque, no call: who remembers it? It was however the most dreadful massacre of workers in Paris since... the Commune. Fog covers that night of remembrance] (*PN*, p. 41). As noted earlier, this memory was tenaciously alive in left-wing and anti-racist organisations;[19] in 1984, Didier Daeninckx would bring awareness of it to a much wider audience with *Meurtres pour mémoire*.[20]

Like Daeninckx, Vilar highlights a continuity of state aggression against those perceived as outsiders: the Jews, the Algerians, and the 'étrangers de l'Internationale — ces immigrés' [foreigners of the *Internationale*, those immigrants] among the Communards (*PN*, p. 38). And once the metro has closed at 1 am, all nightwalkers are transgressive and suspect to the forces of law and order; good citizens are supposed to be in bed before taking the early metro back to work (p. 85).

Saloff's photographs complement perfectly a text devoted to the off-kilter, the uncanny, the attractive yet disturbing nature of Paris at night, like the rue Watt, which Boris Vian and Léo Malet (the anarcho-retro-surrealist) (*PN*, p. 106) have already written about, and which Vilar reaches towards the end of his long walk through 'Paris-Nuit, Paris-Mort, Paris-Noir' [Night-Paris, Dead-Paris, *Noir*-Paris] (p. 105). The rue Watt passes under the railway lines near the Seine, badly lit, filthy, with the trains overhead making a deafening noise ('un bruit d'enfer' [a hellish noise], p. 106). Empty ('pas un chat' [no cats]) and unsettling: 'Qui se cache derrière les colonnes métalliques? Cette ombre? Faut-il se retourner, s'enfuir?' [Who is hiding behind the metal columns? And that shadow? Should I turn back, flee?'] (p. 106), this is one of the gothic spaces of the modern city: 'sale, et très belle, et très inquiétante' [dirty, and very beautiful, and very troubling] (p. 111).

The eighty-six colour photographs of *Paris la nuit* range across famous and little-known views, large scale and small scale, characterised by the dominant use of dull yellows and grey-ish greens.[21] Statues and buildings appear coloured rather than illuminated, with the source of light unclear and often with little variation in intensity. Where there is a street lamp or illumination, it is a point of white intensity that does not radiate beyond itself. Images of bridges across the Seine and the river beneath can only be described as painterly: broad stripes of yellow reach vertically down through the blackness below the bridge, the rippled plane of the water resembling the thick application of paint in horizontal brush strokes on a canvas. Familiar statues of the place de la Concorde or the Tuileries are solid, massive presences in their glaucous colours; we are far from the reassuring luminosity of 'Paris by night'. Saloff himself commented that he wanted to show the grandiose and monumental decor of Paris using its distinctive neon and artificial lighting with exposure times of one to seven seconds, which created strange colours and a dream-like atmosphere.[22] And while one reader disliked them: 'en couleurs (première erreur), un rien clinquantes et abusant des effets de filés' [in colour (first mistake), rather cheap and garish and overusing blurring techniques to suggest speed',[23] Vilar points to the disturbing power of these 'ombres mises à vif' [raw shadows]: 'Quelques-unes des photos de Saloff évoquent pour moi ces documents des services de police au moment du constat, quand on fixe le lieu du *crime* sur pellicule, à fin d'enquête' [Some of Saloff's photographs suggest those documents of the police services, when they make the record, and fix the *crime* scene on film, for the investigation] (*PN*, p. 119). Text and photographs combine to write a gothic *noir* in the darkness, reimagining the night in Paris.

La femme, la mort, Paris

'Tandem', published in the *Les Fous du vélo*, the third issue of *Tango*, blends the theme of the bicycle with cultural references to the writings of the Argentinian novelist Julio Cortázar. André Breton's *Nadja* and *L'Amour fou* haunt many a story of the nocturnal drifting through Paris of a male narrator and a woman of madness and dreams, but so does *Hopscotch*, Cortázar's great non-linear narrative, as well as his short story 'Manuscript Found in a Pocket', where the male narrator chooses to follow a woman on the metro if certain conditions he sets for himself are met.

In front of the statue to Frédérick Lemaître, Victor sees a very beautiful woman dressed in rather old-fashioned clothes holding a small cat. She is called Sybille, 'ce qui naturellement aurait dû m'alarmer, mais non' [which of course should have alarmed me, but no], and her first question is to ask him his star sign (*T*, p. 33). It certainly alerts the reader to the importance of signs, oracles, and fate in the narrative. Sybille's cat, who joins Kamenev, Zinoviev, and Radek in Victor's flat, is called Theodore W. Adorno; she is clearly as steeped in, and generated by, the Frankfurt School as Victor is, as exemplified by the story's epigraph: 'L'image de la femme et l'image de la mort s'unissent dans une troisième image qui est celle de Paris. Walter Benjamin' [The image of woman and the image of death intermingle with a third, that of Paris. Walter Benjamin] (p. 33).[24]

'Paris d'octobre' is a serialised story in the newspaper *Le Matin de Paris*: twenty episodes, one for each of the twenty *arrondissements*. 'Paris est un feuilleton noir' [Paris is a *noir* serial], writes Raymond Pronier in his introduction to the series, explaining the challenge that had been issued to the former journalist: to submit once more to the disciplines of the trade and write the *roman noir* of the Paris *arrondissements* day by day through the month of October and in relation to the news of the day. Deadline: 3pm. This is from the outset a rewriting of great predecessors, Eugène Sue's *Mystères de Paris*, serialised in the *Journal des débats*, 1842–43, and Léo Malet's *Nouveaux Mystères de Paris*, fifteen novels each set in a different *arrondissement*, not forgetting Gérard de Nerval's *Nuits d'octobre*, or *Les Nuits de Paris* by Restif de la Bretonne. Victor evokes a large number of other *piétons de Paris* who have celebrated *le Paris populaire*; the brief article accompanying each episode always starts: 'Paris est un grand roman populaire' [Paris is a great novel of the people], contextualising the issues of the *arrondissement* in question. Signs of all kinds are significant here too, starting in the first episode with a classified advertisement in the personal column of *Le Matin de Paris*: 'Pour Paris d'Oct Victor B. ch. Femme folle de Paris. R.V. mardi et 20 autres jours' [For Paris in October: Victor B. seeks Parisian mad woman. R.V. Tuesday and 20 other days].[25] He receives a reply from 'Lady L'Arsouille'.

In both 'Tandem' and 'Paris d'octobre', a game of references and their links structures the narrative as Sybille and Lady L'Arsouille each present Victor with a challenge, either to identify the meeting places according to the logic of the game, or to identify the logic itself. Fatality and fate are structured into the story from the outset through these femmes fatales. Having declared her love for him, in the cafe where they have listened to tangos on the jukebox and briefly danced in recognition of Cortázar's death the previous day, Sybille sets the parameters of their game, following Cortázar's 'Manuscript Found in a Pocket'. The itineraries of their bicycle rides together and of the sequence of meeting places take them through the *quartier* and surrounding areas — Père Lachaise, the 'boulevard du Crime', the Cirque d'hiver — interspersed with Victor's complex ruminations on the various historical and cultural connections of each, to the next encounter. He comments that she often behaves as if trying to shake off an imagined tail, and the story ends with her death, of course, pursued by armed police who shoot her when she produces her gun. 'Les flics tirèrent les premiers, comme on leur avaient appris à le faire' [The cops fired the first shots, just as they had been taught to do] (*T*, p. 37). Her body floats in the canal. Apart from their game, and the intriguing fact that she carries a gun in her bag, he knows nothing about her, and she is as unstable as she is elusive, resembling now Rita Hayworth in *Gilda*, now Louise Brooks in *Loulou*, now Faye Dunaway in *Bonnie and Clyde*, reinforced by a series of Vilar's drawings of different women illustrating the story, the first unmistakably Lauren Bacall. Sybille is also dispersed and, one might say, multiplied through a proliferation of means of communication: advertisements in the personal column, telegrams, graffiti on buildings, messages on tarot cards: 'Nous nous parlions peu, toute la ville me parlait d'elle' [We spoke rarely, but the entire city spoke to me about her] (p. 37). But then the connection is broken, she is not at the logical point of rendez-vous: 'Je restais jusqu'à la nuit à l'attendre et tout redevint illisible' [I waited there for her until night fell and once more everything was unreadable] (p. 37). She only reappears to meet her violent death below his window. Paris is a forest of signs to be deciphered and interpreted, a book to be read, and Sybille is another scriptor of the space, an interpretative key without which it is unreadable.

The game plays an equally structural role in 'Paris d'octobre', but with a much more complicated set of parameters articulated across its twenty episodes. Lady L'Arsouille responds to Victor's *annonce* in the personal column with a postcard of the Pont Neuf, giving him a rendez-vous in the first *arrondissement*. He watches as she places a bag in the Seine, finding a doll inside that a specialist in the passage Véro-Dodat identifies as a speaking doll produced by Jumeau, a famous nineteenth-century doll maker. A card is pinned under its possibly bloodstained velvet dress: 'Rue Daunou, tomorrow'. Having become a partner in his game, she will now dictate the meeting places across Paris according to a logic he only understands at the end: the Père Lachaise cemetery in the twentieth *arrondissement* where all the individuals who have been named, usually in street names, at the various meeting places, are buried. He wondered at one point why she suggests a meeting at the Théâtre Sarah Bernhardt, using the old name of the Théâtre de la Ville that was removed by the Germans under the Occupation. Once the logic of the game has become clear, he realises it is because in this *arrondissement* there are no street names of individuals buried in the Père Lachaise cemetery, but Sarah Bernhardt is. Le Vieux (Léo Malet's Nestor Burma), whom Victor consults frequently in the course of the story without naming him (although there are enough references to his agency, his hat, and his pipe to make it clear), had worked it out fairly quickly.

The game is therefore structured by death as it converges on the final shootout in the cemetery, just as the narrative is governed by the thematics of the *roman noir*, death, and fate. Paris here is twenty different crime scenes: 'la perspective d'un beau crime par jour s'intègre [...] dans l'idée qu'elle se fait du look femme fatale' [the thought of one fine crime a day fits [...] into her idea of the look of a femme fatale], comments Victor as she exults in the thought of assassinating Soviet leader Gorbachev.[26] She steals back the now mended doll, leaving a stolen Picasso in exchange; in the flat she leaves a Duchamp stolen from a contemporary art exhibition: the unadorned postcard of the Mona Lisa signed by Duchamp and inscribed 'LHOOQ Joconde rasée' [LHOOQ Mona Lisa shaved].[27] Like Fantomas, she comes and goes as she pleases. She proves to be as elusive (or multiple) in appearance as Sybille, with a complete change of look for each meeting, copied as a mannequin at an exhibition where it/she is decapitated and stabbed, and reproduced in various iterations of an identikit portrait that, by the thirteenth *arrondissement*, is finally beginning to look like her. For she is also a quarry, stalked and pursued by various would-be attackers: two punks, a man with a Walkman, a motorbike rider whom she kills with a flourish in the second *arrondissement*, and by the police who want her for murder. Each episode is illustrated by a photograph, the majority attributed to Vilar and featuring in his exhibition in Reims later that month entitled 'Quelques lieux en quête de crime'.

'Et puis, dans Paris, tout le monde suit toujours quelqu'un un peu' [and then, in Paris, everyone is always following someone, to a certain extent], comments Victor having climbed out of the empty canal St Martin in the tenth *arrondissement* where he had fallen escaping from the attentions of 'les petits punks flingueurs' [the little killer punks].[28] His comment is easy to apply to the cultural practice of writing on Paris, with its dense population of walkers, writers, photographers, and fictional characters, as well as the crowds of public figures recorded in street names and buildings who have shaped its cultural identity, and in a genre that in France is so conscious of its own artifice as cultural production (this particular episode is entitled 'Canal Plus', the name of a French television channel). As well as meeting regularly with Nestor Burma, Victor evokes Henri Calet, Pierre Courteline, Fantomas, and Diane Arbus; Lenin and Trotsky playing cards in the Café du Lion in the fourteenth *arrondissement*; Boris Vian singing about la rue Watt in the thirteenth: 'une rue désolée, une rue à crime' [a desolate street, a street for crime] close to the site where 'Le Vieux a jadis dénoué une brumeuse et sale affaire' [the old man once resolved a foggy, nasty affair].[29] In the sixteenth *arrondissement* he meets with his fellow writer and journalist Noël Simsolo to discuss a programme on Atget for France-Culture; having crossed the Pont Bir-Hakeim where Marlon Brando also walked in *Dernier Tango à Paris*, Victor dodges a bullet that kills a pigeon: 'Balle perdue ou référence littéraire? Une fois de plus, c'est la mort d'un pigeon, rue Beethoven' [Stray bullet or literary reference? Once more it's the death of a pigeon, rue Beethoven], *Dead Pigeon on Beethoven Street* being a novel derived from a German television film directed by Samuel Fuller.[30]

Lady L'Arsouille is a descendant of Milord L'Arsouille (the name of a famous Parisian cabaret), a petty criminal associated with the carnivals and fetes held in the open spaces along the 'boulevard du Crime', and often confused with Lord Seymour Conway, half-brother of Lord Richard Seymour Conway. Richard Conway's illegitimate son Richard Wallace, of Wallace Collection fame, endowed Paris with fountains, one of which Lady L'Arsouille steals and leaves for Victor outside his door. In Paris, everything is connected: 'Paris d'hier, Paris d'aujourd'hui tout se mélange [Yesterday's Paris, today's Paris, it's all mixed together], explains le Vieux.[31] An allusion to Cortázar's *Hopscotch* in 'Tandem' adds another way of reading the city; children have drawn the game on the pavement outside Victor's building: 'c'était presque trop mais nous vivions des temps de crise et aucune précaution n'était à négliger' [it was almost too much but we were living in a time of crisis and no precaution should be neglected] (*T*, p. 34). *Hopscotch* is renowned for its non-linear narrative: two different orders in which the chapters might be read are suggested, and the reader can also construct their own, rendering explicit the active role of reading in the construction of the text, a fortiori in the construction of Paris as the reader strolls through it. *Hopscotch* is recognised as a precursor of the hypertext, an appropriate metaphor for these referentially-structured fictions full of connecting links that inflect the direction of the story. Paris is a vertiginous, citational space, a space of the imaginary appropriated by novelists and filmmakers, one that can be scratched to reveal its secrets.

Bastille-Tango

Vilar's writings could be cited as documentary evidence of the extent to which Paris underwent some very rapid changes in the 1980s and 1990s. The drastic changes to the place de la Bastille and Bercy are themes that recur across Vilar's texts; Raymond Pronier and others give an even fuller picture in their half page articles.[32] The description of Bercy in 'Paris d'octobre' and *Paris la nuit*, is revealing: part of the site has been cleared for the construction of the new Stade omnisports; Victor and Lady L'Arsouille regret the ugly construction, but continue on to the little tree-lined streets of wine cellars, and enter the abandoned Auberge de la pomme d'or. In 'Paris désolé', published ten years later, Vilar reacts to the destruction of the whole site, including the famous *auberge* that provokes his final comment that he is tempted by exile, the strength of which can be measured when juxtaposed with Victor's frequent comments that he could not exist outside Paris. If some slippage between Victor and Vilar is permissible at this point, one might say that the comment on the rue Watt — 'une rue désolée, une rue à crime' [a desolate street, a street for crime] — could be applied to Paris itself in 'Paris désolé', where not only Paris, but the observing self is swept away by the criminal destruction.[33]

If there is one word to link the various themes of *Bastille-Tango*, Vilar's fifth *roman noir* published in 1986, it is *disparition*, with its double meaning of disappearance and death, and, in the Argentinian context, state murder. Disappearances here relate to the German Occupation, the Algerian War, the iconic buildings on the place de la Bastille, the 'disappeared' of Argentina during the rule of the military, and the deaths and murders that occur throughout the novel as an Argentinian hit squad pursues exiles to stop them testifying at the trial of nine senior military personnel of the junta years.

Set in 1984–85, *Bastille-Tango* opens days after the work starts on demolishing buildings on the place de la Bastille to accommodate a new opera house being built as part of the bicentenary celebrations in 1989. The old Bastille railway station, long unused, and the Paramount cinema (formerly the Lux) will disappear, and a restaurant, La Tour d'Argent (carefully distinguished from a very expensive and exclusive restaurant of the same name in the fifth *arrondissement*) demolished and its façade rebuilt a few metres away. In 'Paris désolé', Vilar's criticism is not that buildings of architectural merit have been demolished, but that the sense of a *quartier* is destroyed.[34] He also regrets the historical insensitivity that led to the demolition of the Tour d'Argent. The façade was reconstituted because this was the only building remaining on the square that had been there at the time of the storming of the Bastille. However, it is no longer authentically there, since only the name still connects it to the Bastille. For Vilar, something real has been lost in the ending of that living link to history.³⁵ In *Bastille-Tango*, the violence of the process of destruction, as the buildings are reduced to rubble, 'le massacre' as the character Maleo calls it (*BT*, p. 129), is an important part of the narrative.

Bastille-Tango is informed by the internationalist politics of *Rouge*, supporting the Latin American bloody struggles against military dictatorships, and by the cultural politics of the magazine *Tango*: the working-class culture of the right bank with its *bals-musette* and tangos (and the musical culture of Argentina, so many of whose exponents are exiles in Paris), Paris, especially Paris at night, and *Paris noir*, the Paris of death, darkness, paranoia, and madness. The *quartier* of the Bastille provides evocative spaces, such as the passage du Cheval blanc off which leads a labyrinth of courtyards that historically housed artisans' workshops and where several of the characters live and work; and the rue de Lappe, famous in the 1950s and 1960s for its cafes and *bals-dansette* that in the 1980s was being both gentrified, with art galleries moving in, and celebrated for its past with the legendary *bar dansant* Le Balajo at its centre.³⁶ Vilar is one of the writers who contributed to *La Rue de Lappe*, short stories by leading *roman noir* authors with drawings by Eloi Valat, who also contributed many drawings to *Tango*.³⁷ *Bars dansants* in *Bastille-Tango* include Le Balajo, the equally legendary Trottoirs de Buenos Aires, and the fictional La Boca in the passage du Cheval blanc, named after a *quartier* in Buenos Aires associated with the tango, whose Japanese owner, Rita, insists the tango was created in Japan. In the first chapter, Victor takes a photograph combining three elements he has seen on the place de la Bastille during his night-time walk: a poster of a drawing of a naked man undergoing torture, a poster advertising a concert given by Susana Rinaldi, the well-known tango singer, and a brick wall that has caught his eye after studying the torture scene: 'un mur de briques sales, juste à côté, usé, taché d'autres souffrances' [a wall of dirty bricks, just next to it, worn, marked by other suffering] (*BT*, p. 10). His artful composition offers an early configuration of the narrative threads:

> Je photographiai la Rinaldi laissant, dans le coin gauche du cadre, la main crispée de la victime, cramponnée à l'extrémité de l'accoudoir. J'eus cette idée fugace que cet espace de briques ravagées entre ce visage et cette main, entre le cabaret et la cave, était ce que je pouvais saisir de plus pertinent. (*BT*, p. 10)
>
> [I photographed Susana Rinaldi and left the clenched hand of the victim, clutching the end of the armrest, in the left corner of the frame. I had the fleeting idea that this space of severely damaged bricks between this face and this hand, between the cabaret and the cellar, was the most relevant thing that I could capture.]

These are elements that will reverberate through the narrative: physical assault, through torture, rape, and murder, on the bodies of Argentinians; tango as common ground between Argentinian and French popular culture; and the material presence of unglamorous Paris, bearing the marks of the forces of time and change, a vector of narrative in its own right. The juxtaposition of these three fragments generates a narrative of politics in the city, of politics of the city.

Reflection on chance juxtapositions runs throughout Victor's commentary on Paris and on the events of the action, the end of his relationship with the Argentinian exile Jessica and the demolition of the cinema. Another series of questions relates to whether events (the deaths, the road accidents) are accidents or murders. But juxtapositions are also created: Victor has to manoeuvre into position to capture just the hand of the man in the shot. The role of the investigator-enquirer, who sees, who records, who interprets, and crucially, who doubts, is central, for this is a novel that, in a context of the emotional pain and immense suffering of traumatic political violence and personal passions, explores the aporia of sight and knowledge, the epistemological limits of their interactions. What one knows and what one sees are mutually dependent, incompatible, and mutually undermining. There is always a doubt, says Le Soir's cinema expert when asked to pronounce on film snippets of scenes of torture, which he says are images of sadomasochistic pornography (he recognises some of the actors). Images detached from their context become generators of an infinite number of new stories, without the anchoring role of the context, which proves to be very slippery in this novel.

There is a large cast of characters for these interlocking narratives of *quartier* and political murders. Some are familiar: Marc, the editor of *Le Soir*, and Villon the left-wing police officer who seems to have been demoted since the massacre at Beaubourg. The others are mainly Argentinians, some of whom are in political exile from the dictatorship, including Jessica, a former militant activist who is intending to testify at the trial that will open in April 1985, and her brother Julio, the projectionist at the Paramount; Oscar, who put up the posters of the tortured man and, later, one of a naked Jessica being tortured; Edgardo, a tango musician; Ruben, a writer and former Montonéro.[38] Marti, who has been in Paris for much longer, is an artist. They are all living and working in various courtyards (six in total, named after the first six months of the year) of the passage du Cheval blanc. La Boca is one of the important spaces in the novel where they all congregate. The rue de Lappe is another. Ida, who worked in the Paramount cinema when Victor was a child, is a 'semi-clocharde' [virtual beggar] in the area, living outside or, at one point, in Victor's studio. Maleo, a very transparent incarnation of Léo Malet with his pipe, cap, and intention to write *La Méprise de la Bastille* (a novel Malet planned but never wrote), has a kind of bric-a-brac shop and, being much older than the rest, remembers what he considers to be real tango singing in the area, from the music hall star Mistinguett. Other important figures include Jacob, a lawyer working with the political exiles.

If, as is frequently suggested, what is happening to the buildings on the place de la Bastille is a massacre carried out by killers, mass murder seems an appropriate word for the elimination of most of the characters. Edgardo is run over and killed. Julio disappears and Jessica identifies his decapitated corpse in the canal from a tattoo on his shoulder. Jacob is electrocuted when a radio falls into his bath. Ruben shoots himself. Marti and Ida fall totally, and fatally, in love at first sight one evening in La Boca. Because of his passion for Ida, Maleo will kill them both, in the art gallery owned by Jessica's boyfriend Baxter on the rue de Lappe — where Marti's ideal maps of Paris and Buenos Aires are being exhibited — and then kill himself at home, as is discovered much later. Oscar is tortured and murdered by Villon and Jessica. Villon then has a total breakdown, and Jessica dies falling from the top of the Colonne de juillet in the place de la Bastille. Eyewitnesses can only be certain she was alone, unsure whether she lost her balance or jumped. In addition, the words and music of tango songs reinforce the sense of sadness and exile, suffering, violence and pain, and eroticism; each chapter has an extract of a song, mainly by Argentinians in exile in Paris, at its head. For the 'Cour d'avril':

> Comment la nuit a-t-elle pu devenir d'un coup la mort.
> Devenir hurlement
> Devenir sueur et gémissement? (*BT*, p. 201)[39]

> [How has night turned suddenly into death. | Into a howl | Into sweat and groaning?]

For the 'Cour de mai':

> Dans les rues de Trelew et dans les autres rues de ce pays
> Connaissez-vous un seul endroit où ce sang ne coule plus à présent?
> Vos lits n'en sont-ils pas imprégnés, amants? (*BT*, p. 257)[40]

> [On the roads of Trelew and on the other roads of this country | Do you know a single place where this blood is now no longer flowing? | Aren't your beds soaked in it, lovers?]

The fate of Argentina's 'disappeared', as evoked in the image Oscar is plastering over Paris, strikes a chord with both Victor and Villon: 'Si [Oscar] y tenait vraiment, je pouvais enchaîner sur les Escadrons de la Mort ou l'AAA, sur les enlèvements, sur les Ford Falcon, les "disparus". [...] Jessica ou pas. Je sais depuis toujours qu'on disparaît dans les villes' [If [Oscar] really wanted me to, I could go on to talk about the Death Squads or the AAA, with the kidnappings, the Ford Falcons, the 'disappeared'. [...] Jessica or no Jessica. I have always known that people disappear in cities] (*BT*, p. 25).[41] It is difficult to avoid the suspicion that Victor is referring to the Occupation and the deportations of Jews who just disappeared from Paris life. Villon makes it explicit: his mother was hidden in 1942 by a neighbour who was surprised by the reactions around her: 'On arrêtait les Juifs, personne ne voyait rien. Ils disparaissaient, et c'était comme s'ils n'avaient jamais existé' [Jews were arrested, no-one saw anything. They disappeared, and it was as if they had never existed] (p. 114). One of Marti's 'ideal city' maps which fuse Paris and Buenos Aires reinforces the point: 'Marti dessina une place de Mai avec une caserne tout près et vite une autre chose ronde pas loin qu'il appela Vél' d'hiv'' [Marti drew a Plaza de Mayo with a barracks just near and quickly another round thing not far away that he called the 'Vél d'hiv'] (p. 163). Victor and Villon are therefore on a political quest to demonstrate to all what they know to be happening, that after the Occupation, after the Algerian war, people are once again being 'disappeared' on the streets of Paris and the disappearances are again invisible, disguised as accidents and suicides.[42]

Proof of the operation of a death squad led by a man called Ortiz is gathered from a variety of sources including testimony from Julio and Jacob, and is confirmed as much as anything by their deaths. Oscar finally leaves Victor a cassette tape with a full confession: he was one of those who tortured Jessica and he has now given details about the exiles and about Victor to Ortiz, which means Victor is in danger too. Yet

Marc, to whom Victor takes the tape for publication in *Le Soir*, refuses to publish it, on the grounds that there is not one single date or verifiable fact. Unreliability and undecidability hamper all Victor's efforts, as images, statements, and events could be variously interpreted. Do the sections of films that Julio and Victor retrieve from the Paramount display extreme eroticism or extreme suffering?[43] Does the presence of a rather sinister man also searching through the sections of films, who seems to bear a resemblance to Ortiz and who might be Ortiz's brother, confirm that damaging evidence of torture is hidden there? In fact, much of all this unravels: the police had dismissed the hit squad theory in Julio's case in favour of a gang killing. The cinema expert knows Julio as someone who traffics illegal pornography and snuff movies. The lawyer Jacob is not as honorable as had been thought and several exiles were about to remove their cases from him; accidental electrocution is again more plausible. Even the image of the man standing behind Ortiz in the unbearable photographs of Jessica's rape and torture seems less like Oscar once Oscar's story of Ortiz being in Paris is thrown into doubt. Villon remains convinced to the bitter end, his descent into destructive paranoia and obsession underlined by his increasingly dishevelled and filthy appearance, his certainty that his fellow officers' incredulity in the face of the evidence is explained by their politics ('tous fachos') and history (he reminds Victor that it was the French police who arrested the Jews in Paris). Victor realises that Villon has lost touch with reality when he insists Marti and Ida were also hit squad victims; furthermore, Ortiz is proved to be in Argentina, and many of the formerly persecuted are testifying at the trial, quite safely. Proof about the mysterious deaths that have driven the narrative disintegrates.

What remains certain is the reality of the body — of Jessica's scarred and tortured body — and of the erotic encounters, including one between Rita, Jessica, and Victor, an interlude of uncomplicated pleasure. It is through the tango, the fusion of eroticism and suffering, that Jessica expresses the reality of what she has been through. Pushing Baxter away, for failing to match the intensity and ferocity of her dancing, she continues alone:

> Jessica l'ignorait, désormais. Ella dansa quelques secondes ainsi, les yeux clos, murée dans le grand silence du tango, évoluant, tendue et nerveuse, seule comme jamais. Le bandonéon reprit souffle, l'accompagna, attentif, inquiet.
>
> Un instant, je crus qu'elle allait continuer. Qu'elle allait jeter ses chaussures, se défaire de sa robe sous laquelle elle était évidemment nue et danser comme cela, exhibée et farouche comme elle m'avait dit une nuit qu'elle aimerait faire, nue et obscène pour le tango. 'Obscène jusqu'au bout, avec mon sexe et mon cul violés, avec les traces de brûlures de cigarettes sur mon ventre, avec ma peau fatiguée, usée. Faire ça pour moi, pour exorciser.'
>
> Jessica s'immobilisa, vacilla. J'eus peur. Elle resta ainsi, figée, paumes plaquées sur ses cuisses. Longue prostration. Puis elle se redressa. C'était fini. (*BT*, p. 219–20)
>
> [After that, Jessica took no notice of him. She danced on for a few seconds, eyes closed, installed in the great silence of the tango, moving around, tense and edgy, alone as never before. The bandoneon took a breath again, accompanied her, attentive, anxious.

For a moment I thought she was going to continue. That she was going to throw off her shoes, remove her dress under which she was obviously naked, and dance like that, on show and untamed, as she had told me one night she would like to dance, naked and obscene for the tango. 'Obscene to the end, with my violated sex and arse, with the traces of cigarette burns on my stomach, with my tired, worn out skin. To do that for myself, to exorcise it.'

Jessica stopped moving, then swayed. It frightened me. She stayed like that, frozen, the palms of her hands tight on her thighs. Bent over for a long time. Then she stood up. It was over.]

What becomes increasingly pronounced in Vilar's later novels is tangible here. A sophisticated handling of representation and genre, and its 'contorted political intrigue' in Keith Reader's words, is no barrier to the writing of trauma.[44] The whole novel makes the oscillation between true or false, real or imaginary, diegetically important, pointing to the illusory nature of these dichotomies in multiple ways, and demonstrating that truth is inseparable from the construction of coherence. Nonetheless, Jessica's extreme suffering is powerfully conveyed, as is that of Villon sitting on the floor, rocking, incoherent, next to Oscar's battered body where either he or Jessica strangled him to death in the derelict building where it all ends, as the bulldozers start their attack on the building. '"Tueurs" siffla quelqu'un entre ses dents. Je laissai dire' ['Killers,' someone hissed between their teeth. I paid no attention] (*BT*, p. 365).

Notes to Chapter 3

1. 'Bibliographie des auteurs', in *Paris perdu: quarante ans de bouleversements de la ville*, ed. by Claude Eveno with Pascale de Mezemat (Paris: Carré, 1995), p. 319.
2. Victor is of course frequently circulating through Paris on a bicycle rather than on foot.
3. Léon-Paul Fargue, *Le Piéton de Paris* [1939], suivi de *D'après Paris* (Paris: Gallimard, 1964).
4. Giovanni Macchia, *Paris en ruines*, trans. by Paul Bédarida with Mario Fusco (Paris: Flammarion, 1988).
5. See the comments on Paris and narcissism in Atack, 'Streets and Squares, *quartiers* and *arrondissements*', p. 88.
6. The last in the series of exhibitions on international avant-garde art: Paris-New York (1977), Paris-Berlin (1978), Paris-Moscow (1979).
7. Walter Benjamin, *Paris, capitale du XIXe siècle: le livre des passages*, trans. by Jean Lacoste (Paris: Le Cerf, 1997), p. 361.
8. Stierle, Karlheinz, *La Capitale des signes: Paris et son discours*, trans. by Marianne Rocher-Jacquin (Paris: La Maison des sciences de l'homme, 2002).
9. Roger Caillois, 'Paris, mythe moderne' [1937], in *Le Mythe et l'homme* (Paris: Gallimard, 1972), pp. 150–71.
10. Jean-François Vilar, 'Paris énigmes', *Les Vacances*, ed. by Brigitte Ouvry-Vial and others, special issue of *Autrement*, 111 (January 1990), 19–21.
11. Ibid., p. 19.
12. Ibid., p. 20.
13. Each guide was a small brochure inserted in the photobook. That in *Paris la nuit* is by Anne Lorenzo.
14. Jean-François Vilar, 'Paris mode d'emploi: "Les Passages couverts de Paris" ou "La Lumière de l'insolite"', *Rouge*, 974 (19–25 June 1981), 31.
15. There were six volumes in all. The others were: *Gares et trains* by Marc Riboud and Jacques Réda, *Marchés et foires* by Sabine Weiss and Clément Lépidis, a legendary writer on popular Paris,

Jardins et squares by Edouard Boubat and Bernard Noël, and *Fontaines et bassins* by Janine Niépce and Hubert Juin.
16. *Contre-cultures 1969–1989: l'esprit français*, ed. by Guillaume Désanges and François Piron (Paris: La Découverte/La Maison rouge, 2017), pp. 162, 164–66. The photographs of *Paris la nuit* were exhibited in the FNAC Étoile in October 1982, and a 'réalisation audio-visuelle' exhibition in the Centre Kodak in 1983 <http://michelsaloffcoste.blogspot.com/1982/10/1982-10-30-paris-la-nuit.html> [accessed 26 February 2020].
17. See also Pierre Marcelle, 'Last Exit from Bercy', *Tango*, 4–5 (Spring-Summer 1985), 47–48.
18. 'Cadavres exquis' refers to the surrealist game prosaically named 'Consequences' in English, creating the surreal through the arbitrary juxtapositions; *La Septième Face du dé* [The Seventh Side of the Die] is the title of surrealist Georges Hugnet's book of poems and photographs, with Duchamp's *Why Not Sneeze, Rose Sélavy?* on the cover.
19. See the discussion above, in the Introduction.
20. Didier Daeninckx, *Meurtres pour mémoire* (Paris: Gallimard, 1984).
21. This is the only volume in the series to have no black-and-white photographs. The photographs in the other volumes are mainly black-and-white, with a few in colour.
22. As described on his website (dated 30 May 1983): <http://michelsaloffcoste.blogspot.com/1982/10/1982-10-30-paris-la-nuit.html> [accessed 26 February 2020].
23. <http://lediteursingulier.blogspot.co.uk/2010/09/jean-francois-vilar-paris-la-nuit.html#!/2010/09/jean-francois-vilar-paris-la-nuit.html> [accessed 1 July 2013].
24. The Benjamin quotation comes from *Paris, capitale du XIXe siècle*, pp. 42–43.
25. Jean-François Vilar, 'La Poupée phonographe', *Le Matin de Paris*, 1 October 1985, p.19.
26. Jean-François Vilar, 'Etes-vous fou?', *Le Matin de Paris*, 4 October 1985, p. 13.
27. Jean-François Vilar, 'Le Retour de la Joconde', *Le Matin de Paris*, 9 October 1985, p.16.
28. Jean-François Vilar, 'Canal Plus', *Le Matin de Paris*, 11 October 1945, p. 20.
29. A reference to Léo Malet's *Brouillard au pont de Tolbiac* (1956).
30. Jean-François Vilar, 'Mort d'un pigeon', *Le Matin de Paris*, 18 October 1985, p. 24.
31. Jean-François Vilar, 'Je mourrai', *Le Matin de Paris*, 21 Octobre 1985, p. 26.
32. For the twelfth *arrondissement*, Raymond Pronier, 'Les Finances à Bercy' (*Le Matin de Paris*, 14 October 1985, p.16), outlines the construction of the new offices for the Ministry of Finance; for the fourteenth, Raymond Pronier,'Les Petites Gens et la rénovation' (*Le Matin de Paris*, 16 October 1985, p. 18), presents 'l'heure du coup de balai sur les vieilles maisons et leurs occupants. Car pour "rénover", il a été décidé de détruire' [the moment of the sweeping away of the old houses and their occupants. Because in order to 'renovate', it has been decided to destroy].
33. Jean-François Vilar, 'Rififi rue Watt', *Le Matin de Paris*, 15 October 1985, p. 18.
34. See Keith Reader, *The Place de la Bastille: The Story of a Quartier* (Liverpool: Liverpool University Press, 2011), for discussion of the sense of community.
35. Jean-François Vilar, 'Paris désolé', in *Paris perdu: quarante ans de bouleversements de la ville*, ed. by Claude Eveno with Pascale de Mezemat (Paris: Carré, 1995), pp. 205–19 (pp. 205–06).
36. See Claude Dubois, *La Bastoche: une histoire du Paris populaire et criminel* (Paris: Perrin, 2011) for extensive discussion of this establishment.
37. Jean-François Vilar, 'Le Dernier des apaches', in *La Rue de Lappe* (Paris: Eden Galerie, 1987), pp. 75–100. On handing out a copy of *La Rue de Lappe* in the Bibliothèque nationale de France a few years ago, the librarian exclaimed in joyous recognition at the title that his parents used to go dancing there.
38. The Montonéro movement was an urban guerrilla group in Argentina in the 1960s and 70s.
39. From 'Minuit ici' by Edgardo Canton and Julio Cortázar.
40. From 'Le Chant du coq — gloires' by J. Cedrón and J. Gelman. Trelew is the site of a 1972 massacre of prisoners who had escaped and were rounded up and gunned down at the airport. In the novel, the fictional Jessica is one of the few who survived the shooting.
41. The 'AAA' was the Argentine Anticommunist Alliance.
42. Reference is made to the Moroccan politician Mehdi Ben Barka disappearing from the streets of Paris; reporting to Victor that his colleagues tell him the 'disappeared' do not exist, Villon comments: 'j'ai l'impression d'entendre ce genre de chanson depuis que je suis gosse. A propos

des Juifs. Puis des Arabes' [it feels like I've been hearing this kind of story since I was a kid. About the Jews. Then the Arabs] (*BT*, p. 300).
43. The unsettling photographic negatives published in *Tango* in Vilar's 'Bastille-Opéra' bear the same difficulty. See above, Chapter 1.
44. Reader, *La Place de la Bastille*, p. 141. He also salutes the 'disabused piquancy characteristic of the novel as a whole' created by the juxtaposition of the language of gentrification of the rue de Lappe and the 'laconic bourbon-soaked cynicism of the *roman noir*' (p. 142).

CHAPTER 4

Paris Crime Scenes II: History and Memory

Les Exagérés

>   La Lamballe est morte ici!
> Plus aucune borne, plus de trace de sang. Mais ce coin de Paris sans qualité restait un théâtre du crime. Pour moi du moins. Pour le cinéma? Je n'y connaissais rien. Il n'y avait pas le moindre effort à produire. Rasée ou pas, la prison de la Force était de l'autre côté de la rue. Il ne s'agissait pas d'une reconstitution mentale. La mémoire des rues se moque des souvenirs. Un massacre de septembre était possible dans ce coin de Paris, n'importe quand.
>   (*E*, p. 71)
>
>   [Lamballe died here!
> No marker, no trace of blood left. But this undistinguished corner of Paris was still a crime scene. For me at least. For the cinema? Don't ask me. There wasn't the slightest effort needed. Razed or not, the Prison de la Force was on the other side of the street. Not a case of mental reconstruction. The memory of the street has no needs of reminders. A September massacre was possible in this corner of Paris, any time.]

'La Lamballe' is Marie-Thérèse de Savoie-Carignan, princesse de Lamballe, who died on 3 September 1792. She was a companion, confidant, and, according to some, lover of Marie-Antoinette, stabbed to death by a crowd after a summary judgement in the Prison de la Force, in what became known as the 'September massacres'. Her head was then put on a pike and waved for Marie-Antoinette's benefit outside the window of the room in Le Temple where she was being held. Victor and Adrien Leck, his friend the film director, are standing at the undistinguished street corner where the Prison de la Force once stood, because Adrien is soon to start work on a remake of *La Princesse*, a film of the 1950s about the princesse de Lamballe, that several characters remember from their childhood. While Adrien is drawn to setting his scenes in parts of Paris that appear in keeping with the period, Victor is adamant that it has to be filmed where it actually happened. This is an immediate, deeply lived knowledge requiring neither effort nor imagination, though both will be in play in the course of the novel. The Prison de la Force is materially present in its material absence, a crime scene that is both held in the street's memory and a harbinger of the future.

Les Exagérés (1989) was the first of Vilar's novels to be published in the prestigious Fiction & Cie list edited by Denis Roche. Set in the latter half of 1986, published in the year of the bicentenary of the French Revolution, its complex meditation on history, historiography, and memory is integral to the plot, where crimes of passion are developed in the context of a film about insurrection and massacres being shot in a Paris subject to terrorist attacks. 'Les Exagérés' is the name given to the followers of Jacques-René Hébert, journalist and founder of the revolutionary newspaper *Le Père Duchesne*, and leading protagonist of the insurrection of 10 August 1792 and the Club des Cordeliers. Leck's film will re-enact this insurrection that led to the incarceration of Louis XVI and the proclamation of the Republic on 22 September 1792.

The novel opens in the Musée Grévin, the Paris waxworks museum. Victor has been there every day for the past three months for a personal project, researching the wax models, but he is on familiar territory. His grandmother Judith brought him here regularly as a child, he knows all its nooks and crannies. And he is the one to notice something has changed in one of the tableaux of the Revolution: the head of the princess, usually glimpsed through a window at the back of the display, is missing, stolen, he is sure, for the 194th anniversary of her killing. A disappearance which is followed by others: having had the brilliant idea of replacing the missing head with that of the actress Anna Fried since she had played the princess in the 1950s film — the heads of celebrities whose fame had waned were kept in the reserve — they find that her head is also missing. The heads of the guillotined are just one of the elements circulating through the novel.

The Musée Grévin is a particularly productive site for a novel where questions of historiography, of performance and representation are both thematic and structural components of the story. It houses historical tableaux such as the Salle de la Révolution, as well as models of the celebrities of the day. There is also the Cabinet fantastique, where Georges Méliès gave magic shows, and the Palais des Mirages, a small theatre. A complex building over several floors, with concealed doorways and staircases, it is one of the many puzzle spaces of Vilar's fiction, 'un musée à multiples doubles fonds' [a museum with multiple double drawers] (*E*, p. 116) but one that has given Victor, from a young age, a double view of performance and its production: 'Ici j'avais découvert en même temps le spectacle et ses coulisses, la fascination devant les tableaux et l'accès à leur secret.' [Here I had discovered at the same time the spectacle and the wings, the fascination in front of the tableaux and access to their secret] (p. 114). His grandmother's friend in the museum worked all the special effects in the Palais des Mirages; young Victor watched him at work and heard the surprise and wonder from the audience. Being given a guided tour of the museum by Victor, Adrien comments:

> Une drôle de vision de l'Histoire, tu ne trouves pas? C'est quoi? De belles images édifiantes?
> — C'est là que j'ai commencé, dis-je.
> — M'étonne pas. La scène, la coulisse, la machinerie, les loges et la sortie des artistes, celle de secours qui est souvent la même, la rue... ce n'est pas un mauvais endroit pour se déniaiser. (*E*, p. 116)

['A strange view of History, don't you think? What is it? Fine uplifting images?'

'That's where I started,' I said.

'I'm not surprised. The stage, the wings, the machinery, the boxes and the stage door, often the same as the emergency exit, the street... it's not a bad place to lose one's illusions.']

These anecdotes from his childhood bringing together the spectacle (performance or tableau) and the stage machinery offer a revealing insight into one of the central relations of the novel between appearance and process, as he explains on refusing the offer of salaried employment as a 'grand reporter' travelling the globe for *Le Soir*: 'Le seul grand reportage qui m'intéresse, c'est de savoir comment fonctionne ce coin de Paris, celui-là ou un autre, cette ville tout entière. Bien la voir. Trompe-l'œil y compris' [The only major reporting that interests me is to know how this corner of Paris works, this one or another one, this city as a whole. To see it properly. *Trompe-l'œil* included] (*E*, p. 31). The spectacle of Paris is a multi-dimensional one, visible and invisible, the product of work and being worked on, always a work in progress that is at one and the same time historical, political, and architectural, imaginary and imagined. And also personal: the point of view of the one who looks is of course structural to what is seen.

The Musée Grévin is a crossroads, personal, historical, and theatrical, its connections reaching into film, literature (the mannequin of the young woman adjusting her stocking cited in *Nadja*), and crime (*Histoire d'un crime* was one of its first narrative sequences of tableaux).[1] It also resonates powerfully with the dark, gothic roots of the *roman noir* and the troubling thematics of mortality and crime of its contemporary descendants. Wax and clay mannequins, lifeless and lifelike simulacra, doubles that are always more than an imitation, embody an uncanny presence in their own right. And a death, sometimes. One figure in the museum, the body modelled by Julie, a leading character, and still waiting for its head (Brigitte Bardot), is found brutally mutilated with deep cuts, both a crime and an *annonce*, an advance warning of a crime to come:

> Il y a cette expression usée, le teint cireux des morts. Je sais sa pertinence, j'ai vu quelques cadavres. C'était ça. Un corps cireux, un peu blanc, avec des plaies terribles. Corps décapité, profane, comme l'avait été celui de la princesse que ne tarderait pas à incarner Julie. Dans cette effigie de cire violée se trouvaient réunies beaucoup d'histoires passées et à venir. (*E*, p. 117)

> [There is that worn expression, the waxy complexion of the dead. I know how close it is, I've seen a few corpses. That was it. A waxy body, rather white, with dreadful wounds. A decapitated body, profane, as had been the body of the princess that Julie would soon be bringing to life. In this effigy of violated wax many stories, past and future, were brought together.]

Death masks, modelled heads, wax, clay, and wooden bodies are sites of intersection and supports for the historiographical and emotional lines of the narrative.

The plot is as intricate as the multiplicity of these elements suggests. Arriving at the Musée Grévin, Victor sees Jérôme making a mannequin for a Bardot figure, with Julie as the model. In the next chapter, Victor wakes up in a strange bed, after a fairly drunken party that Jérôme took him to. He is in Mona's bed, in the flat she shares with Julie, her twin sister, and later meets Stan (Stanislas Fried), a tramp-like individual who turns out to be the son of Anna Fried. He learns Adrien cast Julie as Lamballe after he saw her on stage as Lucile Desmoulins in Büchner's *Danton*, and the main story in the novel turns around the making of the film. The actor cast as Hébert drops out through injury, and Victor is roped in to replace him. Mona is cast as a woman in the crowd, a 'femme du peuple', who heckles and harangues Lamballe as the royal family and their entourage are taken on 10 August from the Tuileries to the Assemblée. Like the museum, the film carries important emotional aspects of the novel — Anna Fried's bitter resentment of the remake and Mona's dislike of her sister both have serious consequences — as well as being a focus of interrogation for questions of representation and historiography.

In *Bastille-Tango*, Jessica sardonically comments that Victor will no doubt end up as a Paris tour guide. In *Les Exagérés*, where the relations of past and present are even more complicated and tangled, Adrien has the impression that Victor has been revising the night before, as he explains the finer points of historical detail of the restaurant, Le Robespierre, where they are meeting for lunch. Victor's remarkable erudition when it comes to the politics, history, and architecture of Paris, is one of the ways that *Les Exagérés* twists together history and memory in its evocation of the past in the present. Victor's commentary throughout the novel makes clear the heterogeneous nature of the presence of the past, through commemoration, architecture, and the archive, each of which involves a range of practices.

The forthcoming state commemoration of the bicentenary is the reason for Adrien's film; a wealthy devotee of his work wants to give him the financial means to produce a film that will be commercially successful. Adrien's focus on the events of 1792 is, however, in direct opposition to the official celebration, arguing that 1789 was the end of the *Ancien Régime* and the shift towards a constitutional monarchy, whereas it was the insurrection of 10 August, the 'grande date refoulée' [great repressed date] (*E*, p. 67), that led to the proclamation of the republic and the execution of the king. The Musée Grévin and the various plaques on the walls of Paris, idiosyncratic in their choices as they are, embody another form of commemoration, as do the efforts of enthusiasts — while there is no 'comité pour la defense de la mémoire de la Princesse de Lamballe' [committee for the defence of the memory of the princesse de Lamballe] (p. 32), there are certainly others. Commercial interests also stage history: Le Robespierre is in the partially reconstructed house of the Duplay family where Robespierre stayed from July 1791 until his death, and has a range of artefacts, including a head, displayed around the dining area where Robespierre-themed dishes are served (p. 64). And Victor is an avid collector of the tourist trinkets and souvenirs sold at the museum. Libraries and bookshops are equally important sites: Victor spends days in the Bibliothèque historique de la ville de Paris during the shooting of the film, and plunges into second-hand and specialist bookshops to gather material, including any books, images, and postcards, that he can find on Anna Fried in her heyday. He frequently consults the famous volumes by Jacques Hillairet on the streets of Paris.² To this can be added an original sheet from *Le Père Duchesne*, a gift from Stan, and Victor's many quotations of Hébert's words. His work in the archives allows him to map the layout of many important buildings — Marat's printing press for example — when they only partially remain, and he is continually searching for others, such as Hébert's home, and the workshop of Curtius, maker of wax figures and uncle of Marie-Thérèse Grosholtz, better known as Madame Tussaud, pleasingly locating it on the boulevard du Temple, otherwise known as the 'boulevard du Crime'. Even more pleasing is the fact that Madame Tussaud, having left both France and Monsieur Tussaud and travelled around England, finally settled in London, in Baker Street. Sherlock Holmes is a passion Victor shares with Stevenson, the friend his grandmother used to visit at the Musée Grévin, operator of the machinery of magic tricks and sculptor of the fine figure of Anna Fried that has disappeared (the body as well as the head, it transpires). Stevenson's room is overflowing with Holmes memorabilia (yet another mode where history and memory, erudition and commerce intersect) and he is delighted that Victor has failed to note discrepancies in Conan Doyle's use of a simulacrum and a wax model of Holmes in stories after Holmes's supposed death at the Reichenbach Falls.

If the spectacle of history is staged in these multiple modes, the complexity of the staging, as both spectacle and narrative, is then also engaged in the main plot as well as its byways, such as the Sherlock Holmes mysteries. The spectacle appears unified and seamless, but behind the scenes we witness a machinery of multiplicity and contingency. Copies proliferate: the historically famous characters copied by models and by celebrities, in the past or more recently, are further mirrored in the actors and characters in the film (Anna and Lamballe, Julie and Lamballe, Lamballe and 'la femme du peuple', Julie and Mona, who will take over Julie's role at the end). Script production is fraught with tension: Joachim, the script writer, produces script after script, battling with historiography (none of the historians agree on what happened, he complains) and with the director as Adrien rejects Joachim's efforts and also rewrites across his own profusion and confusion of notes. As in these filmic spaces, so in life outside: reworking and reinvention are the norm, as first Victor then Stan visit the 'marchand de cannes' [walking stick shop] (a nod to Aragon's *Paysan de Paris*), as Anna's life offers a complex replay of *Sunset Boulevard*, and as Victor's metacommentary underlines the labyrinth of chance and necessity. Late at night, fed up with the multiplying messages on the answerphone and endless trails of clues, he stares at his own wall of notes, 'les portraits, les plans, les parcours épinglés au mur' [the portraits, the maps, the trajectories pinned to the wall], and points to the irrationality being played out in all this: 'Aucune leçon à attendre. Seulement un recoin de folie douce à découvrir. Qui m'amusait' [No lesson to be expected here. Just a little corner of gentle madness to find. Which amused me] (*E*, p. 202).

This is not so much an instance of reflexive fiction as one that refracts endlessly across its surface and across other surfaces. Victor never fails to be amused either by the distorting mirrors in the museum's Grotte des singes, but it is the Palais des mirages that captures more precisely the dazzling interplay and infinite regress of narrative surface and depths:

> On ouvrit les portes du Palais des Mirages. Une salle octogonale, avec, à chaque angle, des statues exotiques montées sur des cylindres tournants. Les murs étaient tapissés de miroirs multipliant à l'infini tout ce qui se présentait dans leur champ. Il suffisait de tourner les colonnes, de faire descendre des cintres quelques éléments de décors, de jouer subtilement des éclairages: on était dans un temple à Bali, dans une forêt enchantée, ou dans les jardins de l'Alhambra. (*E*, pp. 111–12)

> [The doors of the Palais des Mirages were opened. An octagonal room with, in each corner, exotic statues mounted on moving cylinders. The walls were lined with mirrors multiplying to infinity everything in their field of vision. All they needed to do was to turn the columns, lower pieces of scenery, introduce subtle changes to the lighting and you were in a Bali temple, an enchanted forest, or the gardens of the Alhambra.]

Les Exagérés is not just an *exercice de style*. The experience of death by anticipation is terrifying, be it by the relegation of one's model to the *réserve* for Anna, a brutal sign of the end of her years of beauty and fame; seeing one's death simulated in the stabbing of a mannequin body double, as Julie did; or undergoing the simulacrum of an assassination by guillotine, as Victor does in his role of Hébert, or by the murderous violence of the crowd, experienced by Julie as the princesse de Lamballe. Personal and family memory is also a powerful factor. Having discovered Stevenson's connection to his grandmother Judith and his own past, Victor visits him in hospital and cries on reading, after his death, the letter 'un grand-père adoptif trop parfait' [a too perfect adoptive grandfather] has left for him (*E*, pp. 343, 344). Recalling his visits to the museum as a child, he lists each separate memory, starting 'je me souvenais', the Perecian echoes no doubt intentional (p. 40).[3] Judith was an immigrant to Paris, which she embraced with rapture, communicating her enthusiasm to Victor. Her husband died in the camps — no further details are given, but it is difficult not to be reminded of the Holocaust when Victor shudders at the sight, for he does see it, of the victims of the September massacres, the pile of naked bodies on a Paris street.

The denouement reveals how far love and hatred have been driving events. Stevenson and Anna stole her head and body, which he lovingly restored, from the *réserve*; he was furious at such shabby treatment and Anna utterly refused to acknowledge this kind of death by disappearance of her own self at her most beautiful. Stan stole Lamballe's head, in order to replace it with a finer copy, Grosholtz's original, by way of apology for the theft from the *réserve*. Filial duty towards his now mad mother drives him finally to destroy the completed film.

Intimations of mortality and fear of inevitable death are threaded through this story of decapitations and massacres, of murders and their simulacra. The relationship between Victor and Anna, who not infrequently have talked whole nights long on the phone, ends disquietingly in his empty studio at night. Anna is present, but dispersed across mechanical and mechanically achieved simulacra: images of her pinned to his walls, photos he has taken of her in the film *La Princesse*, her wax model which he now owns and is caressing, and her voice on tape saying: 'Une nuit, il n'y aura plus que mon image, et vous, et moi, moi absente' [One night, there will be nothing more than my image, and you, and me, and me absent] (*E*, p. 344).

Past, Present, and Future: Hopscotch and Goose Games[4]

Police officer Villon is in a bad way in *Les Exagérés*. Sacked by the police after a trial for murder, shunned as a torturer by his left-wing colleagues, shunned by his right-wing colleagues for having killed a fellow officer (not the most obvious descriptor for Oscar, torturer to the junta, but certainly one that places the right-wing officers very firmly on the right), he spends his days in one dingy room playing a computer game, his only excursion for a long time being to a psychiatrist, a condition of his extremely lenient sentence. Victor visits him regularly, this 'loser ontologique' (*E*, p. 185) as he calls him, accompanies him outside when he is working to overcome his agoraphobia, and listens to his achievements as he progresses through the game of *La Cité* (p. 75). It involves working one's way through a maze of streets and rooms with the aim of getting to the end before losing all one's lives: a *mise en abyme* of the city as puzzle, shifting and changing around a little figure as it moves forward. It offers one way of reading Paris in these texts, as a three-dimensional labyrinth of multiple spaces of all kinds, including the imagined, the imaginary, the fictional, and the historical, all to be negotiated on pain of death. The citational structure of *Étant donnés* opens out to the whole city. It triangulates well with the constant invocation of the *jeu de l'oie* and Cortázar's *Hopscotch*, where, as we have seen, non-linearity shakes the narrative elements into multiple possible configurations. Paris is not so much a book as a game book, a complex landscape of buildings, people, texts, and events that Victor has to work his way through in order to follow and identify and construct a coherent pathway through it. The *jeu de l'oie*, a game of movement and chance on a structured board, recurs as an expression of the logic that Victor — as gamester, character, narrator, and metafictional commentator — tries to puzzle out, piecing together narrative fragments, places, or events, as so many 'squares' that may or may not be pertinent. And it is at the metafictional level that the game is mobilised to remind us that narrative space and narrative time are inextricable. As in *Bastille-Tango*, where the names of the courtyards ('janvier', 'février', and so on) provide the chapter headings indicating the months of 1985 as they move towards the trial in April and beyond, the chapter headings in *Les Exagérés* follow the order of the tableaux in the Salle de la Révolution in the Musée Grévin (*E*, p. 148). It is like a moebius strip where three-dimensional spaces and narrative time collapse seamlessly into one another as we progress, knowing they are also squares on the one-dimensional board, the individual logic mapped out by each *jeu de l'oie*.

While the novels' coherence, and their magnificent readability, rely on many features of realist fiction and the generic sensibility of the contemporary *roman noir*, the non-linearity of the games of narrative logic builds on the relationship between chance and necessity familiar from the surrealist trope of *le hasard objectif*. In this profoundly historicised account of Paris, the relationship between space, time, and narrative is thematised as a disruptive one, with sudden deviations in space and with present, future, and past entangled in a range of different processes, not least that of photography, and thus aligning Vilar's framework with Walter Benjamin's conceptualisation of history — Benjamin being a constant point of reference in this textual thematics.

'Cher Nestor Burma', the letter from Victor to Léo Malet's detective, mentions several different kinds of spatial and temporal turbulence as part of the fabric of Paris, such as the discontinuities of the flux and reflux of its multiple histories:

> Il suffit de gratter un peu, de prendre le vent de la rue et toutes les histoires reviennent. Elles s'inventent, se renouent. Et ce ressac va tellement vite, frappe tellement fort, qu'on se sent forcé de faire face, de continuer le jeu.[5]

> [You just have to scratch a little, take the measure of the street and all the stories return. They invent themselves, they all join up. And this violent countermovement goes so fast, strikes so hard, that one feels forced to face it, to continue the game.]

The fusion of producer and performer in the person of the *flâneur* in the co-presence of street and film set, in front of the Hôtel du nord,[6] is one example: 'Le coin est encore plus beau que dans le film. Il est tard. Il fait nuit. Nous sommes devant *et* derrière la caméra. On y est vraiment et c'est à nous de jouer' [This part is even more beautiful than in the film. It's late. It's dark. We are in front of *and* behind the camera. We're really there, and it's our turn to play].[7] Or the dislocations of time attendant upon the coming to life of surrealist realities and metaphysical dreams, and the tenacious commitment to certain indelible marks of history:

> Car nous sommes des rêveurs tenaces, des guetteurs vigilants. Nous trouverons toujours de séduisants cadavres alanguis au milieu des mannequins raides du passage du Caire. Ils ne nous blufferont pas avec le Centre Omnisport de Bercy, qu'ils n'osent même plus appeler 'Vél' d'Hiv' parce que notre manière à nous d'avoir nos montres à l'heure fait que parfois les choses s'arrêtent certains jours de 1942. Nous savons où est la rue aux Lèvres, celle aussi de Tous les Diables.[8]

> [For we are tenacious dreamers, vigilant watchers. We will always find seductive languid corpses in the middle of the stiff mannequins of the passage du Caire. They will not deceive us with the Centre Omnisport of Bercy, that they do not dare to still call the 'Vél d'Hiv', because our way of keeping our watches accurate means that sometimes things stop on certain days in 1942. We know where the rue aux Lèvres is, as well as the rue de Tous les Diables.]

In line with Benjamin's comment on the photographer at the crime scene, the descendant of the augurs, forensically examining it for future crimes, photography in Vilar's fictions is temporally hybrid: a record of the past, a record to be read and deciphered for future actions or knowledge. Photography operates across a complex schema: to photograph is to work in the mode of the future anterior, of what will have been. The image that results from the technical process reveals what was, the 'ayant été', and what was not apparent or was even invisible, as in Cortázar's story 'Blow-up' ('Las babas del diablo') where the photograph reveals a very different story from the one just witnessed. In 'Tandem', Sybille's use of tarot cards reinforces the thematics of deciphering signs and puzzles for future actions and destinies, just as Victor pores over his photographs of the day to discern the systems and logics at work, to deduce where he should go the following day.

As photographer and *flâneur*, Victor is central to the process of historicisation. Kristin Ross writes that mysteries 'are woven into the interaction of the narrator's consciousness with the texture of the city', and 'his *trajet* [...] serves as the structure for a whole network of interrelated histories'.[9] He is also a collector of objects, images, memories, histories, and fictions, demonstrating that the fictional is indeed structural to Paris: 'Le Paris de tous les jours est réellement épais de toutes ces fictions-là' [Everyday Paris really is thick with all these fictions], wrote Vilar of the Hôtel du nord and the boulevard du Crime in *Les Enfants du paradis*, just as fictional figures, Michel Poiccard, Maigret, Nestor Burma, Nadja, take their place alongside historical ones such as Kiki de Montparnasse, or Lenin and Trotsky playing cards and drinking coffee in the Café du Lion.[10] Victor's Paris is, like Stan's rooms in the Palais Royal with its crowd of full-size mannequins of Revolutionaries, alive with figures of many different eras, a mobile space of changing buildings and artefacts. A collection is changed by what is added to it; his reading in the archives and of his bookshop purchases open new perspectives and new lines of enquiry to be followed. And in his eclectic collection of objects, texts, images, stories, events, and anecdotes, the raw material of historiography, where fiction also has epistemological value, juxtapositions and trajectories forge relationships that owe little to linearity or chronology.

Benjamin's complex reflection on past and present, and his conceptualisation of the relations between them, famously rejects traditional historiography, the quest for 'how things really were', the modelling of history as an evolutionary progress through 'homogenous empty time'.[11] Victor's rejection of the 'patrimonial' tradition of 1789 in favour of the repressed history of the insurrection and proclamation of the Republic in 1792, his juxtaposition in the present of the 1986 terrorist attacks and the 1792 massacres are Benjaminian in inspiration: 'Le passé téléscopé par le présent' [Telescoping the past through the present].[12] Of Lenin and Trotsky's conspiratorial meeting in Paris in the 1920s, Victor remarks: 'Un temps que je n'ai pas connu mais qui est quand même le mien' [A time I haven't known but which is nonetheless mine].[13] Like the hero of Cortázar's story 'The Other Heaven' ('El otro cielo'), who moves seamlessly between 1930 and 1870 in the Parisian passages, Victor walks through a kaleidoscope of temporal 'fragments'. It does not always include a physical presence: the old Café du Lion is now something cheap and modern, 'un rade clinquant' [a cheap and gaudy bar].[14] The old political press next door has gone. If it is not easy to work out where they once were, it does not matter: 'Qu'importe car, d'une certaine manière, *tout est encore là*' [No matter, because, in one sense, *everything is still there*].[15] The *flâneur*-historiographer actualises the political past in his political present.

The *roman noir* of the 1980s is well known for grappling with politics and history in the wake of the post-68 *néo-polar*. A major strand of the cultural politics of the 1970s was the revisiting of the years of the German Occupation and the Vichy government, from new academic archival analysis to popular culture. The *mode rétro*, a term given originally to films that undermined binary moral judgements about fascism and Nazism with a sexualised nexus of sado-masochism and desire, and that turned clear-cut differences into ambiguous complicities, soon embraced novels and films that took French behaviour and relations with the occupier as their subject. As has been noted, Vilar wrote lengthy reviews of some key works for *Rouge*, and references to Jewish experiences appear in all his novels. The scandal of the deportations of Jews from Paris became increasingly prominent through the 1980s.

Didier Daeninckx's *Meurtres pour mémoire* is an iconic text of the period, using the structures of the *néo-polar*. Cadin, a police officer, investigates the murder of a young man in Toulouse. The solution involves a further investigation of events on 17 October 1961, the murderous police attack on the Algerian demonstration in Paris, and of the deportations of Jews from Toulouse during the Occupation. The same senior government official was directly involved and responsible for both, and for arranging the murders that Cadin investigates, committed to prevent his past actions becoming public knowledge. The model of collective national repression of the painful memories of the Occupation years is thus overlaid with active state suppression of knowledge about state crimes. The figure of the detective-historian is now centre-stage, and in Cadin's case, reading the signs in Paris that point to the occulted past. At the end of the novel, he sees a torn poster in the metro, under which a notice announces the deportations of Jews. Even though it is not authentic, amending an anti-communist poster of 1941, it is still a powerful metaphor for buried history, and for the cover-up of state crimes on the streets of Paris.[16]

There has been extensive academic analysis of the complex modelling, in films, novels, memoirs, and so on, of what is usually represented as a brutal return of deadly truths. Henry Rousso's ground-breaking *Le Syndrome de Vichy*, published in 1987, offered a detailed analysis of the 'memory work' of Vichy across the post-war decades, setting this firmly within the context of a psychological syndrome, as public debates about Vichy are framed by terms such as 'incomplete mourning' and 'repressed memories'. His analysis also incorporated a post-Barthesian study of public discourse as myth, standing in the place of the displaced material. Richard Golsan wrote of 'bombes à retardement', Charles Forsdick of the 'oubliettes de l'histoire'.[17] More recently, Max Silverman has taken the metaphor of the palimpsest to read in detail a range of films and fictional texts where the hidden material of the past 'shows through' the later surfaces as a result of a variety of voluntary and involuntary processes, as with Daeninckx's multi-layered image of the torn poster in the metro.[18] Michael Rothberg has proposed the notion of 'multi-directional memory' to address the complex relationships between memories of different pasts, whereby memories are seen to unlock rather than displace or further cover up the memory of radically different painful events.[19]

Vilar too is handling a very diverse range of memories in his works, from the Revolution, the Commune, the 'Semaine sanglante', the inter-war period of Stalinist/Trotskyist conflict, Jewish deportations from Paris and the Holocaust, and the Algerian War, material that is interwoven with references to large numbers of artists and writers and their works. Benjamin used the image of a pair of scales to represent the relation between past and present, the former on one side, with a large mass of fragments and details, the latter on the other side with two or three heavy weights.[20] The past in Vilar's work is certainly characterised by a proliferation of detail, which in itself distances it somewhat from existing frameworks of past/present and memory, in that it is not so much past actions as the evidence and knowledge of the past that are the focus.

The metaphor of the palimpsest occurs regularly in Vilar's writings ('il suffit de gratter un peu'). But as we have seen from the discussion of the citational structure and *Étant donnés*, these texts are more citational than palimpsestic, in keeping with Compagnon's metaphor of the mosaic.[21] The layering of the palimpsest implicit in the multiple levels of the constructed city, or the scratching at a surface, is an important aspect within this wider process. Nevertheless, the use of citation and fragment is the primary historiographical methodology here: what dominate in Vilar's texts are the jigsaw puzzle of fragments, the coincidences and juxtapositions of 'objective chance', and the citational structure of *Étant donnés*, one that is fundamental to the small and large spaces of buildings and cities. The citation, the element prised from its context as a way of escaping the continuities of historicism, facilitates the intricate telescoping of past and present in a range of fictional and non-fictional discourses in Vilar's work. While the proliferation of detail and fragment is found on both sides of the scales here, unlike for Benjamin, there is an underlying political constant for each, which is not an organisational principle but a continuity of political oppression. What the Parisian landscape reveals, from the introduction of street lights to the massacres of the Commune or the Algerian war, is the imposition of order, the 'mise au pas' (the compulsory 'falling into line') of the working class who are controlled and shunted around in the reordering of the topography of Paris's streets and buildings in the nineteenth and twentieth centuries, where they are so often brutally murdered.

The insistence upon the importance of the exact place of past crimes — *c'était là* — in extant or long disappeared sites may seem to contradict the affinity with Benjamin's historiography, given the latter's rejection of the search for 'what really happened'.[22] But the crime scene is an integral part of the structure in the *roman noir* and, unlike those of Atget (in Benjamin's view), Victor's crime scenes are always peopled, he sees the pile of bodies outside the Prison de la Force, any body floating in the canal embodies all those victims of previous massacres and assassinations, and the *téléscopage* is not restricted to historical crimes. Walking along the rue Watt, thinking of Nestor Burma, Boris Vian, and Lenantais (murdered there in Malet's *Brouillard au pont de Tolbiac*), Victor formulates slightly differently the thesis that place matters:

> Le coin suggère toujours autant l'attaque nocturne, le traquenard atroce. La scène est en place, elle n'attend que les acteurs. J'ai pris quelques photos, mais savez-vous? Je surveille d'assez près ce genre d'inventaire : *Il y a bien longtemps qu'on n'a pas tué, rue Watt*. L'idée me vint donc, et je vous concède

qu'elle est strictement farfelue, que depuis vos démêlés avec les anciens du Foyer Végétalien et l'écho qui leur a été donné, on ne peut plus tuer *n'importe comment* ici. Comme si les fictions ou les vieilles histoires marquaient de manière indélébile certains lieux, exigeant qu'on y fasse preuve d'une certaine tenue.

Il faut avoir du talent pour assassiner, rue Watt.[23]

[This area always provokes thoughts of a night-time attack, a dreadful trap. The stage is set, it waits for nothing but the actors. I took some photos, but do you know? I keep a close eye on this kind of inventory: *No-one has killed anyone in a long time, in the rue Watt.* The idea then came to me, and I admit it is quite far-fetched, that since your run-in with the veterans of the Foyer Végétalien, and the resonance that had, it is not possible to kill *any old how* here. As if the fictions and old stories marked some places indelibly, imposing the need to show a certain correctness of behaviour.

You need talent, to murder in the rue Watt.]

As we have seen throughout Vilar's work, fiction is as material as history in the apprehension of its marks on the present.

Notes to Chapter 4

1. Pictured in *Silent Partners: Artist and Mannequin From Function to Fetish*, ed. by Jane Munro (Cambridge: Fitzwilliam Museum; New Haven, CT, & London: Yale University Press, 2014), p. 155.
2. Jacques Hillairet, *Dictionnaire historique des rues de Paris*, 2 vols (Paris: Minuit, 1964).
3. Cf. Georges Perec, *Je me souviens* (Paris: Hachette, 1978).
4. 'Chacun ses marelles, chacun ses jeux de l'oie' [To each his games of hopscotch, to each his goose games] (Vilar, 'Cher Nestor Burma', p. 119).
5. Ibid.
6. The setting of the famous film of the same name. The hotel façade was famously rebuilt on set for the film, though the building is revered for the connection.
7. Vilar, 'Cher Nestor Burma', p. 119.
8. Ibid. The Vélodrome d'hiver was demolished in 1959 and the Stade omnisports de Bercy was inaugurated in 1984. The street names are from the Exposition internationale du Surréalisme of 1938; Léo Malet was one of those participating.
9. Ross, 'Parisian noir', p. 100.
10. Vilar, 'Paris désolé', p. 212.
11. Benjamin, *Selected Writings*, IV, 395.
12. Benjamin, *Paris, capitale du XIXe siècle*, p. 488
13. Vilar, 'Cher Nestor Burma', p. 119.
14. Ibid.
15. Ibid.
16. See Margaret Atack, 'From *Meurtres pour mémoire* to *Missak*: Literature and Historiography in Dialogue', *French Cultural Studies*, 12.3–4 (2014), 271–80.
17. Richard J. Golsan, 'Memory's *bombes à retardement*: Maurice Papon, Crimes against Humanity and 17 October 1961', *Journal of European Studies*, 28.1–2 (March-June 1998), 153–72; Charles Forsdick, 'Direction les oubliettes de l'histoire: Witnessing the Past in the Contemporary French *polar*', *Crime and Punishment*, ed. by Atack, pp. 333–50.
18. Max Silverman, *Palimpsestic Memory: The Holocaust and Colonialism in French and Francophone Fiction and Film* (New York & Oxford: Berghahn Books, 2013).
19. Michael Rothberg, *Multidirectional Memory: Remembering the Holocaust in the Age of Decolonization* (Stanford, CA: Stanford University Press, 2009).
20. Benjamin, *Paris, capitale du XIXe siècle*, p. 485.

21. Compagnon, *La Seconde Main* (see above, Chapter 2).
22. See Benjamin, 'On the Concept of History' [Theses XIV and XVI], in *Selected Writings*, IV, pp. 395, 396.
23. Vilar, 'Cher Nestor Burma', p. 119.

CHAPTER 5

❖

Criminal Art

The title of this chapter, taken from the work of the street artist Bando, sums up the transgressive appropriation of the street that defies all the rules of law and order, in line with the situationist custom of *détournement*, of using slogans, quotations, and other practices to re-direct the environment away from the images and words of society's ideologies dominating it.[1] This political art practice exploded onto the streets of Paris in May 68, as did the poster images of the Atelier populaire des Beaux Arts produced by artists of the *nouveau réalisme* and *figuration narrative* movements. The awareness of the city as a political and ideological space to be fought over is fundamental to Vilar's writings and to the public art of contestation in city spaces and on city surfaces; through his visual and textual work on the demolitions of the place de la Bastille, together with that of Pierre Marcelle, he participated in this cultural and artistic work on the fabric of the city which was a significant dimension of cultural and aesthetic reflection in the 1970s and 1980s.

In the two novels to be discussed in this chapter, *État d'urgence* (1985) and *Djemila* (1988), the city is appropriated as theatre and practice of murderous political confrontation. The topoi of the street as crime scene and of the three-dimensional space of *Étant donnés* are both mobilised. In these novels, which involve the compact well-defined cities of Venice and Djemila, it is the city itself which is the theatre of crime. Venice is a spectacular, if infernal, stage for violent conflict between the police, mafia, and Red Brigades (Brigate rosse).[2] Vilar commented on what one might call a negative practice of *détournement*: 'On peut détourner tous les édifices — c'est la perversion. Il n'y a que le roman qui peut le raconter' [It's possible to hijack any building — it's perversion. Only the novel can tell its story].[3] He is referring to the redirected use of Drancy in Paris, a housing estate before the war that became a transit camp for Jews initially taken to the Vélodrome d'hiver and then deported to Auschwitz, and Terezin, the fortress and walled garrison town in Czechoslovakia, that became notorious as the 'model' concentration camp.[4] But as a reminder that *détournement* can be cruel, it is a remark pertinent to the operatic installation of terror on the Venetian canals at night in *État d'urgence*. In contrast, Djemila is a well preserved classical ruin in northern Algeria, open to the skies, several civilisations compressed beneath its stones. In its almost abstract purity, it is described as 'l'épure de toutes les villes possibles' [the blueprint of all possible cities], and its massive Roman theatre where the central narrative confrontation of the Algerian war takes place, is 'un théâtre absolu' [an absolute theatre] (*D*, p. 64).

Street art engages with the fabric of everyday living, contests the orthodox, and writes other agendas into the public space.[5] The *affichistes* of the *nouveau réalisme* movement took the street into the art gallery with their torn posters, ready-mades of the street that they removed and worked on to comment on the political, social, and aesthetic fabric of urban life: 'La peau des murs est le plus vieux journal du monde' [The skin of walls is the oldest newspaper in the world].[6] A special issue of the art journal *Opus International*, *L'Art H̶o̶r̶s̶ S̶u̶r̶ D̶a̶n̶s̶ C̶o̶n̶t̶r̶e̶ La Ville?*, featured work in and of the street by a range of different artists. Anne Tronche discusses Ernest Pignon-Ernest who created an important installation piece: silkscreen prints of the famous photographs of the murdered Communards on the steps of the Charonne metro station in 1971, commemorating both the deaths of the Commune of 1870–71 and those of 8 February 1962,[7] and who also displayed images of wretched men injured and exploited at work on the walls of Calais, Le Havre and Bordeaux, explicitly aiming thereby to escape the contradictions of the art market which reinstates the commercial value of the individual artist as quickly as the image works to critique it.[8] Giovanni Joppolo describes the photographs by Marc Petitjean of the destruction of a cafe in a building cleared to make space around the new Centre Pompidou as registering 'Petits Crimes quotidiens et anonymes' [Daily, anonymous little crimes]. His argument is close to that of Vilar in 'Paris désolé', that there was no particular architectural merit to the building, but the fabric of social human interaction was wantonly destroyed and mourned.[9] Deidi von Schaewen's photographs of sliced-through *immeubles* and their floor-patternings, cut through by the traces of staircases and chimneys, offer a different perspective on the ephemeral art objects created by demolition: 'Murs en cours de démolition: ce sont souvent les plus éphémères. De là vient sans doute leur intensité. [...] Ce sont les "objets trouvés" des villes, des œuvres d'art inattendues, des monuments éphémères, des statues occidentales et populaires, des souvenirs' [Walls in the process of being demolished: these are often the most ephemeral, which no doubt is the source of their intensity. [...] They are the 'found objects' of cities, unexpected works of art, ephemeral monuments, statues of lesser value and of the people, memories].[10] Vilar weaves street art into *Bastille-Tango*, with references to Miss Tic and Blek le Rat, who both began working in the 1980s, and with the creation of a group of three graffiti artists Mi noche triste — named after a well-known tango and all young Argentinian exiles — who produce large-scale colourful images at night of a violent and sinister Buenos Aires: 'Pour le moment, c'est notre truc. Mettre des bouts de Buenos Aires dans Paris' [For now, this is our thing: putting bits of Buenos Aires in Paris] (*BT*, p. 178).

In 'Bastille-Opéra', his visual and textual piece in *Tango* on the demolition of the Paramount, Vilar's photographs highlight the interaction of art and demolition as inscriptions appear on the walls of the partly demolished buildings of the place de la Bastille. Pierre Marcelle, who wrote the quotations on the walls, recorded the process in *La Démolition*, a kind of autofictional diary, where many photographs of the demolition site and his multiple literary inscriptions all around it are woven into a story of his relationship with a woman called Marianne, the various friendships he makes during the project, and Vilar's involvement, at times helping to direct from afar the writing of these large inscriptions, at times serving as co-photographer.[11] A portrait of Vilar illustrates the review of *État d'urgence* in *Libération*; credited to Marcelle, it is taken in front of the Gracq quotation, 'dans la fiction tout est fictif' [in fiction, everything is fictional].[12] In *La Démolition* and in 'Bastille-Opéra', quotations from Balzac, Botho Strauss, Chandler, and Gracq progressively take over the space serving as a kind of intradiegetic commentary and dialogue, if an enigmatic one, but one where a reading of the city, against its newly minted ruins, remains an imperative. Sophie Calle's *Suite vénitienne* was also published at this time, and Marcelle notes being given a copy by Vilar.[13] It is a complex multi-media art book where the artist follows a man, unbeknownst to him, from Paris to Venice and back again. Her exploration of the arbitrary rules involved in the construction of works, of intertextual dialogues, and of the deployment of text and image to approach the texture of urban spaces from many angles is close to Vilar, as is her *flânerie* exploring the labyrinth of the city.[14]

The city as art object is, then, a powerful strand at this time in the exploration of the imaginary of the urban and the everyday. The cities in the two novels discussed here are quite different; Victor is a minor character in *État d'urgence,* and does not feature in *Djemila*. The city is apprehended without the photographer at its heart, but is still a complex mosaic of multiple histories, stories, and images that inflect the narration of the *noir* violence. As Anne Tronche wrote in relation to Anne and Patrick Poirier's photographs of archaeological ruins: 'la vérité du visible n'est en fait que la somme d'imaginaires' [The truth of the visible is in fact only its sum of imaginaries].[15]

État d'urgence

État d'urgence exemplifies Vilar's definition of the *roman noir*: 'Le roman noir, parce que c'est la crise, se joue dans un état d'urgence. Il parle du monde maintenant' [The *roman noir*, because it's the crisis, takes place in a state of emergency. It speaks of the world today].[16] It is a novel of baroque set pieces where the resurgent Red Brigades, the mafia, and the state, both police and judiciary, are pitted against each other in complex, complicitous dark dealings and violent clashes. A story of murders and hostages that references Aldo Moro, Andreas Baader, and the devastating bomb attack of the extreme right in Bologna, *État d'urgence* trades in ambiguities: ethical ambiguities of journalists, the police, and the left; ambiguities of identity and appearance, with carnival masks a variant on the many performances of deception and disguise; ambiguities of behaviour, with betrayals, denunciations, and double crossings.[17] The Red Brigades take Venice hostage at carnival time, and turn the carnivalesque days and nights of misrule into a nightmare of violence. The city is written into this tale of terror and murder as both the grandiose set for spectacular terrorist action on the canals, and as a complex protagonist imbued with rich and diverse cultural scripts.

Venice is a city steeped in death, drowning in death, threatened with annihilation from the rising waters, and from the international rescue efforts that fund work on the beautiful canal fronts at the expense of the sixteenth-century buildings of the working-class areas that are crumbling away (*EU*, p. 200). The imbrication of city, death, and woman that Benjamin saw in Paris takes many forms here, firstly through the historical feminisation of the Venetian Republic, 'la Serenissima', derided also as 'the whore of Europe' with its long tradition of courtesans (p. 44), as well as through various elements of the plot, including the oblique mobilisation of the trope of *Étant donnés* with the recumbent dead female figure at its centre. The very entrance to the city is, we are told, the former site of public executions (p. 67). This is a city of many contrasts, where the symmetries and reflections of its beautiful architecture co-exist with a stinking Grand Canal full of shit (p. 89), and dank, sinister, hidden passageways characteristic of the gothic novel (pp. 21–22, 92, 197). That it once was a plague city is also recalled, as one woman wears hideously disfiguring makeup for the carnival, and sinister Brigadists turn up disguised as plague priests. Venice is a mosaic of spaces: a museified tourist centre forcing Venetians out, the polluting industrial estates of the Mestre area, the cemetery on the island of San Michele in the lagoon, and, as the city that gave the word to the world, the segregated area where Jews were once obliged to live: the ghetto. *État d'urgence* also pays attention to class differentiation, through observation and anecdote, listening to the story of the gondoliers who can no longer work in the traditional manner, eliminated by the *vaporetti*, or little speedboats, or registering the mass of workers leaving the centre for Mestre at the end of the day: 'Pas de masques, pas de déguisements, rien que des imperméables bon marché en plastique, colorés et transparents' [No masks, no disguises, only cheap, transparent, coloured plastic macs] (p. 48), in a novel where class and appearance are itemised in detail, from the huge variety of carnival disguises and costumes to everyday wear of both men and women. The Brigadists proclaim their wish to tear off the masks of the carnival, misrule in name only, to reveal the face of the bourgeoisie enriching itself beneath, an analysis with which Adrien Leck, the narrator, has some sympathy (pp. 44, 74, 75).

It is hard to imagine a more theatrical space than Venice, the whole notion and presence of spectacle being central to its identity. There is no part of the narrative that is not working with the 'already imagined', as each of its eight chapters underlines the thematics of story-telling, of women, murder, and death, with epigraph quotations from Wim Wenders, Hitchcock, Godard, Samuel Fuller and Nicolas Ray, and also Fritz Munro (a fictional film director in Wenders's *State of Things*), concluding: 'Toutes les histoires parlent de la mort' [All stories speak of death] (*EU*, p. 68). Setting the novel during the carnival intensifies the thematics of layered identities, play-acting, and deception. Furthermore, Leck is a famous film director, regularly asked for autographs and photographs, Laetitia Vanese a prominent judge (who is shot by the Mafia in the opening episode), and Gozzi a high profile police commander, which means that press reporting and photographs, television reports and images repeating the narrative events are integral to the action. At one point, Leck is kidnapped with Arno Rieti, a reformed Brigadist and the subject of Leck's current film project. The filmed interview he was forced to give replays endlessly on television. Self-conscious performance is Gozzi's hallmark also, as he cultivates his 'look', dressing like a cop in a *film noir* and imitating Bogart's famous gesture of rubbing his thumb across his lips, while the journalist Oreste points out the attraction of the violent *fait divers* in Venice: 'Voilà le genie du terrorisme, ricana-t-il en désignant les badauds. Avant tout, c'est un spectacle excitant' [See the genius of terrorism, he laughed sarcastically as he pointed to the onlookers. Above all, it's an exciting spectacle] (p. 80).

Awareness of Venice as an imaginary city, a cultural space imbued with multiple imagined existences, is underlined from the outset: 'Je distinguai quelques masques: silhouettes furtives sous la colonnade du Palais, rires étouffés, ombres des ombres d'autres têtes. Venise, où je n'étais que depuis quelques heures, ressemblait déjà un peu trop à ses images' [I made out a few masks: furtive silhouettes beneath the Palace's colonnade, stifled laughter, shadows of the shadows of other festival heads. I had only been in Venice a few hours, and already it was resembling its images rather too closely] (*EU*, p. 7), and reinforced by many hidden and not so hidden references. The name of Fabio Rieti is no doubt behind the choice of the names of police officer Fabio and the former Brigadist Arno Rieti. He was well known as a street artist who, in 1979, painted a mural, *Le Piéton des Halles* [The Pedestrian of Les Halles], on the side of the electricity generator of Les Halles, a mural that became gradually hidden from sight as buildings went up around it, until the generator building itself was demolished. He also designed the Italian poster for Visconti's *Death in Venice*.[18] Leck and Carla, the wife of his producer Stefano, make love on the tomb of 'la Dame Stretter', Aurélia Stretter being a central character in Marguerite Duras's *India Song* and *Son nom de Venise dans Calcutta désert*. Smaller spaces create allusions too: a shopping-centre recalls Chirico, and the Gesuiti college reminds Leck of Chéreau's production of *Toller* with its dirty, worn walls and fascists killing workers, a hint in miniature of the fighting between all the various forces that dominate the final pages (p. 51).[19]

The smallest space is also a spectacular imagined city, a maquette of Venice created by Dr Soto who is in charge of Laetitia's treatment in the hospital where she lies in a coma. At his home Soto has built a perfect, detailed replica of the whole of Venice. An insane totalisation of Venice with very sinister overtones, it incorporates the tropes of the street crime associated with Atget and *Étant donnés*: an installation recreating the city and metonymically connected to a woman suspended between life and death, as indeed is the city itself.

Venice is recreated with a 'précision terrifiante' [terrifying precision] (*EU*, p. 120), yet, after ten years' work — and it will take another ten to finish it — it is not accurate: changes in the city mean that it has already become a historical record, the little angel on top of one of the churches now looks like 'un vieux lépreux aux membres déformés, au visage troué de plaies immondes' [an old leper with deformed limbs and a face pitted with foul wounds] (p. 122). Moreover, there is none of the scaffolding and repair works that are a feature of everyday life in Venice. It might be a fraud, says Soto, but it is a city of the imagination: 'Je rêve cette ville, monsieur Leck. Mes rêves ont de la mémoire. Voilà ma méthode' [I dream this city, my dreams remember things, that is my method] (p. 123). Leck is reminded of his friend Victor's comments on Atget's project of photographing the whole of Paris before its destruction. Most disturbingly of all, this obsessively detailed maquette, detailed down to the worn brickwork, is empty. There are no people, 'il avait voulu une cité fantôme' [He wanted a ghost town] (p. 121). The maquette is not only a fixing of a city before it is swept away, it is also enveloped in some very dark themes. Suggestions of rottenness combine here with infernal nightmares of annihilation. For its creator, 'cette ville se meurt, comment fixer un grouillement d'agonie?' [this city is dying, how do you pin down the writhings of the death throes?] (p. 122). 'Grouillement' would be a normal term for the wrigglings of worms on a corpse; together with the leprous angel, the reality of this beautiful city is the horror of rotting flesh.

As with *Étant donnés*, the rotting female body of this perfect maquette is approached in several stages, through the gates to the street, across an expanse of untended garden, full of rusting, useless objects, through the ground floor and up the stairs to the vast attic and its extensive model. Leck wants to lift the roofs — a final obstacle — and peer inside the buildings of this ghost town where the people have disappeared:

> J'eus alors la conviction qu'en soulevant le toit des maisons, qu'en écartant les murs où méticuleusement l'usure de chaque brique était reproduite, on ne pourrait que découvrir des appartements, des chambres, des meubles, les plus infimes traces mortes de toutes ces vies absentes. J'eus peur. (*EU*, p. 123)

> [I was convinced that, lifting the roofs of the houses, moving to one side the walls where meticulously the worn state of each brick was reproduced, one could not fail to discover flats, bedrooms, furniture, the tiniest dead traces of all those absent lives. It frightened me.]

Lifting the roofs of houses to look inside is the very famous gesture of Asmodeus, the fallen angel in Lesage's novel *Le Diable boîteux*, reinforcing the 'précision infernale' [infernal precision] of the construction (p. 123). Venice is indeed dying: the beautiful mask reveals rotting flesh, in true gothic fashion, and the city is being pulled into the underground of devil and hell, in a *mise en abyme* of the Dantesque journey into a concentrationary hell at the mercy of the Red Brigades later in the novel.

People disappearing from cities is always sinister in Vilar's novels. Disappearance is signalled in *État d'urgence* by its epigraph, from the director Wim Wenders, quoting Cézanne: 'Tout est en train de disparaître. Il faut se précipiter si on veut voir encore des choses' [Things are disappearing. If you want to see anything, you have to hurry].[20] The fear of the mass disappearance of spectators, in a grim recall of the Holocaust, and of Venice itself in an apocalyptic explosion, is at the centre of the final episodes that draw together key strands of the text: dramatic performance, the hybrid space of the imaginary city, the concentrationary, and murder. Carla is taking the part of Eurydice in the play *Les Enfers* to be acted on the canals, and invites all her and Stefano's guests to watch, including Leck and Victor, who has arrived to help out on the film preparation. On the boats, in the darkness of night, they leave the centre behind and head towards the industrial zones of Mestre. The setting is L'Arsenale, the huge dockyard founded in the eleventh century that by the fourteenth century was a producer of ships on an industrial scale, and mentioned by Dante in the *Inferno*. The city is the theatre set for this grandiose production in which Dante and Monteverdi (*Orfeo*) are combined with many visual and auditory markers of the Holocaust, reinforced by the deafening noises of dogs and industrial hammering that accompany the boats, blaring out from loudspeakers, and projectors and lights from the watchtowers raking the darkness. The guests are dragged off the boats and over wasteland surrounded by guards with dogs, projectors on watchtowers, one synthetic voice declaiming 'vous qui entrez. laissez toute espérance' [abandon all hope, ye who enter here], surrounded by 'ombres blanchâtres', 'silhouettes décharnées, vêtues de pyjamas informes' [whitish shadows, fleshless silhouettes dressed in shapeless pyjamas] (*EU*, pp. 213, 214). The Brigades and their large cast of extras have indeed, as promised, taken Venice hostage. The guests are made to stand in line, beaten if they protest or try to leave. It seems at one point that all the guests and spectators of this Dantesque re-enactment of the camps will be 'disappeared' into the darkness of the tunnels, but in the end it is Eurydice's murdered body alone that floats back out towards them: 'Carla Calonna était étendue sur le velours rouge, contessa alanguie et figée, spectulairement nue et morte' [Carla Calonna was lying on the red velvet, a languorous countess in her fixed pose, spectacularly naked and dead] (p. 220).

The theme of the Holocaust has been threaded through the story, from the first mention of the Venetian ghetto. Joachim, the script-writer, denounces the conductor Oscar Langer as a Nazi who let most of his orchestra be deported. Joachim was deported to Belsen as a child, a fact to which Stefano scathingly refers: 'Ses livres sont formidables [...] mais c'est quand même un petit juif pleurnichard. Rescapé des camps, alcoolique et antizionist: très chic!' [His books are superb [...] but he's a whining little Jew. Survivor of the camps, alcoholic and anti-zionist: very chic!] (*EU*, p. 87). Leck is Jewish, and he recalls his trip to Prague with his currently estranged Czech girlfriend Sarah, whose family was deported to Terezin; she pointed out to him the names of the 77,927 Czech victims of the Holocaust, including Kafka's sisters, on the synagogue next to the Jewish cemetery (p. 114). The murdered Oscar will be found on the tomb of Ezra Pound who was imprisoned for his pro-Nazi propaganda.

As figures of armed Brigadists line the bridges and canal sides, this is a spectacle that not only aligns them with the extreme violence of the camps, but also demonstrates again the articulation of past and present that is governed by the crises of the present. One could perhaps see an earlier association between the red star of the Brigades (famously used in the photograph of the kidnapped Aldo Moro), that they draw with aerosols over the doors of intended targets, and the yellow star that Joachim defiantly pins to his chest alongside his disparate collection of badges. While obeying different logics, the one as a sign of a group, the second to mark Jews as other, there is a disquieting iconographical similarity in their use to designate a target. The articles in *Rouge* on left-wing terrorist action, often written by Bensaïd or Vilar, argued strongly that it was a kind of gangsterism, quite divorced from the interests of the working class and caught up in the logic of its own violence. Working with the mafia to achieve their ends further proves the point here. Arno's critique of his previous armed activism also echoes their position, that they were caught in the logic of their violence, losing sight of any political progress for the class they were defending (*EU*, pp. 33, 35, 173).

The novel ends in central Venice, as a giant oil tanker manned by Oreste and the Brigades brings both modern industry and extreme violence into the museum-city. They threaten to blow the tanker sky high, and Venice with it, if their demands are not met, which would engulf the city in a 'marée noire', a black tide of oil, rhetorically extending the metaphors of dirt, gangrene, rot, and humidity already threatening Venice from below. Alphant concluded her review of *État d'urgence* with the judgement that the *roman noir* is at one and the same time the most realist and the most exaggerated ('outré') of genres, but arguably no more so than the melodramas of the gothic novels and B-movies that have been so frequently invoked.[21] These dramas of violence have also been dramas of allegiance and hatred, of murders motivated by loyalty and betrayal, in a city where citizens of the Republic posted anonymous denunciations into the mouths of stone lions' heads set in the walls (*EU*, p. 202). The leitmotif of 'no *possible* morality' in a world in crisis plays out here across notions of guilt, innocence, and repentance. Arno is a *pentito*, working with the police and the judiciary, though carrying out his own revenge killings; among other double games, police officer Gozzi is working with the mafia; and Leck has taken mafia money for his film. Langer's pleas of innocence, that he was only interested in music, cuts no ice with Joachim, and is echoed by Leck's plea to his kidnapper Oreste, that he just makes films and tells stories, and should not be killed for that. 'Guilty' is what the Brigadists and extras scream at the frightened guests by the canal. Guido refuses to help a former Brigadist because of their violence against the people of Italy, but has little answer to Leck's charge that as a former communist, he should realise revolutionaries can become criminals (pp. 223–34).[22] Leck's world-weary comment, faced with Gozzi's complicity, 'Ma vie est ce qu'elle est. Il y a longtemps que je n'ai plus d'éthique' [My life is what it is. I have had no ethics for a long time] (p. 253), could be applied to them all.

Djemila

Djemila is the name of a dead city, of a dead woman in Algeria, and of her daughter, who is a central figure in this political story of murky complicities and collusions, mainly but not exclusively of mainstream and extreme-right politicians. Djemila is an ancient ruined city in the Constantinois region of Algeria whose beautifully preserved theatre is a crime scene; Djemila Assedine is the name of a nationalist leader who died under torture during the Algerian war; her daughter, Ouria, takes the name 'Djemila Sariat' for her false papers on her arrival in Paris. She has turned to François Sinclair, a well-known university lecturer who appears regularly on television, and whom she met in Algeria on a visit he made to the area after the war, because when he was an officer in the French army during the Algerian war he took a stand against torture, publicly proclaiming that her mother had been tortured and killed in army custody. 'Djemila' is a common Algerian first name, but also inevitably recalls the famous cases of Djamila Boupacha, tortured and tried for planting a bomb, and Djamila Bouhired, tortured after her capture and condemned to death in 1957.[23] In some ways a companion piece to Daeninckx's *Meurtres pour mémoire*, *Djemila* tackles murder in the context of both the Algerian War and the French Resistance. It is a story of the murder of extreme-right thugs and an 'establishment' cover up, investigated by an extreme-right journalist, where what was received as a heroic denunciation of torture in Algeria during the Algerian war is shown to be much more complex, as a murder in the present resonates and disturbs received views of murder in the past.

Vilar's novel opens with Djemila in Paris shoplifting in a supermarket and attacking the guard who tries to arrest her. Losing her identity card in the struggle means he turns up later with a friend at Sinclair's house, driven in part by racist anger against a young Algerian woman. They attack and humiliate Sinclair's son Barthélemy (known as 'Barth'); a gun goes off and both are shot dead. This, and its cover up by Sinclair and his friend and police commissioner Jonas, is the *fait divers* that drives the narrative. The two men bury the bodies in remote woodland, but as Djemila, also present, knows, crimes cannot be buried: 'Pas un seul instant elle n'a cru que tout serait réglé après quelques pelletées de terre, dans un petit bois, une nuit. Rien ne se règle jamais comme ça' [Not for a moment did she believe that all would be solved by a few shovels of earth, in a small wood, one night. Nothing is ever solved like that] (*D*, p. 49). The narrative combines the reverberations of these murders in the present with the account of what happened during the Algerian war in Djemila. The guard and his friend are both members of the extreme-right Mouvement national; their friend, Bobo, takes his concern at their disappearance to the Mouvement's journalist Fourier (an obvious reference to Alain Fournier, the writer who used the pseudonym A.D.G. and contributed to the extreme-right publication *Minute*) who starts investigating what he soon believes to be an establishment cover-up.[24]

The political groupings in the novel are rather sardonically presented in an episode that is a parody of the television discussion programme created primarily for entertainment. Its presenter Lucas brings together an unholy cocktail of activists, an amalgam of clichéd positions on the left and the right with their various loyalties and disloyalties to past commitments. The four from the left are: Sinclair; Brice (a Resistance comrade of Sinclair and editor of the left-wing daily *La Tribune* and a 'conscience malheureuse' [unhappy consciousness]); a 'soixante-huitard reconverti dans le polar' [68 activist who now writes crime fiction], veteran of the rue Gay-Lussac battles of 10 May, but now 'repenti'; and a former communist now involved in overseas aid. Facing them from the right are: Vrignot (the editor of *Halte!*, the Mouvement national paper); an ex-OAS member; the secretary of the Maréchal Pétain fan club; and a Maurras groupie. Sinclair insults the May 68 veteran, outperforms the OAS man by invoking the love of country he had learned from outlaws and immigrants in the Resistance and from fighting 'quelques salauds parfaitement nationalistes' [some perfectly nationalist bastards], and humiliates Vrignot who uses the occasion to accuse Sinclair of murder (*D*, pp. 71–73). Since this accusation is based at this stage only on suspicion, Sinclair triumphs, Vrignot flees the set only to be savagely beaten later that evening on the orders of the Mouvement national leader Massart, both to remove an incompetent editor and to accuse Sinclair of the violent attack.

Sinclair is a performer, whether in the lecture hall, on television, or in the theatre. Lecturer, writer, and dramatist, he is modelled on Maurice Clavel who was Vilar's philosophy teacher in school, and author of a novel *Le Jardin de Djemila*.[25] His Resistance pseudonym was 'Sinclair'. His well-known passion for Kierkegaard appears here no doubt in Sinclair's injunction to his students: 'Soyez inquiets' [Be anxious] (*D*, p. 8), that Djemila dismisses as an empty formula. In the course of the narrative, Sinclair recalls his time in Algeria and the capture of Djemila, as well as his later return to the ruined city and first meeting with Djemila's daughter. After the television programme he manages to get visas for them both to return to Algeria and to the city of Djemila, where the novel ends.

Fourier has embarked on an investigation of Sinclair, researching his past in the archives and interviewing many who knew him in the Resistance — when he was apparently a hard man ('un dur à cuire', *D*, p. 56) — and in Algeria, where the consensus is that he was an excellent soldier and leader of men, but that the episode with Djemila is less than clear. Having captured her and handed her to his unit, he then set out on a routine patrol; that seemed strange, as did the fact that all of his unit were killed in an ambush shortly afterwards, meaning no-one could challenge his account.[26] Described as disloyal to his men, forging for himself a heroic posture, having realised, says one, that the wind was about to turn, this is a far from flattering picture. Fourier's suspicions of a murder cover-up in Paris are of course true: having disposed of the bodies, police officer Jonas will then kill the driver Bobo in an apparent hit-and-run accident; Brice, the *Tribune* editor, deflects two young journalists who have unearthed Fourier's inquiry and mistakenly believe Fourier to be embarked on an invented smear campaign against their hero Sinclair. Brice and Jonas both fought in the Resistance with Sinclair, and Fourier's accusations of a Resistance mafia of the powerful are not only well grounded, it is precisely because of his extreme-right allegiance, allergic to these figures of the intellectual left, that his investigation is so dogged.

Equally murky are the machinations of the powerful politicians of the state and the extreme right. The Mouvement national leader Massart orders the killing of Fourier, who is planning some personal blackmail having discovered Barth's written account of killing the two men with his father's old war-time gun. When Fourier's little recording-machine is discovered in his pocket after his death, with all the grisly details on it, and finds its way to the desk of the Minister of the Interior, Massart's schemings are exposed. The novel is set after the 1986 legislative elections, which the right had won, and in the run-up to the 1988 presidential election. Massart and the extreme right are riding high in the polls, and the minister, in consultation with his socialist predecessor, uses the evidence of the murder of Fourier to silence Massart, while giving him full permission to continue to proclaim his views on

Algeria, the OAS, Vichy, the Holocaust, immigrants, and Jews as loudly as he likes: 'Tu consolideras un vieux fonds de commerce d'irréductibles imbéciles qui se reconnaîtront parfaitement en toi. Les autres, ceux qui estiment que tu dis bêtement trop fort ce qu'ils pensent benoîtement tout bas, nous reviendront' [You'll shore up the old stock of irreducible idiots who will see themselves in you. The others, those who think you say stupidly too loudly what they complacently think very quietly, will come back to us] (*D*, pp. 153–54).

Earlier in the novel, Djemila has seen Sinclair writing about the city: 'Un vague essai. Une chose sur les villes, la topographie et le théâtre. Donc, sur la fatalité' [A vague essay. On cities, topography and the theatre. Therefore, on fate] (*D*, p. 38). If 'fate' hints at Benjamin's photographer at the crime scene, working like the augurs to identify the forces at work, this site weaves in also the elements of *Étant donnés,* projected across the ancient city. On their first meeting, Sinclair and Djemila had walked around it, with its Numidian, Roman, Christian, and Islamic traces, having passed the garden full of fragments of statues and the museum that they decline to enter. This city is its own multi-layered installation, a potentially functioning machine with all the working spaces intact: 'Tout y est, le dispositif idéal' [Everything's there, the ideal system] (p. 32). He points out the sacrificial altar in the forum where the victim would lie. The surrounding scenery also recalls the waterfall and hills behind the body in Duchamp's installation, often compared to his drawing of hills, 'les cols alités' [the bedridden mountain passes]:[27]

> De chaque côté, des maisons, des monuments. Pas le moindre effort mental de reconstitution à faire, tout est là. Au loin, plus bas, des gorges où l'on devine des torrents, les collines tourmentées.
> — Pas une ville morte. Une ville imaginaire.
> Peut-être le modèle, l'épure de toute ville possible. (*D*, p. 31)

> [On either side, houses and monuments. Not the least effort needed to reconstitute it, everything is here. In the distance, lower down, gorges where there will be torrents, tormented hills.
> 'Not a dead city. An imaginary city.'
> Perhaps the model, the blueprint of every possible city.]

The last scene of the book returns them to the theatre where he recounts his shooting and capture of Djemila and where her daughter now, scratching at the soil — completing the fragmented scenario of *Étant donnés* — unearths bullets just below the surface. Did he kill her here? He says not, though he is now referred to as 'le tueur' (*D*, p. 166), confirming the strong suspicion that his whole denunciation of torture has been smoke and mirrors, a view that has already been suggested in Paris by the Minister of the Interior to his socialist precedessor. Fourier's investigative scratching ('J'avance lentement, je flaire, je gratte' [I move forward slowly, I sniff, I scratch], p. 62) laid bare the *fait divers* that the three former members of the Resistance covered up, and that the politicians cover up in their turn, the government minister to ensure the extreme-right gains no credibility, and the socialist, who stops Brice publishing Sinclair's (false) confession to Barth's murders, to protect the (unmerited) reputation of a man of the left.

Is there some dramatic way out for 'le tueur frappé de soleil' [the killer struck by sunlight] way up at the top of the theatre and difficult to make out? If so, Sinclair does not take it:

> Il pourrait y avoir comme une détonation tragique, le bruit alarmant d'un suicide correct, ou d'une exécution, une fin en bonne et due forme, Sinclair, le théâtreux, aurait dû savoir faire. Il avait les moyens personnels et le cadre grandiose, donné. Rien. Pas la moindre anecdote finale. Il s'en va et c'est tout, quitte médiocrement le théâtre où il est devenu importun. (D, p. 166)

> [There could be something like a tragic gunshot, the alarming noise of a decent suicide, or of an execution, a correctly observed ending. As a professional of the theatre, Sinclair should have known how. He had the personal means and the grandiose setting, given. Nothing. Not the smallest final anecdote. He goes away and that is all, a mediocre departure from the theatre where he has become a hindrance.]

The showy performer of the left fails either to perform repentance or to give a repeat performance as an assassin. One might say that the crime scene has seen off the criminal — it is the daughter, returning to her own name 'Ouria', who now moves into a more certain future. There is no resolution for the ethically compromised Sinclair, not even the performance of one.

The cities of Djemila and Venice are each described as a 'ville fantôme' in different contexts, the first by a reviewer who suggested that this 'ville fantôme du passé algérien' [ghost city of the Algerian past] had an allegorical value.[28] In the 1980s, the absence of the Algerian war in official memory became a strong cultural theme, and the metaphors of the haunting past and the unquiet dead were strongly suggestive of an immaterial presence of the past that persisted and continued to unsettle. This is very different from Leck's description of the model of Venice as a 'ville fantôme', ghost town in the sense of a deserted town. But in both texts, it is the materiality of the past and absence which is striking. Like the chemical reaction of light on photosensitive film, there is an elemental imprint of the event on the place where it took place. Leck's reaction when faced with the maquette is caused by the fear of seeing the dead traces of the absent, 'les plus infimes traces mortes des toutes ces vies absentes' [the very tiniest traces of all those absent lives]. Absence leaves a mark, even, horrifyingly enough, a dead one. The past does not so much haunt the present in Vilar's fictions, it is rather reactivated to be grappled with, and the place where that happens is part of its reality. Venice and Djemila are both imaginary cities but not ethereal ones; the material solidity of these complex arenas is fundamental to the scenarios of the present and of the past in the present.

Notes to Chapter 5

1. *Criminal Art* is a large-scale mural in the bright colours and 'dancing' letters of the tag movement. A photograph of the mural can be viewed at <https://www.artranked.com/topic/Criminal#&gid=1&pid=25> [accessed 2 February 2020]. See also, 'Bando, Manhattan-Saint-Germain des Prés', *Le Pressionnisme 1970–1990: les chefs-d'œuvre du graffiti sur toile de Basquiat à Bando*, ed. by Marc Restellini (Paris: Pinacothèque de Paris, 2015), pp. 44–51.

2. The Red Brigades were an extreme-left group using violence to achieve revolutionary aims. It was involved in the kidnapping and murder of prominent legal, political, military, and business figures, kneecapping and firebombing of factories and warehouses.
3. Vilar, in *Jean-François Vilar: 95% de reel*.
4. See Claude Lanzmann, *Un vivant qui passe: Auschwitz 1943-Theresienstadt 1944* (Paris: Gallimard, coll. Folio, 2013), the transcript of Lanzmann's interview with Maurice Rossel, who inspected the camp as a Red Cross delegate in 1944.
5. See Gillian Jein, '(De)Facing the Wall: The Traditions, Transactions and Transgressions of Street Art', *Irish Journal of French Studies*, 12 (2012), 83–111.
6. François Dufrêne, quoted in Alain Jouffroy, *Les Pré-voyants* (Brussels: La Connaissance, 1974), p. 132.
7. For a photograph of this street installation, see the 'Politique partout' section in Jean-Louis Pradel, *La Figuration narrative: des années 1960 à nos jours* (Paris: Gallimard, 2008), [n.p.]; and Jérôme Gulon, *Ernest Pignon-Ernest: le lieu et la formule* (Grenoble: Critères, 2012) p. 19. The latter includes a photograph of the prints on the steps of the Sacré-Cœur in Montmartre, built to mark the end of the Commune (p. 16).
8. Anne Tronche, 'Pignon sur rues', *L'Art Hors Sur Dans Contre La Ville?*, *Opus international*, 65 (Winter 1978), 13–16. She also notes a 1971 exhibition of his work at the Salon de la Jeune Peinture, where he related his silkscreen prints of a man's damaged body to the numbers of killed and injured at work in France during the exhibition: 156 deaths and 8,400 injured (13 deaths and 700 injured each day).
9. Giovanni Joppolo, 'Petits crimes quotidiens et anonymes: Marc Petitjean', *L'Art Hors Sur Dans Contre La Ville?*, pp. 45–47.
10. Deidi von Schaewen, 'Murs', *L'Art Hors Sur Dans Contre La Ville?*, p. 13 (*occidental* with the meaning of being of lesser value was used in the precious stone industry).
11. Pierre Marcelle, *La Démolition* (Paris: Denoël, 1985). It has also been read as a novel: see Margaret Cook, '*La Démolition* de Pierre Marcelle ou le crime du signe', *Tangence*, 38 (December 1992), 55–64 <https://doi.org/10.7202/025738ar38> [accessed 29 August 2019].
12. Marianne Alphant, 'Vilar en flâneur noir', *Libération*, 7 March 1985, p. 28.
13. Sophie Calle, *Suite vénitienne* (Paris: L'Étoile, 1983).
14. See Nigel Saint, 'Space and Absence in Sophie Calle's *Suite vénitienne* and *Disparitions*', *Esprit créateur*, 51.1 (Spring 2011), 125–38 (pp. 126, 127).
15. Anne Tronche, 'Anne et Patrick Poirier ou l'espace-temps conditionné', *L'Art Hors Sur Dans Contre La Ville?*, p. 38.
16. Vilar, 'Noir c'est noir', p. 11.
17. In March 1978 Aldo Moro, former prime minister of Italy and president of one of its large political parties, Christian Democracy, was kidnapped by the Red Brigades. The five bodyguards and policemen protecting him were killed. A photograph of him in captivity, against the backdrop of a Red Brigades flag with the red star, was released a few days later. His body was found in the boot of a car in May 1978. The whole drama was highly mediatised throughout. Andreas Baader was one of the leaders of the German Red Army Faction, an extreme-left organisation that carried out kidnappings and murders, bank robberies, and bombings. Several of them, including leaders Ulrike Meinhof and Baader, were arrested in 1972. Meinhof was found dead in prison in 1975, officially the cause was suicide. In October 1977 Baader and two other members of the Faction were found dead in their cells, and were judged to have killed themselves. This has remained controversial. Gerhard Richter produced a series of paintings entitled *October 18 1977* (1988). 'The fifteen works in *October 18, 1977* evoke fragments from the lives and deaths of the Baader-Meinhof group and reflect Richter's distrust of painting's ability to accurately represent the world, a recurring subject of his work. Their slurred and murky motifs derive from newspaper and police photographs or television images' (MOMA website on the occasion of an exhibition of these paintings in 2019 <https://www.moma.org/collection/works/79037> [accessed 25 May 2020]). A bomb at Bologna railway station, planted by extreme right-wing terrorists, killed eighty.
18. See also Wilson, *The Visual World of French Theory*, pp. 29–31, for his involvement in the collective

painting *La Datcha* (1969) depicting Louis Althusser, Roland Barthes, Michel Foucault, Jacques Lacan, and Claude Lévi-Strauss.
19. *Toller* is a play by Tankred Dorst about the playwright Ernst Toller, for a few months president of the Soviet Republic of Bavaria that saw violent political battles between its defenders and right-wing forces. Chéreau directed it in Milan and Paris in the early 1970s.
20. Wim Wenders, *The Logic of Images: Essays and Conversations*, trans. by Michael Hofman (London: Faber & Faber, 1991), p. 1. The quotation appears in a response to a questionnaire dated 1987, so Vilar will have had a different source.
21. Alphant, 'Vilar en flâneur noir', p. 28.
22. Leck uses the term *stalinien*, of course. In one not very subtle touch, one of the guards in the Auschwitz scenario is described as 'kominternien' (*EU*, p. 213).
23. Djamila Boupacha was defended by Gisèle Halimi and publicly supported by Simone de Beauvoir; together Beauvoir and Halimi wrote *Djamila Boupacha* (Paris: Gallimard, 1962). Jacques Vergès defended Djamila Bouhired, and with Georges Arnaud wrote *Pour Djamila Bouhired* (Paris: Minuit, 1957).
24. Vilar resigned as President of the Association 813 amis de la littérature policière in 1987 in protest at the participation of A.D.G.
25. Lefebvre, 'Grand Prix du roman noir Télérama-Fayard', p. 10.
26. A plot that has structural affinities with *Passage des singes*.
27. Duchamp's 'cols alités' is also a word-play on *causalités*.
28. [Anon.], [review of *Djemila*], *Boum Boum*, 1–7 (April 1989), consulted in 'Recueil Vilar: dossier de presse', Bibliothèque des littératures policières.

CHAPTER 6

All That is Solid Melts into Air

Victor is a walker, a cyclist, a *flâneur*, and a traveller, always within the boundaries of Paris. A large number of Vilar's texts, fictional and in the authorial first person, insist that life outside Paris is unthinkable, and any excursion, such as Victor's rapid trip to London in *Les Exagérés* to visit Madame Tussaud's and check on the heads, exceptional. *Les Fous de Chaillot* (1997), Vilar's contribution to the Tourisme et polar series, which gathered short stories from a wide range of countries and regions, is typical: a journey in time and space around and through the Palais de Chaillot.[1] But at the same time Vilar writes increasingly about Prague and Czechoslovakia.[2] Two very different works, *Sherlock Holmes et les ombres* (1992) and *Nous cheminons entourés de fantômes aux fronts troués* (1993), the first a photobook, the other his longest and final novel, combine Prague with London and with Paris, and introduce a very different kind of wandering to the *flâneur* of Paris, a shift in space accompanied by complex shifts in time, as each story involves intricate connections to different pasts. Both works take *le noir* into territory where the characters seem to become detached from their previously grounded realities. In *Sherlock Holmes et les ombres* this is achieved through multiple narrations of the first Sherlock Holmes story, 'A Scandal in Bohemia', in a context that accentuates the irrational and the strange, and a particular combination of different historical moments, including the 1930s and the Holocaust. *Nous cheminons* focuses very directly on the political history of Trotskyism. Its configuration of politics, violence, utopian aspirations, and betrayals, woven around the three key dates of 1938, 1968, and 1989, and the cities of Paris and Prague, involves confusions and dislocations that ultimately remain enigmatic. Both texts are inflected with an undeniable melancholy.

At a time when many novels were turning to the past of the Occupation years, Vilar sought to 'restituer un minimum de mémoire romanesque' [restore a minimum of fictional memory] to the 1930s, the years when the catastrophic rise of Nazism and, from a Trotskyist point of view, the equally catastrophic consolidation of Stalinism led to slaughters and executions on a mass scale.[3] He singled out Stalin's policy of 'class against class' for bitter criticism, because it identified the social democrats as the primary enemy, and also involved seemingly unthinkable alliances with the national socialists, indirectly helping them extend their grip on power. He passed over the errors of the Trotskyists, 'je n'ai pas la mémoire cruelle' [I do not have a cruel memory], too focused, he believed, on their own concerns with the IVth International.[4] In 1997 he wrote the postface to a republication of

Jan Valtin's extraordinary memoir of his militant life from the first decades of the twentieth century.[5] Valtin was imprisoned by the Americans (for attempted murder, a murder ordered by the Communist Party that he could not bring himself to carry out), and by the Gestapo for whom he turned double agent on the orders of the party. In his own account, and in Vilar's commentary, he is a man of principle who does unprincipled things — for example the party ordered him to denounce his mentor, whom he respected, and he wrote a comprehensive and damning report. The contradiction between the political realities in Germany (for example that contrary to party views, the working class was not solidly for the German Communist Party) and the heart and soul commitment to the cause and the belief in the unassailable wisdom of its party becomes increasingly unbearable; when the party turns on him, he escapes to America, for dissent or doubt are punishable by death. Valtin exemplifies the process already identified in Dashiell Hammett, '*moral* in this century without any *possible* morality'.[6]

'All that is solid melts into air' is a famous phrase from the *Communist Manifesto*, one that initially expressed what Marx and Engels argue is a primary feature of the power and economic base of the bourgeoisie, namely its destructive energy, eliminating old systems, producing new markets, new demands. This is a structural feature, defining of the bourgeois epoch, and one that is ultimately destructive of its own power:

> All fixed, fast-frozen relations, with their train of ancient and venerable prejudices and opinions are swept away, all new-formed ones become antiquated before they can ossify. All that is solid melts into air, all that is holy is profaned, and man is at last compelled to face with sober senses, his real conditions of life.[7]

Marshall Berman's well-known study of modernity took this poetic and evocative phrase as its title to explore the resonance between the fundamental social and political instability that it encapsulates and the structures and insights of modernism from the nineteenth century onwards, arguing that it suggests we are 'at once subjects and objects of the pervasive process that melts everything solid into air', one that is also essential to us. If stability means a withering-away, then 'to say that our society is falling apart is only to say that it is alive and well'.[8] There are many points of contact here with Vilar's descriptions of the operation of the Communist Party of the 1930s, where the militants like Valtin, like Vilar's protagonist Alfred Katz, are both agents and victims of an inexorable process that constantly evaporates political realities to replace them with illusions, most notoriously in the Moscow show trials. Berman extends the phrase to discuss the relationship with the past in the 1970s:

> My second symbol is implicit in the title of this book: *All That Is Solid Melts Into Air*. This means that our past, whatever it was, was a past in the process of disintegration; we yearn to grasp it, but it is baseless and elusive; we look back for something solid to lean on, only to find ourselves embracing ghosts. The modernism of the 1970s was a modernism with ghosts.[9]

Vilar's processes of disintegration affect the present as much as the past, and his historiography is quite different. The past is not made of elusive spectres, it is a dynamic part of the present. Valtin's life is paradoxically both close and distant, part of living memory and also written into thousands of history books;[10] more importantly, the whole notion of revolution is tainted with barbarity: 'Révolution, Cause, camarades, prolétariat, Internationale sont des mots devalués, usés, ils ont comme un goût de cendre. On sent pourtant que, sous la cendre, couve la braise' [Revolution, Cause, comrades, proletariat and International are devalued, worn words, as if they had a taste of ashes. But we can feel that under the ashes the embers are smouldering].[11] Just as Hammett's fiction lays bare a crisis we share, engagement with the past is integral to the Trotskyist political project.

'Gothic Marxism' is the term Margaret Cohen forged to discuss aspects of Marxism, surrealism, and the work of Walter Benjamin that are embraced by *le noir*, prompted by the *Guides noirs*, guide-books to 'the irrational, illicit, inspired, passional, often supernatural aspects of social topography'.[12] Vilar's model is not one of a hidden, repressed, unconscious reality, although there is clearly much overlap between Cohen's discussion of Benjamin, Breton, and Paris and Vilar's exploration of these same texts. 'Gothic Trotskyism' seems a term ideally placed to identify the distinctive drawing together of *le noir* and the militant commitment of Trotskyists past and present that Vilar consistently places in dialogue with surrealism. *Sherlock Holmes et les ombres* and *Nous cheminons* both deploy the thematics and iconography of *le noir* to explore the tragic illusions, misapprehensions, betrayals, murders, and disappearances that characterised the 1930s and 1940s, in tension with the present day. Breton met Trotsky in Mexico in 1938, a meeting that Vilar argued was a great opportunity for a revolutionary coming-together of the political and cultural avant-gardes, but that never materialised.[13] It is one of the many events of 1938 to feature in *Nous cheminons entourés de fantômes aux fronts troués* [We make our way surrounded by ghosts with holes in their foreheads], whose title is a quotation from Trotsky's wife Natalia, referring to their situation in Mexico as their friends and comrades throughout the world are killed. There are various kinds of ghosts in both *Nous cheminons* and *Sherlock Holmes*, that each construct a labyrinthine network of narratives and time frames, retrieving the past, and displaying once more the 'lambeaux sanglants de nos pauvres rêves' [bloody rags of our poor dreams] in a very uncertain present and future.[14]

Sherlock Holmes et les ombres

Vilar's text in *Sherlock Holmes et les ombres* enfolds and develops 'A Scandal in Bohemia', the first of the Sherlock Holmes stories to be published in the *Strand* magazine in 1891, which relates how Irene Adler — an 'adventuress' and famous opera singer — outwits Holmes, hired by the King of Bohemia to retrieve from her a photograph of the two of them together. Holmes fails, but everyone accepts her statement that she would never think of using it against the king. As a story, it lends itself well to exploitation in the contemporary crime genre. Artifice, disguise, and performance are essential to Holmes's quest for the photograph that Irene Adler refuses to hand over. Sherlock disguises himself as an unkempt groom, and later as a non-conformist clergyman. Irene disguises herself as a young man in order to follow the clergyman and verify that it is indeed Sherlock Holmes of Baker Street. Even with her cheery 'Goodnight Mister Sherlock Holmes', he fails to recognise her. His own acting skills are much in evidence too — the 'clergyman' is 'taken ill' and has to be taken into Irene's house to recover, but he also deploys large casts when necessary, as bystanders and firefighters, all actors, act in his scene of a sudden fire at Irene's home. The interrogation of illusion and reality can draw directly on this systematic deployment of artifice.

Christian Louis's photographs have their own dynamic in the complex interaction between text and image here. There are forty-three black-and-white photographs in total, some half-page, the majority full-page, and some of which carry over to about one third of the adjacent page. It is a large format photobook, as tall as and a few centimetres wider than the classic *bande dessinée* book. The majority are studies of places, not people, though most have a single human figure present, on the streets, in passageways, at railway stations and on railway tracks. These are urban images, of street corners, of a part of a bridge, of an alleyway in Wapping or a passageway leading out of an inn. They exemplify the several meanings of 'les ombres' of the title (shadows and other worldly shades): in the deep shadows cast by buildings and walls; in the dark silhouettes and shapes of human figures against the light; and, in the final photograph of the book, one of the figures in an unidentified interior that could be a cafe or waiting room is a blurred ghostly presence. They are photographs of everyday life today — the black cab in the middle distance moving away from the camera, the boys walking along railway tracks — that often invite questions: what is this man doing, crouching down in a dark passageway looking obliquely towards the camera? Is the out-of-focus man with sharp features and white hair, walking along a street with some purpose, caught throwing a backward glance, the same one? There are occasional direct connections between an individual photograph and Vilar's text, but in general the relations between text and image here are thematic and structural, not illustrative. The impulse to speculate about the scene in the image and its relation to the text is one of the points of contact between text and image here, and indeed anticipates the structure of the exhibition catalogues discussed in the next chapter.

'Rewriting Scandal in Bohemia' would be one possible subtitle for Vilar's contribution, for the plot of Conan Doyle's story is retold several times, each time differently. The narrators are collectors of Holmes memorabilia and exegetes of Conan Doyle's text, who collectively raise inevitable questions about the nature, status, meaning, and boundaries of an 'original story'. This is story-telling in infinite regress. The narrator, who will remain unnamed, overhears a customer in a second-hand shop in London enquiring after material relating to Irene Adler, which causes him to remember that, years earlier, in Prague, in the company of Egon Erwin Kirsch (a famous journalist, and here presented as a Holmes fanatic), he heard a young man make a similar enquiry in another second-hand shop. After the narrator's succinct résumé of the story, Egon provides a very different account of it, finds incoherences throughout — accusing Watson of being a very unreliable narrator — and embarks on a speculative pursuit of the truth, involving marriage records in London, the birth of a child, the migration of Irene's Jewish family to the United States, and her later return to Prague. He entrusts to the narrator his extensive notes of a meeting in 1930 with the country's president, who described meeting an English scientist at the turn of the century, who was clearly Sherlock Holmes in disguise. The final re-telling of Irene's story comes from Jan Adler, the customer of the opening scene, who was indeed the one in Prague in 1938. Considering Conan Doyle's story to be full of implausibilities, and stressing the ability of both Holmes and Irene to deceive, he nonetheless distances himself from the hypotheses of other exegetes since he personally knew Irene: she was his grandmother (old, and vague on the details of her own past). His account therefore is of tracking down the details of her past and Holmes's attitude towards her. Like Holmes, then, the journalist and the grandson are seekers after the truth, battling through a mass of lies and deceptions, happy to use disguise themselves when necessary, expert, they believe, in distinguishing verified realities from implausible flights of fancy.

Andrea Goulet's study of the links between the nineteenth-century scientific imagination and early crime fiction in France has demonstrated the difficulty of disentangling reason from unreason in analytical and criminal investigations. Watson's comment that Sherlock's intricate deductive reasoning would have had him 'burned as a witch' in earlier times highlights these blurred boundaries of science as rational process and science as dazzling or intimidating wonder that underscores so much early crime fiction from Edgar Allan Poe onwards:

> Scientific inquiry [...] expanded to include notions of deep geological time, while carrying positivism into the realm of the occult, so that rationality and Spiritism (along with their literary analogues of reason and the fantastic) emerged as interrelated entities rather than oppositional poles.[15]

Sherlock Holmes et les ombres sits squarely within this problematic, and not only with the figure of Holmes embodying both reason and unreason in various guises — his opium and cocaine use, his reason-defying deductions — but also with the Holmes fanatics with their unreasonable accumulation of empirical 'evidence'. Jan Adler shows the narrator his 'cabinet of curiosities' (which turns out to be a house-full rather than a cabinet), overflowing with scientific and preserved biological deformities and stuffed pre-historic remains: 'de quoi troubler un matérialiste' [reason to upset a materialist] is the narrator's reaction (*SH*, p. 19). Louis's photographs reinforce this monstrosity of the scientific and the scientificity of monsters, with his images of exhibits in London's Natural History Museum, the dramatic presence of the huge tyrannosaurus rex skeleton, decidedly gothic flying dinosaurs like large wingless skeletal bats throwing intricate shadows on the vault-like walls and display cases, or their smaller relatives, stuffed crocodiles in display cases completing the triad of land, air, and water creatures retrieved from deep time. This archeological parade of the scientific and the monstrous in museum vaults and 'cabinet of curiosities' is matched in the present by the exploration and excavation of the dark underbelly of the city, the subterranean layers of Prague, the 'ville palimpseste' (p. 30), where the long encounter between Egon and the narrator takes place.

Through the shadows and shades of Sherlock Holmes, and the 'zones d'ombre' (the obscure parts) of his stories, this is a dialogue of the dead as much as of the living. Goulet has shown how skulls played a special role in early crime fiction, combining the enthusiasm for excavation with the shiver of mortality.[16] A white statue of a seated Darwin, taken through the rounded shape of the dinosaur skeleton in the Natural History Museum, a shape echoed in the cloister-like arches above it, has an undeniably strange, spectral quality compared to the physicality of the huge bones. Their sojourn in the realm of the shades of memory and memorabilia seems to contaminate the Holmes enthusiasts; the narrator points to the 'teint blafard' [ashen complexion], the 'peau de spectre' [spectral skin] of Jan Adler, this grandson of a fictional character (*SH*, pp. 73, 77). The narrator himself seems closer to the living dead than the living, an elderly retired journalist judged professionally 'useless' (p. 58), unable to master modern communication methods, living in a bare hotel room that he describes as his 'terminus'. He is about to move into a flat he compares to a 'caveau' [vault] (p. 76), an empty space that is metaphorically closer to the sepulchral vaults and subterranean labyrinths of the dead and the preserved than to the spaces of Holmes and the collectors, crammed full with objects of all kinds.

Darwin's search through the processes of evolution for the origins of species, displayed in the skeletal presences in the Natural History Museum, has its fictional counterpart in the genealogical search for the origins of the Adler family. 'A Scandal in Bohemia' is a quest for a missing photograph, the indisputable proof that there had been a relationship between the king and the singer. *Sherlock Holmes et les ombres* is a quest for Irene Adler and material relating to her, for proof of her existence and knowledge of what really happened. Jan Adler produces an index card, with photograph attached, from Terezin, the model concentration camp, where she died, building on previous references to anti-semitism: the Jewish ghetto in Prague, the Adler family's emigration to America in the nineteenth century to escape persecution, and, most explicitly, the narrator's train journey to London from Prague after the Munich Agreement. He stretches his legs at every station to relieve the sense of oppression caused by the cynicism of his employers towards the fate of Czechoslovakia and the hostility of his fellow travellers towards what they see as its irresponsibility in provoking 'Monsieur Hitler'. But his sense of relief will be short-lived: 'L'angoisse s'installa vite: ces wagons bondés, ces convois constitués à la hâte, ces parcours incertains seraient, dans les mois, les années à venir, les éléments dont personne ne pourrait s'éveiller. Ce retour était une fuite illusoire' [Anxiety quickly took hold. These crowded carriages, these convoys put together in haste, these uncertain trajectories would be, in the months and years to come, elements that no-one could wake up from. This return was an illusory flight] (*SH*, p. 69). In addition, these references inevitably pervade the many photographs here of railways stations, railway tracks, and steam trains, which are destabilised by the comment on the convoys quoted above and by Irene's death in Terezin. Ostensibly picturing the trains of Holmes's age, with individuals emerging from the steam recalling the London fogs of so many Sherlock Holmes films, they also evoke a transport system serving entirely sinister purposes; the 'what happened to Irene

Adler next?' generates an awareness of the future that undermines the innocence of these historical tableaux. 'A Scandal in Bohemia' is overlaid by the scandals of modern Bohemia, the betrayal of Czechoslovakia, and Irene's death.

The problematisation of truthfulness and evidence inherent in the many variants on Irene's story is echoed in the photographs, which are hardly aiming for reality but which are still more layered than at first appearance. Several are photographs of reconstitutions of streets and shops, from Beamish, an open-air museum that recreates north-east working life, and from the Granada Television studios in Manchester, where a Sherlock Holmes series was filmed.[17] The photograph on the front cover highlights visually the undecidable nature of the referent. The brooding face of a middle-aged man, with a bald head, heavy rimmed glasses, and a moustache, seated behind the open window of a counter of some sort, leaning forward on his left arm, is both mysterious and sinister, lit from above so that his glasses cast strong linear shadows across his face. The same image is repeated in the book, and the text introduces him. The narrator is in Madame Tussaud's and has been taken in for a moment by the disdainful stillness of the man on the entrance desk: 'Rien qu'un habile mannequin. Un simulacre parfait' [Just a clever mannequin. A perfect simulacrum] (*SH*, p. 70); and indeed it is, unlike Tussaud's policeman and the murderer standing over the body in the bath (pp. 64, 75), clearly photographs of models; it is only the closed fist of this clerk that looks, on close observation, to be of wax rather than flesh, yet it has the uncanny effect of making one wonder about other figures here, such as an old man in a pub, a smiling man apparently checking tickets in the old-fashioned train carriage, a shop keeper in the hardware shop (pp. 70–71, 57, 8). The image of the entrance clerk is an apt choice for the cover of a photobook that has explored the many layers of the staging of representation visually and textually. The uncanny oscillation between original and model both confirms and complicates the indisputable 'there-ness' of the photographic record, since however much we stare, it won't tell us what is there. Mannequin or person? Baker Street or 'Baker Street' courtesy of Granada Television? Solid evidence is as elusive as Irene.

Nous cheminons entourés de fantômes aux fronts troués

Vilar's seventh novel was his second to be published in Seuil's Fiction & cie series. With no paratextual signs of the crime genre, the novel indicated its literary family by printing 'roman noir' on its front cover. Grappling with the crises and upheavals of the modern world through the prism of political and social criminality, from massacre and murder to hostage-taking, tackling the communist and Nazi states and their crimes, with their multiple repercussions in the present, it fits squarely within the contemporary tradition of political crime fiction and its attention to the history of the century.[18] *Nous cheminons* is also a *roman noir* in its gothic sense, a novel of the strange, of the marvellous. In its repeated use of dark labyrinthine spaces, in the panoply of visual references to the uncanny, and its increasingly insistent erosion of the frontiers between waking and dream states, between received causality and order and the powerful working of other logics, with hints of the supernatural and the undead, *Nous cheminons* incorporates many features of the historic *roman noir*.

It tells several interlocking stories across different periods and different countries, and invites reflection on the great political confrontations within and against the left, on political activism, and on history and historiography. The title highlights both the narrative importance of the cruel history of Trotskyism as well as the gothic world of the undead. Trotsky was murdered in 1940, and Jacques Mornand, one of the pseudonyms used by his assassin Ramón Mercader, is a significant character here. *Nous cheminons* is a story of many wanderers: Trotsky and his wife who have finally settled in Mexico, the Spaniard Mercader, who used the identities of the Belgian Jacques Mornand and the American Frank Jackson. There are exiles from communist Czechoslovakia like Solveig, the journalist sent to interview Victor after his release; and Victor himself, returned from the Middle East, travels between Paris and Prague, as well as between three historical moments: 1938, 1968, and the present, 1989. The year 1938 was a momentous one in this century of wars and revolutions: the year of the Anschluss, Germany's annexation of Austria; of the Munich Agreement and the dismantling of Czechoslovakia as agreed with Germany by the Western powers; of the meeting of André Breton and Trotsky in Mexico, which resulted in the publication of the *Manifesto for an Independent Revolutionary Art*. In Paris, 1938 saw the founding of the IVth International (breaking from Komintern, the IIIrd International founded by Lenin); the killing of Rudolf Klement, a well-known militant and follower of Trotsky whose decapitated corpse was fished out of the Seine; the assassination of Ernst vom Rath, an official of the German Embassy, by Herschel Grynszpan, which triggered Kristallnacht in Germany, the night of multiple and sustained attacks on Jews and their property. It also saw the famous Exposition internationale du Surréalisme where visitors passed Dali's 'taxi pluvieux' [rainy taxi] in the courtyard, where mannequins were presented in tableaux on the streets of the 'ville rêvée' [dreamed city], and Duchamp arranged the scenography, hanging multiple sacks of coal from the ceiling.[19] All this is rendered in *Nous cheminons* through the diary kept by Alfred Katz, a German communist activist, follower of Trotsky and poet who is encouraged by Breton and participates in the exhibition. Alfred arrives in Paris in January 1938 and disappears, presumed murdered, in November 1938.

The novel opens in 1989 with an interplay of dates and anniversaries, the calendar, and the almanach, that will continue to bind both the political anniversaries and intimately personal memories: 'C'est un mardi 8 novembre, figurez-vous, qu'on a perdu toute trace d'Alfred Katz. C'est ce jour anniversaire que nous recouvrons notre liberté. Curieuse coïncidence, n'est-ce pas?' [It's on a Tuesday 8 November, do you realise, that we lost all trace of Alfred Katz. It's on the day of this anniversary that we regain our freedom. Strange coincidence, isn't it?] (*NC*, p. 9). But of course *le hasard objectif* has taught us there are no coincidences: this points us from the very outset to the intertwining of the stories of Victor and Alfred. The words are spoken by Alex Katz, Alfred's son, as he and Victor are finally free to pick up their lives after more than three years being held hostage together in the Middle East. Victor had accepted Marc's offer to work as a 'grand reporter' travelling the world, but he did not get far from the airport on his first trip. The taxi that Alex proposed they share into Beirut city centre was surrounded by men with Kalachnikovs. After a debriefing at the Val de Grâce military hospital, where Laurent, first described as a doctor, then as a member of the special services, and then just as 'le flic', enters his life, Victor returns to his flat, having been warned it has been broken into and cleared out during his absence. All his photographic equipment, all his personal belongings have gone, apart from one shabby chair and the cats Radek and Bastille, cared for by a neighbour. The following day, 9 November, the anniversary of Kristallnacht, the Berlin Wall starts to come down. On 17 November, International Students' Day — marking the killing of students in Prague in 1939 in reprisals for protests again the German occupation — commemoration of this anniversary combines with protest against the Czech communist regime in what would become known as the 'Velvet Revolution', that would bring Vaclav Havel to power in December 1989. The novel closes with Victor witnessing the investiture of Havel in Prague, putting an end to years of repression after the previous attempt at freedom and independence was crushed by Soviet tanks on 21 August 1968. As an activist in May 68, Victor vividly remembers the headlines of this invasion, and the self-immolation of Jan Palach the following January.

This, then, is a structure that places large themes of twentieth-century politics centre-stage, focusing on the commitment of individuals in the context of huge political forces: the fall of the Berlin Wall and the collapse of the Soviet Union; Soviet communism and the relation of its Interior Ministry, the NKVD, and Komintern to other significant movements such as the IVth International; the ascendancy of National Socialism in Germany and the national confrontations across Europe that it was provoking; the Spanish Civil War, in its second year in 1938, where the Spanish Communist Party (of which Ramón Mercader was a member) and the Trotskyist POUM had also turned on each other. Politically, the novel raises questions of commitment and betrayal, and of the relationship between politics and art, articulating them through the personal memories and memoirs of militants. More specifically, it interrogates the level of awareness and discrimination of politically active individuals as to which are the defining issues of the day when they are operating in a world in crisis. This is a matter of life and death in the 1930s, but is equally relevant to militancy in 1968. Using the figure of Paul Nizan, the prominent Communist Party intellectual of the 1930s, who is first mentioned (and dismissed) in relation to May 68, Victor remembers the camaraderie, the loves and the hatreds of the moment:

> Les 'Italiens', les trotsks, les maos, les anars, les spontanéistes, les bordighistes, les archéo-situs, les posadistes, les contre tous les courants et quelques autres. Là, c'est l'instant de grâce crépusculaire, la pause, entre la manif historique et prochaine AG-soviet. Le temps de savourer que vingt ans est le plus bel âge de la vie, quoi qu'en ait dit un néostalinien mort bêtement sous l'uniforme, à Dunkerque. (*NC*, p. 100)[20]

> [The 'Italiens', the trots, the Maoists, the anarchists, the spontaneitists, the followers of Bordiga, the archeo-situationists, the followers of Posadas, the

group of those against all the currents and a few others. That was the twilight moment of grace, the pause, between the historic demo and the next Soviet-GM. The time to savour the fact that twenty is the best age of your life, whatever a neostalinist who died a stupid death in uniform at Dunkirk might have said.]

But if, as Vilar suggested, utopias and betrayal go together, Victor's own failure in 1968 relates to the invasion of Czechoslovakia. His lover at the time, Marine, an actress and former member of the Resistance, proposed they drove immediately through the night to join the Czech protestors. Victor's enthusiasm did not however translate into action. After the intensity of May when everyone was hooked up to their transistor radios, there was only indifference to Prague in August:

> Ce mercredi 21 août, chacun vaquait à ses occupations ou se livrait à l'insouciance d'être en vacances. Une saloperie de plus avait été commise, ailleurs, dans un autre monde. A supposer qu'on soit au courant, personne n'y pouvait rien. Je me suis dégonflé. (NC, p. 175).
>
> [That Wednesday August 21st, everyone was going about their own business or enjoying the nonchalant feeling of being on holiday. Yet more villainy had been committed elsewhere, in another world. Even supposing one knew about it, nothing could be done. I chickened out.]

A choice that is echoed in the account of an earlier failure, this time by Paul Lourcet, an elderly television producer who approaches Victor about making a film of his experiences as a hostage. Lourcet, who was close to Alfred Katz, although as a Communist Party member politically opposed to him, must have been about twenty in 1938, Victor guesses. He not only had no interest in the fate of Czechoslovakia, a country stitched together by the Treaty of Versailles, a 'pays en toc' [cheap imitation of a country], he failed the test of Spain: 'L'Espagne ou pas? Ceux qui sont allés s'y battre et les autres. Pour les gens de ma génération, vue par la vôtre, c'est tout à fait discriminant' [Spain or not? Those who went to fight there and the others. For people of my generation, seen by yours, it is a clear dividing line] (NC, p. 277).

This layered historical structure of moments of massive upheaval and crisis is traversed by the characters who effectively hold the interlocking elements together at the level of the diegesis, by the repetition of anecdote and event, but also by the historical, fictional, and metafictional reflections on this lived convergence of present and past. Inevitably such a structure of continuities and discontinuities, of similarities and contrasts invites questions about its epistemological bases, the nature of the models of history and memory being mobilised here. In a letter to Vilar, Daniel Bensaïd argued that the novel's 'ingenious structure' depoliticises history, in suggesting that history is made of patterns and repetitions from which we can learn.[21] He cites other comparisons of Milosevic to Hitler, as well as the 'Appel des 101' after the death of Makome' M Bowole', shot in police custody, which stated:

> Les générations de policiers, accomplissant les basses besognes, se sont toujours donné la main. Les mêmes qui, aujourd'hui, contrôlent au faciès, remplissaient les autobus de la ligne Drancy-Auschwitz, en juillet 1942. Les mêmes noyaient dans la Seine les martyrs algériens d'octobre 1961.[22]

[Generations of policemen, carrying out their dirty work, have always joined forces. The same ones who, today, are using facial profiling for police checks, were in July 1942 filling the buses of the Drancy-Auschwitz line. The same ones drowned the Algerian martyrs in the Seine in October 1961.]

Bensaïd suggested that the use of 'les mêmes', collapsing together such very different times, demonstrates a poverty of political thinking, arguing that the present does not flow out of the past, that it is the strategic point in time where meanings are endlessly tied and untied. And it is the opposite that he finds in *Nous cheminons*, as his letter to Vilar continues: 'Or, j'ai l'impression que la mémoire dans tes livres tend à se faire de plus en plus historienne; que le poids du passé écrase le présent et que son ombre devient envahissante' [I have the impression that memory in your books is tending to become more and more a historian's memory; that the weight of the past crushes the present and that its shadow is overwhelming'], which leads him to conclude that 'Je flaire chez ton Victor quelque chose de cet air du temps, de cet accablement sous le poids de l'histoire monumentale. D'où un livre hanté. Histoire de fantômes' [I detect in your Victor something of this trend, of this burden of the weight of monumental history. Hence a haunted book. A story of ghosts].

The complex deployment of surrealism might be considered to add to this notion of history as a haunted house rather than a living process governed by the complex political fabric of the here and now. As well as the surrealist exhibition and Breton's visit to Trotsky, other scenes reproduce Breton's texts as the earlier Paris novels did with *Nadja*. Together with Solveig Victor follows Alfred and Mila, whom he has just met in the exhibition, on their nocturnal stroll through Paris, a stroll past the Tour St Jacques surrounded with scaffolding that replicates a key passage of *L'Amour fou*.[23] Cohen discusses the importance of 'the ghosts of Paris' in Breton's poetic economy of the surreal: 'The uncanny effects of Parisian places, Breton suggests, derive from effaced historical memories that continue to cluster around the place of their occurrence in invisible but perceptible ghosts'.[24] But the 'traces of the insurrectional past in the uncanny present' would pass unnoticed, she argues, were it not for the surrealist muse Nadja, and quotes Nadja's fearful reaction to the place Dauphine:

> Elle se trouble à l'idée de ce qui s'est déjà passé sur cette place et de ce qui s'y passera encore. Où ne se perdent en ce moment dans l'ombre que deux ou trois couples, elle semble voir une foule: 'Et les morts, les morts!'[25]

> [She is disturbed at the thought of what has occurred in this square and what will occur here again. Where only two or three couples are at this moment disappearing into the shadows, she seems to see a crowd: 'And the dead, the dead'.]

What differentiates Vilar's dead is how material they are in contrast to Nadja's — not the presence of an indeterminate number of dead, but the pile of dead bodies on the Paris street in *Les Exagérés* produced by the September massacres, and contemporary to characters like the père Duchesne who is striding along these same streets. In *Nous cheminons* also, the dead are not so much ghosts as 'ghosted', killed for very specific political reasons, part of the lives of the characters, as Rudolf Klement is, until they are assassinated. One of the chapters in Jan Valtin's memoir is entitled 'Mort en sursis', someone whose death is now only a matter of time, and many of the characters in *Nous cheminons* could be described as the walking dead, heading towards the catastrophes that will claim them. This is compounded rhetorically by the number of characters whose foreheads receive fatal or major injuries, like Blaise, the very sinister communist, one of the rare survivors whom Victor visits, who carries a large star-shaped scar in the middle of his forehead; or Alex, killed in a car crash, speared through his head by one of the metal poles catapulted from the lorry in front. In other words, the relation of past to present in *Nous cheminons* cannot be reduced to a one-way street, given the overlapping dynamic of the multiple narrators and very particular relationship between the narrator in the present and the first-person diary from the past.

At one point Solveig gives Victor a watch with hands that move backwards, imitating the clock of the synagogue tower in Prague, where the hands move in accordance with Hebrew script from right to left. By the end of the novel, forward-moving, chronological waking time seems to have been abandoned, and moving backwards, 'à rebours', is an appropriate metaphor for Victor's progress in the novel, continuing on his way through November and December 1989 while looking backwards at the catastrophe of the 1930s. In other words, Victor's stance is that of Benjamin's 'Angelus Novus', looking backwards as the rubble of history piles up before him. Benjamin's metaphor expresses his hostility to a grand narrative of historical progress; Vilar's structure shows the limitations of the utopian impulse towards positive revolutionary change that motivates his characters. As Nazism increasingly gains the upper hand through a combination of unbridled violence and the grandiose spectacle and glory at Nuremberg, it is clear the militants are not only fighting the wrong enemy, but are being drawn, in the Soviet tactic of hostility to social democrats, into a damaging and damning alliance with the Nazi Party;[26] Bensaïd contextualises these errors by suggesting they too were making the error of historical analogies, counting on the coming war to deliver revolutionary change in the way that the First World War had done, in combination with the 'difficulty of realizing the totally unprecedented nature of Stalinism'.[27] While such contextualisation might be politically helpful, I would argue that it is a different blind spot that *Nous cheminons* highlights. Alfred Katz is clearly a mere foot soldier of the revolution who concentrates on his given tasks, but when he takes a job at *Match* (the photojournal that was the precedessor of *Paris Match*) he is struck by some photographs of men in striped pyjamas in camps behind barbed wire that Nathan, the keeper of the *Match* archives, shows him. 'Quelque chose nous échappait dans la situation. Une donnée nouvelle, inédite, inimaginable encore' [We are missing something here. A new element, unprecedented, as yet unimaginable], he later comments, thinking back to them (*NC*, p. 348).

The development of the personal stories and relationships through these times of turbulence is at the heart of the plot. Victor has no desire to re-equip his studio and return to his work as a photographer. His time is spent in encounters with Gaïl, who had once been Alex's mistress and who gives him Alfred's notebook after

Alex's death. He meets with Solveig, with Laurent who continues to keep an eye on him, with Lourcet and with Gaïl's father, Levine, both of whom knew Alfred.[28] Victor spends much of his time reading Alfred's notebook, which relates his political activities distributing leaflets, his work, his meeting with André Breton, and his subsequent involvement with the creation of the Exposition internationale du Surréalisme. On the opening night he meets Mila, photographic model for Man Ray and occasional prostitute, who has various relationships, including with a Communist Party member Félix. But she chooses to marry Alfred, with Félix as best man, and organises a 'déjeuner sur l'herbe' to celebrate, stripping off for a recreation of Manet's famous painting. She also encourages both men into bed with her for regular threesomes.

The enigmas driving the narrative relate to fictional events (was Alex's death in a car crash soon after their return an accident or murder?) and historical ones (is the death of Trotsky's son Leon Sedov in Paris in 1938 due to illness or murder?), as well as the wish to know how the murderous events of the 1930s and 1940s, and the dismantling of the regimes of Eastern Europe, will play out in the detailed stories of Alfred, Mila, and Félix, and of Solveig and Victor. Biography and identity are also vectors of enigma in these circles where pseudonyms and false identities proliferate. Victor reads out the passage of the notebook where Alfred Katz first encounters the Belgian Jacques Mornand with his American friend Sylvia. 'And we know the rest,' comments Solveig, and indeed we do as the pair, who will end up in Mexico where Mornand/Mercader will assassinate Trotsky, start to ingratiate themselves. Alfred never learns Mornand's real name, but becomes increasingly suspicious and finally denounces him. Laurent gives Victor a potted résumé of Solveig's chequered history, suggesting she had been an informer, as well as bemoaning the frequent impossibility of constructing coherent biographies from police archives. He has been searching for Alfred, and makes no headway with the thousands of index cards. He has fared little better with Victor: 'Vous n'êtes plus qu'un dossier à ramifications multiples que je ne sais pas classer, organiser' [You are nothing but a file with multiple connections that I don't know how to classify or organise] (*NC*, p. 332). The intersecting pathways of these multiple biographies are also a source of bemusement for Laurent, as he realises Victor and Solveig are renting the same room in the rue Gît-le-cœur hotel where Alfred and Mila stayed (the hotel made famous by William Burroughs and the beat poets, whose concierge on the reception desk is engaged with cutting up text for a novel he is working on). Are these 'coincidences gigognes' [coincidences within coincidences], in Laurent's term, meaningless or meaningful, revelatory of something else, in the manner of *le hasard objectif*?

The paintings of Giorgio de Chirico, Raoul Ubac, Paul Delvaux, and Edward Hopper create a referential infrastructure of strange city spaces, detached in the case of the first three from contemporary urban life, neither aimless nor purposeful, but impossible to locate precisely in a narrative sequence of the time and space displayed. Delvaux's *Entrée de la ville* plays an important role in the narrative, as Victor finds this image, of a man holding a map on a large avenue, inserted in Alfred's notebook.

The image seems to suggest there is a key, a possibility, via another image of a map, to navigating one's pathway through the city. There are various marginal comments in the notebook made by Alex, and this might therefore be one of them, a clue to negotiation of the puzzle space of the city, and so it proves, perhaps, although not in the way intended.

Along with the rather dreamlike, pale spaces of Chirico and Delvaux, the narrative includes several sequences offering a different but equally unsettling sense of disorientation. The surrealist exhibition is the model here, as the visitors stumble through the dark 'streets', by the light of the torches handed out at the entrance, peering at the extravagantly-dressed mannequins that were intended to be taken for women in the darkness. Mila reports that Man Ray had wanted her to take part, dressed and standing as if one of the mannequins. This is replicated as Victor and Solveig make their way through the dark, dirty, empty flat in the soon-to-be-demolished Grisette building where Mila and Alfred once lived, and in the underground passages of the Lucerna shopping complex in Prague (built by Vaclav Havel's grandfather) where the final section of the novel takes place. The night-time landscape of streets, monuments, and arcades combines with a subterranean world of the surrealist dream city and the underground city in Prague, inhabited by figures of the uncanny, poised between life and death, like the mannequins and, as we shall see, the figure of the tramp. Solveig describes herself as a 'vagabond' (*tulák* in Czech); her name is a pseudonym, taken from a production of *Peer Gynt*, whose eponymous hero wanders the world while Solveig waits, but Solveig herself is the wanderer here.

Victor too has been uprooted. After the lightless confined spaces of the hostage years, what one might call the internal scaffolding of his life has been destroyed. All his possessions have gone: his photographic equipment and his miscellaneous accumulation of pieces of Paris. Moreover, his local cafe *La Capitale* is closing, and the kiosk outside it, where he gets his morning paper — a most intimate and everyday frontier of the personal and the impersonal — has to look for a new site.[29] New trajectories had been provided by following Alfred but this is a guide that will prove to have been forged: Victor destroys the 'puzzle-labyrinthe' of notes and photographs he has been pinning to his wall to try and make sense of events since his return, as all the clues and anchoring points have melted away (*NC*, p. 393), and as the cats tear the notes to pieces, he discovers the Delvaux sketch is in fact a collage — 'Avant d'en arriver à une perspective classique, Delvaux avait imaginé dans un premier temps des lignes de fuite aberrantes, des édifices piégés' [Before settling for a classical perspective, Delvaux had at first imagined aberrational perspectives, and booby-trapped buildings]. It has a little note underneath it: 'Blaise: un traître — Félix: un délateur, un faussaire' [Blaise: a traitor — Félix: an informer, a forger] (p. 395). The guide to 1938 proves to be a quagmire of falsehoods; aberrational perspectives and booby-trapped buildings are closer to Victor's realities now. After which, following Solveig, he uproots himself to Prague, shedding Paris like shedding a skin. If the implication of the title is that the 'nous' of 'nous cheminons' are 'des morts en sursis', the same is certainly true of Victor whose identity has been progressively taken apart through the text. The fragility of Victor in this text, the elaborate dismantling of all the thematic supports of the character, bring to the fore a structural element, namely that this photographer-subject is frequently the object of others' gaze and attention, that the seeker of knowledge through the maze of clues and uncertainties is often a quarry. Here he discovers in Prague, through a friend of Laurent, that he has been the object of an experiment carried out by Laurent, to understand the psychology of the hostage. The stripping of his flat was a deliberate destabilising tactic. His understanding of everything he has been going through was another kind of *trompe l'œil*, and it is not the only one.

As the diary progresses, Victor stops quoting it; instead there is a shift, firstly to third-person narration, then to first-person narration, but not typographically shown to be a quotation, as in the earlier extracts. Lourcet comments on the troubling merging of identities of Alfred and Victor: ' Peu à peu vous êtes mis à parler en son nom' [Little by little you've started speaking in his name] (*NC*, p. 437). Most of the time, the content distinguishes it from the first-person narration of Victor's life, although one episode demonstrates how the boundaries between Victor and Alfred are being blurred. Alfred has a meeting, of which he is very wary, and sees a stranger walk along who is jumped on by three men, killed and thrown into the canal — it is clear Alfred was the intended victim of this crime he has just witnessed. He moves away, through thick undergrowth to avoid the path, smelling the fresh blood from the nearby abattoir of La Villette, 'Je faillis renoncer, tant j'étais épuisé' [I nearly abandoned the attempt, I was so exhausted]. The next section immediately continues: 'Je rentrai en fin de matinée, fourbu. Du côté de la Villette, le canal était redevenu un endroit paisible, plus du tout un lieu du crime. Solveig regardait un flash d'information' [I got in at the end of the morning, absolutely worn out. At the La Villette end, the canal had become a peaceful place once more, no longer a crime scene. Solveig was watching a news flash] (p. 381). Until the mention of Solveig, the reader could be forgiven for thinking they were still in 1938.

In Prague, Victor walks through the streets listening to the tape of Lourcet's confession, a tape Laurent has found in an envelope addressed to Victor after Lourcet's death. Lourcet was Félix. Lourcet wrote the notebook. On the tape, Lourcet retells the story, this time from his point of view as Félix the communist militant. After the years of the war and the Resistance, he tried to track down information about Mila and her child, discovered she was denounced and deported to Auschwitz, where she died. In 1962, Lourcet met Alex who had just written a best-selling work about his dead parents in which he asks whether his father was a revolutionary hero or a bastard, whether his mother was a whore or a remarkable role model. In the whole work, there was no mention of Félix, so Lourcet writes himself into Alex's story by inventing his father's diary where he does have a major role. But the evaporation of Alfred as narrator has a disintegrating impact on the text itself — an autobiographical pact is broken, for not only is Alfred not the author, he spins out of reach. How should it now be read, now we know Félix is the author? What, of Alfred's thoughts, hopes, emotions, is true in it all? And as

Alfred's voice dissolves, Victor's appropriation of Alfred's voice also dissolves. The relation of Victor to his own biography is overturned.

That appearances are deceptive and unstable is a lesson of all Vilar's works; the focus on the years 1989 and 1938 places the destruction of a previously taken-for-granted landscape as a central force in a narrative that treats the personal and the political as inextricably linked. The fall of the Berlin Wall, the overthrow of Ceausescu in Romania, and the collapse of communism in Czechoslovakia are intimately unsettling. All the landmarks of political life have been swept away, it is the end of Yalta and indeed of the context to the left's easy vocabulary of communism and comrades since 1968. 'La brèche s'est ouverte sur le grand inconnu, pour tout le monde' [A breach has opened up to the great unknown, for everyone] (*NC*, p. 177), as was the case for the cataclysmic events of 1938. The rubble of history piles up with no signposts forward and the landscape has dissolved. This is compounded by the pervasive nature of *trompe l'œil* and simulacra, from the uncertainty surrounding the deaths of Alex or Sedov to make-believe communications such as Victor and Alex's televised messages as hostages, read out under constraint, with any effort to signal their inauthenticity proving invisible to the French audience; or Rudolf Klement's letters supposedly proving his continuing existence, derided as fake by his Trotskyist comrades; or the cultural extravagances of Breton, ce 'maître des simulacres' [master of simulacra] (p. 116). The photographs of Prague that Victor had taken on an earlier visit are dismissed by Solveig as nothing but clichéd reproductions of what the authorities wanted him to see. 'Gratter avec persévérance sur la perverse apparence des choses' [Scratching with perseverance on the perverse appearances of things], in Laurent's phrase, does not necessarily reveal a more authentic reality (p. 292).

One figure with a particular weight in this thematics of movement and confinement, of obstacle and obscurity, is the tramp, who comes and goes, says nothing, and seems to be freighted with mystery and significance. His loose bundle of rags for clothes prefigures the later appearance of Odradek, the strange creature who lives under the stairs and in entrance halls in Kafka's 'Cares of a Family Man'. Victor returns from captivity to find the tramp apparently living on the ground floor of his building. Before leaving Paris, Victor joins the tramp on his bench and is given a cigarette and a drink from this mysterious figure wreathed in cigarette smoke and frosty breath: 'Mon clochard n'avait pas de visage' [My tramp had no face] (*NC*, p. 394). Lourcet is also drawn into this configuration of marginality and mysterious wisdom. Victor goes to say farewell to the dying Lourcet, a moving episode in the chapter entitled 'Odradek est la forme que prennent les choses tombées dans l'oubli, selon Walter Benjamin, que je ne savais trop comment saluer' [Odradek is the form that things take in oblivion, according to Walter Benjamin, whom I was unsure how else to acknowledge] (p. 399). Lourcet is also a physical wreck, disappearing into the shadows of his ill-lit flat. In Prague Victor meets Odradek, the strange star-shaped creature who addresses Victor with his voice of leaves. Victor visits the street near Prague Castle where Kafka lived, and many of the events of the novel have Kafkaesque overtones, especially the Moscow trials, the sense of threat directed at Trotsky and his companion-followers like Alfred as their daily routine takes them into danger, even the fact that Victor cannot grasp how all these interactions fit together and that, like Alex, he could be at risk of random violence. But it is Odradek, 'the form which things assume in oblivion', that Adorno referred to as 'a motif of transcendence [...] or of the overcoming of death' that confirms the strange in-betweenness of the final section.[30]

The final chapter is entitled 'La Lanterne magique' [The magic lantern] and closes in the underground passages of the Lucarna. The Theatre of the Magic Lantern, where the dissident Civic Forum met after the suppression of protests on International Students' Day (17 November 1989), is not within the Lucarna, but political discussions are continuing here, and one room is screening footage of protests outside. This complex underground labyrinth of rooms and streets evokes others, directly and indirectly: the rue de la Vieille-lanterne in the surrealist dream city; Dante's Inferno (Solveig is the guide here); and the labyrinth building of the Musée Grévin with its uncanny life models and the magic shows of its Cabinet fantastique. This is a no-mans-land: 'the zone in which it is impossible to die is also the no-man's-land between man and thing: within it meet Odradek'.[31]

In these final pages, Victor sees Solveig looking like Mila, and is aware of Alfred not far away. Odradek tells him about Nathan, the *Match* archivist, who had left immediately for Prague after Munich, who had taught Odradek about archiving, and who had been put on trial because he remembered too much. Odradek talks to Victor as if he were Alfred, and stuffs all his archives into Victor's pockets. Victor's last meeting is with Solveig:

> Katz et Mila étaient avec nous, ce soir. Félix aussi, Alex et tous les autres. C'était leur dernière nuit. Tu les as conduits où il fallait. [...] Ils font maintenant partie de la cohorte discrète et tenace des ombres de Prague. [...] Elle dit encore: ' — Il y en a qui vont et viennent. Toi, tu reviens. Maintenant, ce sera à Prague'. (*NC*, p. 476)
>
> [Katz and Mila were with us, this evening. Félix as well, and Alex and all the others. It was their last night. You have led them to the right place. [...] They are now part of the discreet and tenacious cohort of the shades of Prague. [...] She also says: 'There are those who come and go. You, you come back. Now, it will be in Prague'.]

It makes sense to describe Victor as a revenant: held away from Paris as a hostage where he experienced a dramatic mock execution (the bullets hitting the wall just above his head), returning to the shell of his home and professional life, being knocked over by a car, which he takes as another attempted murder, like Alex's, even attacking the genuinely concerned motorist by planting his lighted cigarette in the middle of the motorist's forehead. As we have seen, Victor merges with Alfred, including in the narration of Alfred witnessing his own potential murder, and in Prague Victor listens to the demise of Alfred as the actor of his own story, on a recording from a dead man, for the tape of Lourcet's confession ends with his suicide: 'La detonation explosa dans ma tête. Je titubai, glissai.' [The sound of the shot exploded in my head. I staggered and slipped down] (*NC*, p. 438). Time and again, Victor is taken through his own annihilation. In the novel's undeniably non-realist ending, boundaries between different states of being, between life and dreams, present and past, disappear and, in a final resetting of the interrogation of representation, of original and simulacrum, all is swept up in the power of fiction: 'La fiction ne déçoit pas' [Fiction does not disappoint] (*NC*, p. 472).

In Sauvageot's documentary, *Jean-François Vilar: 95% de réel*, Vilar described the new novel he was working on, which was set in Prague. Julius Katz dies after falling out of a building. Suicide or murder? His friend Victor wants to know; how could this happen in 1993? The Holocaust, and particularly Terezin, is at the centre of the story about Julius and two brothers, his father and uncle, the one a communist militant and journalist, the other an apolitical architect, both Jewish. Both will die in Terezin, one in the ghetto town, the other in the small fortress. Julius is a child in Terezin's ghetto town, survives but has no memory of it. As an adult in communist Czechoslovakia, he will do some work with the police. The novel was structured to raise again questions of politics, history, and memory, the history and memory of the Holocaust, and the history and memory of Czechoslovakia's past, working through the political challenge of being moral in a world where there is no possible morality, which is the challenge of the 1930s and 1940s, and of the post-war years of Czechoslovakia under Soviet control. The new novel would move 'd'une histoire privée à la tragédie du siècle' [from a private story to the tragedy of the century]. In the two texts discussed in this chapter, it is indeed the tragedy of the century that is the focus. *Sherlock Holmes et les ombres* creates its complicated stories around a fiction, but one rooted in a place, and will take its central character to the tragedy of dying in Terezin. *Nous cheminons* investigates a decade of tremendous hope and tremendous loss, recording how the moment of revolutionary promise, the coming together of the avant-gardes of art and politics, is destroyed as the thousands of Trotskyist militants are destroyed, by Nazism and by Stalin's communism.

Nous cheminons and *Sherlock Holmes et les ombres* might seem to end without the tangible materiality of the cities of Venice and Djemila, but the accent in these texts is on fictionality. And the fictions of the past are told by an elderly man moving towards death, and by Victor, who displays many characteristics of the walking dead. These are fictions that are not so much haunted by history as bearing the melancholy prospect of death and loss in the present. Their ghosts are ghosts of the fiction, not history. The dead thronging the place Dauphine in *Nadja* create a frisson of horror, an anonymous crowd of ghosts, the past invading the present through a haunting. In *Nous cheminons* and in *Sherlock Holmes et les ombres* they are 'les ombres', shades in the dark zones; Mila, Alfred and Félix, and Victor, all gathered in the pure story-telling of Prague's theatrical underground passages that have become, with the arrival of Odradek, a metaphysical space. In these fictions, it is the present that melts into air.

Notes to Chapter 6

1. Jean-François Vilar, *Les Fous de Chaillot* (Paris: La Baleine, 1997). The Tourisme et polar series was launched by Jean-Bernard Pouy for La Baleine in 1997, 291 titles have been published so far.
2. See: Jean-François Vilar, 'Le Réveil du Golem', in *Métropolis: la ville est un roman 1841–1991* (Paris: Conseil Général Seine Saint-Denis and Denoël, 1991), pp. 20–21; 'Rue de Prague', in *Octobre 1983/1993* (Paris: La Terrasse de Gutenberg, 1993); 'Je ne sais pas', in *Le Cinéma des écrivains: nouvelles*, ed. by Antoine de Baeque (Paris: Cahiers du cinéma, 1995), pp. 131–37; and 'Paris-Prague: aller simple et vague retour', *1968: le devenir de mai*, special issue of *Lignes*, 34 (1998), 82–98.
3. Hervé Delouche and Alexis Violet [Jean-Michel Mension], 'Tapez "noir" pour mémoire' [interview with Jean-François Vilar], *Rouge*, 1538 (16 April 1993), 14.
4. Ibid.
5. Jean-François Vilar, 'Postface', in Jan Valtin, *Sans patrie ni frontières*, trans. by Jean-Claude Henriot, rev. by Philippe Carella (Arles: Actes Sud, coll. Babel, 1997), pp. 873–94.
6. Vilar, 'Noir c'est noir', cited above, Chapter One.
7. Karl Marx and Friedrich Engels, *The Communist Manifesto*, intro. by A. J. P. Taylor, trans. by Sam Moore (Harmondsworth: Penguin Books, 1967), p. 83.
8. Marshall Berman, *All That is Solid Melts into Air: The Experience of Modernity* (London: Verso, 1983), pp. 89, 95.
9. Ibid., p. 333.
10. Vilar, 'Postface', p. 878.
11. Ibid.
12. Margaret Cohen, *Profane Illuminations: Walter Benjamin and the Paris of Surrealist Revolution* (Berkeley, Los Angeles, & London: University of California Press, 1993), p. 1.
13. Delouche and Violet, 'Tapez "noir" pour mémoire', p. 14.
14. Vilar, 'Noir c'est noir', p. 10.
15. Andrea Goulet, *Legacies of the Rue Morgue: Science, Space, and Crime Fiction in France* (Philadelphia: University of Pennsylvania Press, 2016), p. 3. Conan Doyle's interest in and support for spiritualism is well known. See also David Platten, 'Reading-glasses, Guns and Robots: A History of Science in French Crime Fiction', in *Crime and Punishment*, ed. by Atack, pp. 253–70.
16. Goulet, *Legacies of the Rue Morgue*, pp. 116–17.
17. Both institutions are thanked by Louis in his acknowledgements.
18. 'You will find the whole history of the twentieth century in the Série noire', commented its director Patrick Raynal ('Le Roman noir est l'avenir de la fiction', *Roman noir, Temps modernes*, p. 94).
19. Along the gloomy corridors, each of the 'tableaux' was given a street name. There are several photographs of the Exposition internationale du Surréalisme, including the streets, in *Silent Partners*, ed. by Munro, pp. 217–20.
20. Nizan began his angry anti-colonialist polemic, *Aden, Arabie*, with the famous sentence: 'J'avais vingt ans. Je ne laisserai personne dire que c'est le plus bel âge de la vie' [I was twenty years old, and I will not let anyone say it is the best time of your life]. *Aden, Arabie* had been reissued by Maspero, in 1960 with a preface by Sartre. It is also worth noting that the Communist Party is conspicuously absent from this list.
21. Daniel Bensaïd, letter to Jean-François Vilar, May 1993. Three of Bensaïd's letters to Vilar, in January 1992 and May and September 1993, have been posted to the website <danielbensaid.org> [accessed 27 May 2020].
22. 'Appel des 101', quoted in Maurice Rajfus and Alexis Violet [Jean-Michel Mension], 'Présentation de l'Observatoire des Libertés publiques' (1994) <http://quefaitlapolice.samizdat.net/?page_id=90> [accessed 10 November 2019]. Makomé M'Bowolé was shot when in police custody in April 1993.
23. Captured in Brassaï's famous photograph, and on the cover of the novel's original edition. André Breton, *L'Amour fou* (Paris: Gallimard, coll. Folio, 1982).
24. Cohen, *Profane Illuminations*, p. 83.

25. Ibid., pp. 98–100; André Breton, *Nadja* (Paris: Gallimard, coll. Folio, 1964), pp. 94–96.
26. See also Vilar, 'Postface', in Valtin's memoir on his life which discusses this in some detail.
27. Bensaïd, letter to Vilar, May 1993.
28. Levine is one of the hybrid figures in this tale where historical and fictional characters mingle, drawing on Jean van Heijenoort, Trotsky's secretary, who went to America after the war, became an eminent mathematician, and who was killed, like Levine, by his estranged fourth wife whom he was visiting in Mexico City.
29. One of the epigraphs to the novel is a quotation from Breton's *Nadja*: 'Un journal du matin suffira toujours à me donner de mes nouvelles' [A morning paper is all I ever need to give me news of myself].
30. Theodor W. Adorno and Walter Benjamin, *The Complete Correspondance 1928–1940*, ed. by Henri Lonitz, trans. by Nicholas Walker (Cambridge, MA: Harvard University Press, 1999), p. 69.
31. Adorno quoted in Mike Newman, 'Odradek and the Rethinking of Political Method in the Work of Art' <https://research.gold.ac.uk/21412/1/Newman-Benjanin%20Brecht%20Wall%20and%20Odradek%20for%20Oxford_rev.pdf> [accessed 7 May 2020]. Newman is discussing a photograph of Jeff Wall that pursues the dialogue between *film noir* and the everyday in interesting ways. See also the presentation of *Odradek, Tàboritskà 8, Prague, 18 July 1994* at <https://www.tate.org.uk/whats-on/tate-modern/exhibition/jeff-wall/jeff-wall-room-guide/jeff-wall-room-guide-room-6> [accessed 27 May 2020].

CHAPTER 7

Memento Mori

That Vilar collaborated with artists is not surprising; the visual arts are threaded through all his novels. Vilar's writings encompass publications with contemporary artists through photobooks, contributions to the artist's book — a book created by the artist as a work of art — and interpretative texts in exhibition catalogues, including the two that will be discussed in this chapter. As we have seen, photography, film, and painting, in conjunction with architecture, are mobilised to generate the narrative and to place to the fore the interrogation of representation, as well as being a foyer of reflection on sight, perception, quest, desire, and death. From Duchamp's rather macabre *Étant donnés* that opens *C'est toujours les autres qui meurent*, the works of many other artists have been deployed as part of the rich metafictional tapestry that accompanies the various quests of Victor the photographer. The interplay of text and image, of photographs and drawings, including Vilar's own, was fundamental to the magazine *Tango*.

Vilar reflects on Jacques Monory's work through the medium of fiction in his texts for two exhibition catalogues of the artist's work: 'Poses' in *Come-back*, the 1990 exhibition in the Sonia Zannettacci gallery in Geneva, and 'Memento mori', in *Memento mori*, the 2014 exhibition in the same gallery. The deployment of narrative fiction as commentary and illumination constructs a structural affinity between text and images, facilitating the exploration from within of Monory's visual narrative spaces and their recurrent figures. Monory has been the subject of extensive art-historical attention.[1] Most relevant to the work of Vilar is the sustained reflection on realism in art in the 1970s in which Monory was an important figure. I discuss this not only to explore further the political and ideological issues in avant-garde art that were addressed earlier, but also to situate Vilar's fictional discourse on Monory in relation to Jean-François Lyotard's very different approach to Monory and narration.

Vilar dedicates 'Poses', his short story in *Come-back*, to Monory 'dont les images me sont aussi indispensables qu'un journal du matin' [whose images are as indispensable to me as a morning paper] (*P*, p. 4); paintings by Monory feature in *C'est toujours les autres* and other novels, and several of the murder scenes evoked in *État d'urgence* are imbued with the imagery of Monory's scenes: corpse and bullets in a bedroom or hotel room. There are strong thematic and conceptual continuities also between text and art in the photobooks created with Michel Saloff and Christian Louis, and in the artist books of performance artist Pierre Molinier and of

Jean-Paul Ruiz. Ruiz's *Moments noirs* (1992) brought together five wood engravings with handwritten texts by the crime writers Tonino Benaquista, Robin Cook, Daeninckx, and Vilar. Vilar's contribution, 'Arch', is a fragmented piece, visually and textually, as snippets of radio news announcing the Gulf War heard early in the morning, are jotted down in short sentences distributed in little blocks of text across the page, as are messages on the answerphone.[2] The public/private interface is a jumble of recorded voices inviting reflection on distance and proximity, on the ephemeral and the catastrophic. *La Grande Mêlée* (2001) is a small box containing one of Molinier's well-known erotic photographs of the same name, a collage of multiple images of Molinier in his transvestite shaman persona, dominated by bare buttocks and entwined black stockinged legs in high heels (a *mêlée* is a 'confused throng'), and texts by one hundred authors in alphabetical order together with a statement about the rules of the game. One hundred and twenty-six authors were invited to contribute by following precise instructions: 'Write in a rectangle 15 cm high and 9 cm wide what the photograph 'La Grande Mêlée' evokes'. Daeninckx's short text refers to rugby (a *mêlée* is also a 'scrum'): 'impossible now to watch a Five Nations match innocently'; Vilar addresses sexuality and desire, the meticulous organisation involved in the apparent 'bordel' on show (*bordel* meaning both 'brothel' and 'chaos', 'disorder'): 'à un quart de poil de cul près' [to the nearest quarter of an arse's hair].[3]

Jacques Monory

Jacques Monory (1924–2018) was associated with the *figuration narrative* group from its first exhibition, and participated in the famous trip to Cuba in 1967. His large and complex body of work, spanning fiction, film, photography, and above all fine art, comprises a very distinctive set of themes, recurring images, and use of colour. He produced paintings in series, the titles of which often underline his thematics of death and criminality, such as 'Meurtres' [murders], 'Enigmes', 'Noir'. Murder, anxiety, bullets, guns, and the apparatus of killing and catastrophe are dominant themes. Death haunts his work, as Alain Jouffroy points out:

> Pour Monory, la société contemporaine est une ennemie dont il faut contourner les obstacles et les interdits, parce qu'elle est dangereuse, sinon meurtrière pour tous les individus qui recherchent la liberté. Il a donc consacré de nombreux tableaux au thème du meurtre et du suicide, et si ces tableaux ont des accents bouleversants, c'est que, pour lui, il s'agit toujours de conjurer la mort, qu'il voit cachée derrière toutes choses, à tous les coins de rue.[4]

> [For Monory, contemporary society is an enemy whose obstacles and taboos are to be worked around, because it is dangerous, even murderous, towards individuals seeking freedom. He has therefore devoted many paintings to murder and to suicide and if these paintings are at times overwhelming, this is because, for him, it is always a case of exorcising death, which he sees hidden behind all things, on every street corner.]

In this world in crisis, representation is also in crisis, and his work is a complex reflection on the image. Painting is engaged with its time because it is constantly engaged with images that are exterior to it: 'dans l'autoréflexivité qui est un trait permanent de l'art moderne, le nouveau courant apportait la possibilité d'une mise en crise de l'image par la peinture, comme d'ailleurs de la peinture par l'image' [in the auto reflexivity that is a permanent feature of modern art, the new current introduced the possibility of painting putting images into a state of crisis, just as images did the same to painting].[5] Film images are regularly integrated into Monory's paintings as is photography, both as image and as process, since he painted from photographs. Like Vilar, he is attuned to the mechanical means of reproduction, as is evident in his *Toxic no 1, Melancholy*, a painting that conflates, as Sarah Wilson shows, Manet's portrait of Zola and Dürer's *Melancholia*: '[Monory] surrounds her not only with books and reproductions but also the reproductive technology of her age: radio, tape recorder, headphones. Monory embraced popular culture, kitsch, the erotic and, above all, the fictional'.[6] His paintings are distinctive for their use of monochrome blue that carries layers of interpretations: the filmic techniques of 'day for night', a 'blue room' effect suggesting a transition from the negative of the dark room,[7] coldness and distance, often associated with the thematic seam of dandyism, and the artifice of representation: 'La couleur que j'emploie est fausse, ce qui m'intéresse c'est la valeur, le jeu des valeurs. Que je plonge dans un bain bleu glacé ou maintenant dans un technicolor des plus artificiels, image de notre monde artificiel' [The colour I use is false, what interests me is its value, the play of values. Whether I plunge into an icy blue bath or as now into a most artificial technicolour, the image of our artificial world].[8] But this does not mean his paintings are devoid of emotional charge. Bailly sees the coldness of the treatment co-existing with the violence of the affect, and Wilson points to the importance of 'memory and erasure, love and loss, the "romantic space-time of nostalgia'.[9] Monory himself described blue as a 'cruel colour', but also one that for him was the colour of dreams.[10]

The theme of Monory as a 'peintre assassin' is one that recurs throughout critical writings devoted to his work. Motifs of murder and art history fuse in the famous painting *Monet est mort*, which shows Monory, who often represented himself in his work, firing a gun in a clearing towards a small case on a floor of leaves visually recalling Monet's lilies. 'En réalité, Monory a contribué, encore plus fortement que les peintres américains du Pop Art, à tuer la conception occidentale la plus obsolète de la peinture. De cet assassinat, il a fait, ironiquement, romantiquement, son œuvre' [In reality, Monory contributed, even more powerfully than the American Pop Art painters, to killing the most obsolete Western conception of painting. From this assassination, he has, ironically and romantically, created his work], wrote Jouffroy.[11] Clearly a blood brother to Marcel Duchamp. Lyotard wrote on and worked with Monory for many years, publishing an extensive study of Monory's work as vector of the libidinal economy in 1973, and in a further essay ten years later on the 'Esthétique sublime du tueur à gages'.[12] They collaborated on *Récits tremblants*, and Sarah Wilson discussed their collaborations in her important study of visual theory in French philosophy.[13] Lyotard argued that representation and economic production are each segments operating within the libidinal economy; using Monory's work to support this, he presented critiques of traditional approaches to painting as expressive of the complex fantasmatic exchanges of painter and public, and also of traditional Marxist approaches whereby representation is explained in terms of mediations between base and superstructure.[14]

Lyotard's analysis of Monory is part of a wide-ranging debate at the time on art and realism. Two issues of *Art vivant* in 1973 were devoted to hyperrealism and realism, where the photographic, foregrounded in the hyperrealist replication of representation, was discussed in relation to the optical machine and particularly to photography. Jean Clair's introduction, 'L'Adorable Leurre', brings together in his presentation of the issues raised for realism by hyperrealism Breton's *Nadja*, Dürer and the camera obscura (Vermeer's optical device), and Duchamp's elaborate demolition and display of illusion.[15] Lyotard had earlier drawn attention to the importance of the mechanical aid for both painting and photography, but he saw a clear difference between the pre-modern use of the camera obscura and the contemporary use of photography. Arguing quite rightly that contemporary realism, particularly hyperrealism, is always a meta-realism, 'a procedure which, in painting, represents representation', the hyperrealist image is called realist 'because it ostensibly bears the mark of the apparatus (dispositifs) — mechanical, electrical and photographic — by which it is produced'.[16] Displaying the mechanical 'secrets', then, the painter is like Barthes's mythologist, pointing to his mask, in this instance the machines that engineer the vision. Lyotard's stress on the importance of mechanical processes of reproduction is interesting because he distances himself from Benjamin's dichotomy of mechanical process and aura, referring to 'the banalities the philosophers of the *aura* have managed to peddle concerning photographic art'.[17] Yet he himself installs a binary where photography is still a disruptive force; the pre-modern camera obscura is artisanal, unlike the modern camera obscura that puts an end to the wisdom and knowledge anchored in the body of the painter: 'This is the relation which photography displaces. The former professional secret becomes the techno-industrial secret of the photographic apparatus'.[18] The body of the photographer supports the machines, rather than the other way round, 'the complicity with the thing in the expert caress of the brush on the canvas has been suspended'.[19] The economic relations are those of capital and the accumulated energies of political body part, not the libidinal body of the painter, hidden behind his illusion of realism. The painter of realism as manifest illusion is a dandy, as is Monory, one who points to the mask, who has turned his back on nature and, who like Baudelaire, exalts his rejection, disgust, and difference.[20]

Lyotard's article 'Esquisse d'une économique de l'hyperréalisme', illustrated by Dürer and an eighteenth-century camera obscura as well as contemporary paintings, also explores the body of the painter, the painter as machine, and the relation of master and slave-worker to the machine and the libidinal process. He quotes Gerhard Richter, who like Monory was famous for his paintings of projected photographs: 'photography is not a means (un moyen) useful to painting. It is painting that is a means useful to a photograph made with the means (les moyens) of painting'. 'The investment is in the machine,' comments Lyotard, 'namely in the apparatus of the introduction of the photographic into the reproduction of the image and the production-re-production of the painted canvas'.[21]

While the elaboration of the libidinal economy is specific to Lyotard, the dismantling of the epistemological and ideological position of the artist as all-powerful master of the work of art is fundamental to all these analyses. In 'Les Appareils du réalisme', Marc Le Bot focuses on Monory and Valerio Adami, arguing that Monory's paintings, forged from a multiplicity of mechanical and painted images, and with their guns and bullets, capture the fear and the violence of the mechanical eye, the intolerable pressure of the proliferating image in contemporary society and the undecidability of the very nature of the painted image.[22] 'L'image, conçue comme représentation d'un réel déjà systématiquement ordonné, relève de l'idéologie humaniste, qui fut l'idéologie de la bourgeoisie capitaliste. [...] Qui parle de réalisme sans un désir de meurtre, est pris au piège de cette idéologie' [The image, conceived as representation of a reality that is already systematically ordered, rests on the ideology of humanism, which as the ideology of the capitalist bourgeoisie. [...] 'Anyone who speaks of realism without murder in their heart is caught in the trap of this ideology].[23] For Le Bot, photography serves the ideological purpose of reinforcing the notion of reality with the so-called 'objectivity' of the apparatus; however, he sees Monory as questioning this whole problematic: 'Ce que dit donc [...] la peinture de Monory, c'est que la question du réalisme pictural reste aujourd'hui pour la peinture une question-piège, une question de vie et de mort' [What Monory's painting says [...] is that the question of pictorial realism is today a trick-question for painting, a question of life and death]. He argues that the ghosts of objective reality haunt painting today, because they have never stopped asking the urgent questions fundamental to its existence, about the meaning, power, and social function of the image.[24]

Le Bot's argument is an explicitly anti-humanist one, where illusion, order, and mastery see 'God-the-painter' and Man as their ideological underpinnings; similarly, Lyotard identified a 'problematic of the theatre', which he placed alongside Lacan's mirror-stage and the phenomenology of Sartre and Hegel, as the elaboration of the ideological and political 'apparatus' of the subject offers another angle on this 'age of suspicion' in the visual arts. And it is in the name of order and illusion that he sets aside narrative as pertinent to Monory's work, a move which may seem counter-intuitive given Monory's elaborately staged scenes. Lyotard characterises Monory's art as that of the catalogue;[25] his works are organised in multiple series, but, Lyotard argues, his series involve no narration: 'Il n'y a pas d'histoire chez Monory'; 'Le bleu suspend l'histoire et donc il ne se passe rien' [The blue suspends history and therefore nothing happens].[26] Each one is formed of a sequence of paintings, but, when the series is exhibited, especially in the spectator's eye darting back and forth around the exhibition space across the multiple variations on the walls, there is no narrative sequence as such. This certainly contradicts many other critics: Catherine Backès-Clément describes the knowing illusionism of photography-based realism as 'trop représenté pour être vrai, il est le comble de la fiction' [too represented to be real, it is the height of fiction].[27] 'Au début était la narration' [In the beginning was narration], wrote Gérald Gassiot-Talabot in his introduction to *Mythologies quotidiennes 2*.[28] While narrative, with its ideological supports and illusion of universalising order could indeed be critiqued as one of Lyotard's grand narratives, one could also argue that a proliferation of narratives operates differently, and can form a meta-commentary on the certainties of naive realism, as we have seen throughout Vilar's writings.[29] Bailly would see this as indeed fundamental to Monory's art, pointing to its 'essence fictionnante' [fictionalising essence] and its 'onde fictionnante' [fictionalising wave].[30] Certainly in 'Memento mori', Vilar continues to place fictionality centre-stage as he takes figures and elements from Monory's texts and art work to construct a story that is more meditation from a philosopher-killer than it is conventional action, as no doubt befits the title's invitation to reflect on one's mortality.[31]

Vilar's texts in the two Monory catalogues tell stories of death, murder, and violence, using elements from the paintings in the exhibitions as the citational material for plot development, and taking Monory's paintings — which so often stage multiple scenes, either internally or in the variations across a series — into different *noir* narratives.

'Poses'

'Poses' (1990) might be classed as a kind of psychological *noir*, a study of violence acted out in the studio of the unnamed photographer who is the narrator. The studio is the centre of a network of different communications: answerphone, post, unexpected visitors on the doorstep. The photographer is in a state of decline, unwashed and unshaven, losing weight, seemingly existing on a diet of coffee and white wine. He is in a relationship with a woman called Pilar, listening to but not answering her messages, turning her away when she appears on the doorstep. He has occasional meetings with Wagner, the gallery owner who exhibits his work. The supports of the story are thus economically set as a frame for his main activity, the 'research' as he terms it, that he is pursuing through a series of photographs of himself having been shot as a result first, of murder, secondly, of suicide. He has rigged up a kind of set, using ceramic tiles that will look like a bathroom or a morgue. This is interrupted by the unexpected ringing of the doorbell to which, like the answerphone, he refuses to respond. He later picks up a delivery note and collects an unsolicited parcel, a Smith & Wesson Magnum 357 lying on red velvet in a wooden box with six bullets, sent by Elmer Keith (later in the story identified as the inventor of this gun who died in 1984). When these bullets have been used, to verify and adjust the gun's aim, he finds a box of fifty more on the landing outside his door.

There are elements of mystery, then, which intensify an all-pervasive sense of violence. On the radio he hears news of murderous armed conflict in Beirut. As Pilar turns to leave, he acknowledges to himself his urge to kill her; he relates his idea of producing this series of photographs to seeing a photograph in a newspaper of the body of a guerilla fighter on a street in Havana, and then cutting out and collecting all subsequent similar photos; his project, 'autoportrait de l'artiste en cadavre' [self-portrait of the artist as a corpse] sets the tone (*P*, p. 10). The story works in and around the framework created by the paintings in the exhibition, all drawn from Monory's 1989 series *La Terrasse*. A handgun or bullets, or both, feature in all fourteen paintings in the catalogue, and the only human shapes are the target silhouettes used in shooting ranges. The catalogue cover is a bullseye target, a black circle on a white background, peppered with actual holes at the front. In monochrome blue or blue and pink, the strangeness of the scenes and the meticulous display of the practice and technology of killing create an undeniable tension, culminating in the final small image in monochrome blue, in the centre of the page (*La Terrasse no 12*), of a single bullet on a tiled background, the bottom left-hand area covered with a thick smear of a dark blue-black substance.

La Terrasse no 1 shows a revolver clamped into a ballistic testing machine with a remote trigger cable attached, and its handgrip and trigger pull-lever resting on its base. The apparatus is on the inside of a large floor-to-ceiling window looking out onto an empty tiled swimming pool, with a loosely coiled hose lying in it, and a large round table with four long metal tubular legs forming an X on each side in its centre, creating a sense of mystery, of suspense. This image is waiting for something. There is rather lush vegetation — trees, bushes, rocks, and shrubs — on the other side of the pool, and, beyond in the distance, a modern concrete building, in a less startling white than the table, but white nonetheless. A rich pink colour, as if thrown by some invisible pink light, suffuses the base of the ballistic tester and the tiled floor beneath, and more palely, the window sill and the area of swimming pool floor behind the revolver. These are the elements that will be repeated in many variations across the following paintings, as they are presented in different spatial relationships, from different angles, the gun and tester at times in close-up (*La Terrasse no 7*, *La Terrasse no 2*) and in pieces (*La Terrasse no 8*). In *La Terrasse no 9*, the figure of a target silhouette drawing a gun from a holster, with bullet holes peppering the bullseye in the centre of the chest, is barred by a large black X over its torso, and a very small black-and-white photograph, possibly of a swimming pool, is painted in the right-hand bottom corner. Bullets are scattered right across the surface, in tension with its vertical plane, and the top-right hand corner has a few handwritten lines in white, elliptical phrases with no context, including, 'je ne crains rien — je ne bouge pas.... puisse que je ne marche plus...., oui — oui Jonq' Erouas de la tribu des Cym, tout va bien, si ce n'est que j'ai un peu froid' [I fear nothing — I am not moving.... let it be that/since I no longer walk...., yes — yes, Jonq' Erouas of the tribe of the Cyms, all is well, except that I am a little cold] (*P*, p. 9). It suggests Monory's killer double might be speaking from the other side of the wall of death. *La Terrasse no 16* is a memento mori painting, with a rather lumpy, broken, incomplete skull in a white-edged square in the centre of the lower half, with two target silhouettes behind the skull and in front of romantic blue and pink seas and skies. There is a clarity, both painterly and philosophical, to the layering of representations and the stark commentary, intrinsic to their construction, on pleasing romantic images of the infinite.

The staging of death is central to Vilar's text and uses these elements of the *Terrasse* series: the gun, the mechanics of its workings, the mechanics of killing, the tiles, the bullets, and the multiple images of the artist, for Monory appears time and again in his paintings, as assassin, as fugitive, as pursuer, as well as creating the fictional double 'Jonq' Erouas Cym' (an anagram of his name), named in one of the paintings here (*La Terrasse no 9*) and also the main protagonist of his writings. 'Poses' begins with the scene the photographer has created for his series of auto-portraits, taken against a tiled background, and with bullets strewn around. Ketchup simulates the blood on his T-shirt, then the blood on the wall behind. He regularly develops the exposed film to check his progress towards 'l'esthétique de l'identité judiciaire' [the judicial identity esthetic] he is trying to achieve, as found, we are told, in myriad artless images of violent death taken by press, police, and amateur photographers miraculously on the spot (*P*, p. 18).

With the arrival of the real gun, the relation of photography and death takes tangible form, as a ballistic testing machine is ordered and set up on its tripod next to that supporting the camera. A cable is ordered for the tester and each apparatus can be triggered remotely. Stylistically too, the language of photography often overlaps with the language of the gun in French: *mitraillage*, machine gun fire, is the taking of multiple shots with a camera; *rafales*, a hail of bullets, also means multiple shots; and one loads a camera as one loads a gun. With the setting up of the real gun, which is tried out multiple times, first on an old camera shot in its empty lens socket, then on a billiard ball on the pool table from an abandoned game against himself ('entre moi et moi') things move on. He fires on a life-size photo of himself as well as continuing the self-portraits which are increasingly convincing: 'J'étais recroquevillé, douloureux, déjà mort, pris par un dernier spasme tétanique, l'appareil mitraillait la scène' [I was curled up, in pain, already dead in a last muscular spasm, the camera was taking multiple shots of the scene] (*P*, p. 18). The first experiment with the gun, which hits the wall behind him, produces the perfect image: 'Il me semblait qu'un voyeur ignorant les conditions de la prise ne pouvait que s'y tromper. J'avais le visage et l'attitude de quelqu'un qui encaisse une balle en plein corps' [It seemed to me a viewer ignorant of the conditions of the shot could not but be taken in. I had the expression and attitude of someone who'd received a shot right in the centre of his body] (*P*, p. 24).

To achieve this has demanded a fine attention to the process involving two sets of apparatus, the management of the staging in front of the camera and of the technical demands. At one point the staging is too obvious; later, with the gun involved, technological competence becomes paramount: 'La mise au point comptait cette fois plus que la mise en scène' [This time, accuracy counted for more than the staging] (*P*, p. 22). That the technological and cultural processes cannot be separated out is indicated by the title, 'Poses', referring to the multiple poses struck by the narrator in front of his camera, and to the *pose*, exposure, the action of light on film. The body of the photographer, smeared with ketchup, affecting the attitudes and expressions of the dead, or adjusting the moving parts of the two complex objects he is facing, is equally central to the material process. He refers also to an inflammation of his optic nerve and the regrettable effect of this illness, 'amblyopia', that prevents him from distinguishing between blue, pink, and yellow, the primary colours of so many of Monory's paintings, a further twist in the foundational interplay of the material and the imaginary in the photographic process. Merleau-Ponty's famous essay on Cézanne starts with the painter's anxiety that his work on image and representation was no more than a biological quirk, causing him to see the world differently.[32] In showing the process to be at one and the same time conceptual and corporeal, imaginary and technical, 'Poses' responds to the paintings with an equally effective dismantling of the mechanics of representation.

Having been shot once and badly injured, the photographer has just enough time for a few more images. The story ends with him reloading the camera, with the implication this will be final. The alignment of gun and camera to deliver a corpse and an image of a corpse is generated by the understanding of the intimate connections, well established by 1990, between photography and death. 'All photographs are *memento mori*,' wrote Susan Sontag.[33] Barthes's *La Chambre claire* explores in great detail the poignant and paradoxical relations to time and death captured in an old photograph of a young child, 'il est *possible* qu'Ernest [...] vive encore aujourd'hui (mais où? comment? Quel roman!)' [it is *possible* that Ernest [...] is still alive today (but where? how? What a novel!], and of Lewis Payne waiting to be hanged, 'il est mort et il va mourir' [he is dead and about to die].[34] The incontrovertible *être-là* of the photograph as record, discussed by Barthes in relation to a photograph of himself that he cannot remember being taken, that he both does and does not recognise, is echoed in 'Poses' when the photographer takes out the life-size photo of himself for shooting practice, acknowledging both the narcissism of the photographer's self-portrait and its limits — he has no memory of it at all.

'Poses' explores the relations of death and photography, then, visually and textually, from a variety of angles, including interpersonal ones: so that she can have the full measure of 'my lies', the photographer leaves a message on Pilar's answerphone to the effect of how well he is, an aggressive farewell springing no doubt from the same impulse of wanting to kill her. At the same time, 'Poses' is an elaborate reminder, through the images of Monory's work as well as the text, of the mechanical processes involved, clearly in photography, but also in painting. The mechanics of photography — box, lenses, tripod, chemical development — are as important to the narrative as the mechanics of the gun. And, therefore, to these photographed paintings of photographs. Too often the relationship of photography to painting is one of disruption, rivalry, and difference; the photographic image that is the result of chemical reactions and machinery, infinitely reproducible, operating independently of the human agent as an 'optical unconscious' to processes of perception, is thus presented as ontologically different from the painted image. Monory's work has always put that in question, as part of his interrogation of the image and representation; Vilar's catalogue fictions invite us to pay attention more carefully to processes of the visual.

André Rouillé points out how quickly the photographic became an integral part of painting — 'On n'a pas suffisamment considéré l'impressionnisme comme une peinture travaillée par la photographie' [There has not been enough consideration of impressionism as painting worked by photography] — and indeed of perception itself.[35] Le Bot saw how Monory's use of photography placed him in a long-standing painterly tradition.[36] Diana Knight is surely right that Barthes's choice of title, *La Chambre claire*, is overdetermined by the transparent space of the conservatory in the 'missing' photograph of his mother, but the image of the draughtsman using a camera lucida on the front cover of the French edition points the reader firmly in the direction of the technical meaning rather than a 'light room'.[37] In the English translation, the neat reversal of camera obscura to the now inescapably photographic connotations of 'camera' in the phrase 'camera lucida' seamlessly does the job on its own. The 'camera obscura' too was an adjunct to painting for centuries before its use with photo-sensitive paper. The material support of painting, brush, paint, easel, and canvas, involved a range of mechanical devices that tend to fall outside the ideological frame composed of the artist and the unique work of art. Removing this Romantic figure of the artist was a particular focus of avant-garde art, and the use of film, photography, and *bande dessinée* in both *figuration narrative* and *nouveau réalisme* work was deliberate and knowing. Monory projected photographs onto canvases, worked with the serialisation of theme and image, and multiplied images of himself across his paintings and in conjunction with them. In Monory's work, Lyotard's comment that realism is meta-realism applies as much to the artist, governed by these shifting sands of auto-reflexivity and referentiality, as to the image. The controversy around the sequence of paintings *La Fin tragique de Marcel Duchamp* shows how complex and contradictory it can be to work against the powerful image of the artist as sole creator and controller.[38] Yet it is not surprising that Duchamp, whose work integrated the photographic before he abandoned 'retinal art' and stripped things back to mechanical relations, is a constant reference, and particularly the reactivation of Dürer's optical machine in his final, secret, posthumously revealed work *Étant donnés*, with which Vilar began his first *roman noir*.[39]

'Memento mori'

Vilar's story could be described as a meditation on a meditation, weaving together themes and narrative fragments from Monory's work and juxtaposing them with a significant number of paintings. If 'Poses' deploys art, photography, and fiction around a thematics of murder, 'Memento mori' (2014) presents mortality, lived as a catastrophe in multiple guises, in relation to fictionality.[40] It elaborates on the thematics of *film noir* and *roman noir* with a story that features murders, massacres and executions, violent death, long discussions of dreams, eternity, and parallel worlds that are both metaphysical and personal, and in a context of riots, civil wars, and catastrophe. It is a story of Jonq' Erouas Cym, a hired killer who is also an artist, and his companions, a young girl, a tiger, and a monkey moving through the city until they come to the cafe close to an art gallery whose owner exhibits Jonq''s work. A large number of the paintings here include images of guns or corpses or both, and several have the traditional marker of a memento mori painting, the inclusion of a skull. But visually, the painting of the living also 'remembers' mortality and the skull in the skull-like shape of the bald head of Jonq'/Monory, or in the skull-like shape of the bald head and sunken eyes of little monkeys that immediately connote images of early space flights (during which most of them died), or scientific experiments. The very first painting in the catalogue is *Meurtre no 6, 3/6* (1968) (*MM*, p. 3), dominated by a large expanse of blue scalp. The male figure of Monory, at the front of the painting, is seen from above slumped in a sitting position, leaning slightly forwards against an expanse of blue watery tiles, with a line of bullet holes across the surface and shadowed on the tiles. The ill-shapen, almost unfinished hands at his midriff have a small hole forming a small x between them over a dark patch, surrounded by two circles: bullseye. Monory often pointed to death as a constant theme of his work: 'Cet insupportable avènement de la mort, j'essaie de l'agrémenter du faste de la tragédie, le colorer de la froideur du roman noir, du thriller bleuté, du délire glacé d'un romantisme dérisoire' [This unbearable approach of death, I try and adorn it with the splendour of tragedy, colour it with the coldness of the *roman noir*, of the blue-tinged thriller, of the icy delirium of a derisory romanticism].[41]

'A chaque aube, je meurs' [Each dawn I die]' are the opening words of 'Memento mori', spoken by the presenter on a television set that has just turned on automatically, waking up Jonq' (as he is referred to throughout) in the small rented studio flat where he is sleeping. '"A chaque aube je meurs." Comme si Jonq' ne le savait pas' ["Each dawn I die". As if Jonq' didn't know] (*MM*, p. 7). The story is continued with a long quotation from Jonq''s notebook, describing himself as lying on either a stretcher or a camp bed, feeling better than expected given the gun battle of the day before, and gripping an attaché case: 'les deux trous qui le transperçaient ne devaient rien à la fusillade qui avait eu lieu ici' [the two holes that cut through it had nothing to do with the shootout that had taken place here] (*MM*, p. 7). He remembers using the case as target practice, and on the facing page is a black-and-white photograph of Monory in a clearing in a forest aiming at a pale square object on the ground, the small case lying open to his left (*MM*, p. 6). He is taken from the side, leather jacket, pale trousers, fedora, rifle poised, one foot on a chair. In *Technicolor no 1, Monet est mort* (1979), Monory is painted facing the camera. The case itself, with its connotation of Duchamp's *Boîte-en-valise*, contains objects and a copy of Stanislas Rodanski's 1975 novel *Victoire à l'ombre des ailes*, and is carried by Jonq' throughout the story.[42] The mechanics of the narrative are thus established from the outset: the shift between third- and first-person narration; interaction between content of text and image on a regular, though not systematic basis; the doubling and redoubling of the persona of the artist. This last occurs firstly in the text: as well as Jonq', there is reference to 'Jeascuq Myroon' (another anagram of Monory's name), probably but not certainly Jonq's father, who is killed in New York; and secondly in the images of Monory, in photograph and painting, in various signature dress styles. The story of Jonq' the hired gun is at the same time a story drawing on a complex cultural imaginary of dreams, science, and science fiction. A quotation from Edgar Allan Poe's poem 'A Dream within a Dream' — 'All that we see or seem is but a dream within a dream' — is placed as an epigraph and is also a reference to Monory's painting *For All that We See or Seem, is a Dream Within a Dream* (1967). The interface of dream and reality plays out in many ways in the story, not least diegetically: Jonq' wakes up in a room surrounded by details he is not quite sure of, except the constant repetition of 'Each dawn I die', the title of a film he knows well; it is not illogical in the circumstances to wonder if he was dreaming that he was waking up.

Three of these paintings are from the *Vie imaginaire de Jonq' Erouas Cym* series, each a composite in blue monochrome of various images. Catastrophe, Hollywood glamour, compositions that ignore realist conventions of scale and composition, and a personal mythology of death involving the hitman, guns, shooting-range targets, and criminality are enacted in various ways across these paintings and in this resolutely non-realist story as the characters, human and animal, move through the turbulent city. *La Vie imaginaire de Jonq' Erouas Cym no 11* (2002) (*MM*, p. 9) has in its centre a woman in white with her head in her hands, holding one end of a pair of handcuffs, the other under a gun beside her; a Monory figure in evening dress and hat is on the left, in front of cars on a freeway; other sections include the head of a sleeping woman and a small image of a huge explosion. The final one of the series included here, *no 9* (2002) (*MM*, p. 162) shows the dining car of a railway carriage dominated by death because the lines of a bullseye are drawn across it, with a mask-like white skull lying on the floor towards the front, and a 'Wanted by the CIA' poster (recalling Duchamp's famous 'Wanted' poster) in grey in the right-hand bottom corner. The poster has two images of Monory/Jonq', one with dark glasses that have the effect of giving him black empty eyes, visually repeating the black sockets of the skull to his left.

The story elaborates on death and *le noir* to inform the characters' discussions of reality (and obliquely indexing Monory's *Skies, Constellations and Galaxies* series of the late 1970s), for example in the unclear distinction between events in dreams, daydreams, and waking reality, as in Edgar Allan Poe, and in their relation to mortality. To reassure themselves about the risks they are facing, they repeat time and again that it is not possible to die in a dream. Science fiction provides several theories of multiple worlds; notions of Philip K. Dick's multiverse and of parallel worlds are tangibly real for the characters and intersect with the dreamworlds and the waking dreams, which they or others might be in. When 'la Petite fille' wonders how the three policemen Jonq' has just brutally shot could die if you do not die in a dream, Jonq' replies that in their world, they are not dreaming. The science of galaxies and the skies, and mathematical infinities, are also woven into discussions that loosen all sense of a single fixed reality, just as do the paintings that present people and events of different scales and planes cohabiting the same pictorial space. 'J'avais perdu tous mes repères logiques' [I'd lost all my logical points of reference], says Jonq', unable to distinguish between window and screen (*MM*, p. 24).

His grasp of reality is at best tenuous. He is not sure of his date of birth. He consistently fails to remember things, finding for example a man's body on the terrace outside his room, whom he presumes he must have shot, and then a woman's body in his bath, whom again he thinks he must have killed. 'Le souvenir confus', 'de manière confuse, ça pouvait donner ça', 'Rien n'a dû se passer comme ça' [confused memory; in a confused way, it could be that; nothing can have happened like that] (*MM*, p. 18), are just some of the expressions that constantly underline how adrift he is from his own story. He is in a world of déjà vu, of places that are probably familiar from dreams: 'Maintes fois, il lui était arrivé de se savoir dans cette ville qui s'appelait Paris, où il était persuadé d'avoir passé une partie de sa jeunesse, sans trouver le moindre repère' [Many times, he happened to know that he was in the city called Paris, where he was sure he had spent a part of his youth, without finding any landmarks] (*MM*, p. 94). The power of the imaginary in the world he is in is indicated by the many filmic and literary street names ('rue Douglas Sirk', 'rue Paul Muni', 'rue Hopper', 'rue Gaston Leroux', to name but a few), and the diegetic importance of specific films (*Each Dawn I Die, Gun Crazy, Kiss Me Deadly, Scarface*). 'Le noir — film ou roman [...] se devait de servir de grille de lecture au pur spectacle que la presse présentait chaque jour' [the *noir*, film or novel [...] had a duty to provide a reading grid for the pure spectacle in the daily press] (*MM*, p. 122), the point of articulation between private tragedy and the chaos of the world. 'Jonq' vivait le monde, celui de l'illusoire reel, de même que les mondes de ses rêves, éveillés ou non, comme des romans ou des films noirs' [Jonq' experienced the world, the world of real illusion and the worlds of his dreams, daydreams or not, like *noir* novels and films] (*MM*, p. 131), and Monory's *Memento mori* paintings stage the 'fracas du monde' [the commotion of the world] in various ways. Auschwitz, Hiroshima, and Nagasaki, are events that define Jonq''s being: 'c'était un commencement absolu. Mes petites histoires s'articuleraient à l'histoire collective' [it was an absolute beginning. My little stories would be connected to collective history] (*MM*, p. 84). The rubble of Hiroshima is the subject of *Toxique no 2, Hiroshima* (*MM*, p. 119). The *Opera glacé* series that inspired the director Jean-Jacques Beneix for his film *Diva* combines the grandiose opera house and opera singers, with the crash of collapsing buildings or, in the case of *Opéra glacé no 1, '1943'* (1974) (*MM*, p. 43), the monumental staircase of an opera house with a huge central image of the railway lines leading to Auschwitz.[43]

Vilar's article in *Rouge* on Monory's *Catalogue mondial des images incurables* highlighted the powerful combination of fragment and narrative in Monory's work: the juxtaposition of seemingly unconnected and disparate elements, the hyperviolence of the world in crisis, from which there is no escape, with shoot-outs in a bathroom, Hollywood in the bedroom, and Vietnam in the hall. The segments of these fragmented paintings operate like the chapters of a novel, or a personal diary recording the dislocations of living in such violence; the whole is a terrible machine ('une machine infernale'), but one that is rendered with glacially precise realism, which is why Monory's series have such power: 'Incurables comme ce monde pourri que ces toiles bleutées figent, congèlent, et qui augurent mal d'une rémission possible. Leur succession constitue la plus terrifiante et la plus démonstrative des fictions: celle de notre quotidienneté' [Incurable like this rotten world that these bluish canvases immobilise and congeal, and which augur ill for any kind of remission. Their sequence constitutes the most terrifying and clearest illustration in fiction of our everyday].[44] The disquieting painting *Noir no 9* (1990) (*MM*, p. 101), that represents a man trying to get up from a pavement where he must have fallen, as passers-by continue on their way without a glance towards him, has its effect intensified by being a double image, the lower half a reverse mirror image of the upper half, confounding any attempt by the viewer to position themselves spatially in relation to the scene, endowing it with a claustrophobic eeriness.

This aporia of spectatorship recalls Lyotard's argument that Monory's work puts the traditional subject to death, the 'I' who experiences (in the same way that the libidinal economy is incompatible with the 'problematic of the theatre' and the organizing I/eye of the subject/spectator for whom it is staged). Lyotard described Monory at one point as 'incommensurable', by which, according to Bill Readings, he underlines the co-presence of radically heterogeneous spaces in the artwork, disrupting the conceptual spaces of discourse and identity.[45] It is undeniable that Monory's paintings problematise representation, demonstrating the limits and ironies of classical realism. Monory's paintings are often hard to take in at a glance. In *Enigme no 17* (1995) (*MM*, p. 25) for example, the eye is drawn to the staircase towards the right, the body sprawled down it and the dropped gun at the top, to a computer-generated three-dimensional image of a head in the centre of the painting, to a disproportionally large gun to the left, and to a figure in white, bending over, back turned, between them. It takes time to notice, behind the body at the top of the stairs, a couple embracing, standing in the top right-hand corner, the dark coat and hat of the man, the pale hands of the woman on his back, or the disembodied wrist and hand, index finger pointing towards the body, rising from the bottom left-hand corner, or the broken pane of glass against the staircase. The spectator is obliged to decide whether the fragments do or do not fit together, as they contemplate the spatial, thematic, and referential construction, the use of light and colour, the kinds of narrative, conceptual and visual, generating the painting, in order to make some relational sense or, on the contrary, to install a failure of sense as an organisational principle. The sudden awareness of new elements alters the perception and understanding of the whole. The spectator-detective very often has new major clues to weigh up and consider. With a fragmentation of space that is not conceptually open to resolution by the construction of a single coherent meta-narrative, the relations between the elements are relations of incompletion and enigma.

Vilar's text also thematises the break with the epistemology of the Enlightenment: 'ce fut plutôt le système institutionnel dans son ensemble, ce système présenté comme immuable et incarnation enfin trouvée de la Raison, qui était gangrené' [it was rather the institutional system as a whole, the system presented as unchangeable, and an incarnation, found at last, of Reason, that was rotten] (*MM*, p. 68). With the multiple stories of Jonq''s past, the use of Poe, and the indirect introduction of Borges, through the tiger Gros Chat — this figure that appears across Monory's work and in many of the paintings here, first belonged to Monory's *Dreamtiger* series, directly alluding to Borges's story *El Hacedor*, translated as *Dreamtigers* — the narrative elaborates a variety of points of connection with Monory's painterly constructions. The fantastical dream fictions sit alongside the nineteenth-century science fiction that was integral, as we have seen, to the imaginary of the early *noir*. Dr Cordelier, for example, who at times appears on the verge of a rather alarming transformation, is the name of the central figure in Jean Renoir's 1959 adaptation of Jekyll and Hyde, *Le Testament du docteur Cordelier*. And the apocalyptic scenes towards the end are logically described as a 'guerre des mondes' [war of the worlds] (*MM*, p. 172).[46]

The figure of Louis-Auguste Blanqui is a significant pivot between the science-fiction and the historical and political dimensions of the text. A political revolutionary from 1827 onwards, he spent many years in prison where he wrote *L'Éternité par les astres* [Eternity to the Stars] (1872) which, with its themes of infinity, time, space, and eternal repetition, figures prominently in Jonq''s conversations. 'Memento mori' is set in an indeterminate dystopian present where power resides with a 'new-look neo-fascism', and violence and massacres are its stock-in-trade, such as the mass shooting in *Meurtre no 18/1* (1968) (*MM*, p. 25, and see the cover of this book) that takes place on the steps of what could be a theatre or a cinema, but in this text is a student demonstration being gunned down at the university entrance, witnessed by Jonq' from his bathroom through the unstable material that is now window, now screen, now mirror. There is a virtual civil war going on. The present repression has historical precedent in the Commune. Jonq' recalls the Commune and the 'Versaillais assassins', regretting that they have virtually disappeared from collective memory. Yet this is an imposed effacement:

> Les forces de répression chargeaient toutes les affiches de mémoires qu'elles pouvaient découvrir. Elles les chargeaient ainsi qu'on charge un rassemblement d'opposants. Les mitraillaient, montaient à l'assaut des barricades à l'arme blanche, déchiquetaient le papier à mains nues, le sang de leurs doigts meurtris dégoulinaient sur les uniformes dépareillés des communards. (*MM*, p. 94)

> [The forces of repression would mount a charge against all the memory posters they could find. They charged them as a gathering of opponents is charged. They used machine guns, mounted attacks on the barricades with knives, tore the paper into pieces with their bare hands, the blood of their injured fingers dripping on the mismatched uniforms of the Communards.]

This is an image that literalises the political repression of the memory of working-class revolt, recalling both the torn posters of the *affichistes* and the torn poster that ends *Meurtres pour mémoire*, although here the wall imbibes the image and thus resists destruction: 'Imprégnant les murs salis, des yeux crevés fixaient implacablement les soudards, des bouches sanglantes grandes ouvertes hurlaient leur rage' [Soaking into the dirtied walls, gouged out eyes stared implacably at the brutish soldiers, bleeding wide open mouths screamed their rage] (*MM*, p. 94). It establishes several connections with the facing painting *Spéciale no 7* (2001) (*MM*, p. 95), where a statuesque Angèle with black empty eyes stands in the centre, three serried rows of the numbered Communard coffins behind her: political repression, defiant memory, and a disquieting imagery of extreme violence that has not ended. In a section in the bottom left-hand corner, coloured pink, are revealed, we are told later, the remains of fighters killed in a more recent fight (*MM*, p. 155).[47]

As the narrative moves towards the end, the violence and fighting become more and more insistent. The Tour Montparnasse is ablaze, bodies are falling from the upper floors, and then it collapses (*MM*, p. 176). Naked female mannequins are menacingly on the march (*MM*, pp. 176–77). Having taken refuge in the flat of 'la Petite fille', which seems to be a replica of his own flat except for the very large painting of Hiroshima covering one wall, Jonq' finally opens the small case and it is all over, with a large white flash 'qui se répandit, très vite, sur toute la ville et bien au-delà. La fin' [which spread very quickly over the whole city and well beyond. The end] (*MM*, p. 178). Bailly wrote that in Monory's work 'le tueur élégant qui traverse en se jouant un univers de décombres est celui qui survit [...] lui, comme la petite voleuse qui toujours parvient à se sauver, en réchappe toujours' [the elegant killer who crosses a universe of rubble while playing himself is the one who survives [...] he, along with the little thief girl who always manages to run away, always comes out alive].[48] Not this time.

Both these volumes bring together avant-garde art and *le noir*, but in very different ways. 'Poses' is close to the psychological *noir,* the gothic horror of the closed space, charting a process leading inexorably to death.[49] It incorporates one dimension of the critique of the epistemology of the subject inherent in realist painting from the Renaissance onwards, one that we have seen earlier in Lyotard's analyses, and that Lucien Vinciguerra identifies also in Foucault's analysis of *Las Meninas*: that the disappearance, the rendering invisible, of the mechanics of painting was integral to the establishment of the all-powerful seeing subject.[50] One process by which modern art dismantled it was precisely by incorporating the technical and material apparatus of painting that, as we have seen, was brought to the fore in the theoretical discussions of realism in the 1970s. The other disruptive process is from the inside, attacking the homogeneity of space and perspective within the painting, a process that in Monory's case unleashes the 'onde fictionnnante' [fictionalising wave], one that, like the *roman noir* itself, tells multiple stories of murder within the existential anguish of mortality and the murderous havoc of a world in crisis.[51] *Notre quotidienneté* [our everyday].

Notes to Chapter 7

1. See, for example: Jean-Christophe Bailly, *Monory* (Paris: Maeght, 1979), and *Jacques Monory* (Neuchâtel: Ides et Calendes, 2001); Bernard Vasseur, *Monory* (Paris: Le Cercle d'art, 2012); *Monory*, ed. by Pascale Le Thorel, exhibition catalogue (Landerneau: Fonds Hélène & Edouard Leclerc, 2014).
2. Jean-François Vilar, 'Arch', in Jean-Paul Ruiz, *Moments noirs* (St-Sornin-Lavolps: J. P. Ruiz, 1992), [n.p.]. Full details of *Moments noirs* are available at <http://jeanpaul.ruiz.pagesperso-orange.fr/livre/MomentsNoirs.htm> [accessed 29 May 2020].
3. Jean-François Vilar, [untitled text], in Pierre Molinier, *La Grande Mêlée*, ed. by Madeleine Millot-Durrenberger (Strasbourg: In Extremis, 2001), [n.p.]. Millot-Durrenberger, a collector of art photography, founded this publishing house. The object-book was created for the centenary of Molinier's birth (see <https://www.exporevue.com/magazine/fr/inextremis_mmd.html> [accessed 29 May 2020]).
4. Jouffroy, *Les Pré-voyants*, p. 116
5. Bailly, *Jacques Monory*, p. 14.

6. Wilson, *The Visual World of French Theory*, p. 160.
7. Bailly, *Jacques Monory*, p. 30.
8. Jacques Monory, interview in the *Cahiers du cinema* (1977), repr. in Jacques Monory, *Écrits, entretiens, récits* (Paris: Beaux-Arts de Paris, 2014), p. 61.
9. Jean-Christophe Bailly, 'Préface', in Monory, *Écrits, entretiens, récits*, pp. 9–10; Wilson, *The Visual World of French Theory*, p. 159.
10. Quoted in *Jacques Monory*, ed. by Le Thorel, pp. 20, 59.
11. Alain Jouffroy, in the catalogue of the 1984 Monory exhibition in Tokyo, quoted in *25 ans d'art en France: 1960–1985*, ed. by Robert Maillard (Paris: Larousse, 1986), p. 118.
12. Jean-François Lyotard, 'Contribution des tableaux de Jacques Monory à l'intelligence de l'économie politique libidinale du capitalisme dans son rapport avec le dispositif pictural, et inversement', in *Figurations 1960/1973*, ed. by Gérald Gassiot-Talabot, P. Gaudibert, and Marc Lebot (Paris: Union générale d'éditions, coll. 10/18, 1973), pp. 154–238. This essay was republished twice with different titles and prefatory pieces, firstly in Jean-François Lyotard, *The Assassination of Experience by Painting — Monory. L'Assassinat de l'expérience par la peinture — Monory*, ed. by Sarah Wilson, parallel trans. by Rachel Bowlby (London: Black Dog, 1998), and secondly, in Jean-François Lyotard, *L'Assassinat de l'expérience par la peinture, Monory. The Assassination of Experience by Painting, Monory*, ed. by Herman Parret, parallel trans. by Rachel Bowlby (Leuven: Leuven University Press, 2013). Lyotard's essay 'Esthétique sublime du tueur à gages' is included in the second of these editions.
13. Jean-François Lyotard, *Récits tremblants*, illus. by Jacques Monory (Paris: Galilée, 1977); Sarah Wilson, *The Visual World of French Theory*, Chapter 5, 'Lyotard, Monory: Postmodern Romantics' (reworked versions of this chapter are published in both the 1998 and 2013 editions of Lyotard's *L'Assassinat de l'expérience par la peinture — Monory* cited in the previous note).
14. Lyotard, 'Contribution des tableaux de Jacques Monory', pp. 160–63.
15. Jean Clair, L'Adorable Leurre', published in two parts: *Hyperréalisme 1*, special issue of *Art vivant*, 36 (February 1973), 4–5, and *Réalismes/2*, special issue of *Art vivant*, 37 (March 1973), 4–6. The phrase 'adorable leurre' [adorable lure/illusion] are the words used by Breton in *Nadja* to describe the mannequin adjusting her stocking in the Musée Grévin, both an illusion, she is sadly not real, and a lure with her captivating eyes.
16. Lyotard, *The Assassination of Experience by Painting — Monory*, ed. by Wilson, pp. 130, 129 (latter translation amended).
17. Jean-François Lyotard, 'Philosophy and Painting in the Age of their Experimentation: Contribution to an Idea of Postmodernity', trans. by Mária Minich Brewer and Daniel Brewer, in *The Lyotard Reader*, ed. by Andrew Benjamin (Oxford: Blackwell, 1989), p. 189. Earlier in the article Lyotard has a variant of the 'ineffable' tarnished by industrial society, and Benjamin himself is more than critical of the aura and the grand tradition of the noble artist. Lyotard's sense of a hierarchy is however completely justified.
18. Lyotard, *The Assassination of Experience by Painting — Monory*, ed. by Wilson, p. 132 (translation amended). See also Jean-François Lyotard, 'Esquisse d'une économique de l'hyperréalisme', *Hyperréalisme 1*, special issue of *Art vivant*, 36 (February 1973), 9–12 (pp. 10–11).
19. Lyotard, *The Assassination of Experience by Painting — Monory*, ed. by Wilson, p.133.
20. Lyotard, 'Le Dandysme', in *The Assassination of Experience by Painting — Monory*, ed. by Wilson, pp. 137–54.
21. Lyotard, 'Esquisse d'une économique de l'hyperréalisme', p. 11.
22. Marc Le Bot, 'Les Appareils du réalisme', *Hyperréalisme 1*, special issue of *Art vivant*, 36 (February 1973), 6–8, 7.
23. Ibid.
24. Ibid.
25. Lyotard, *The Assassination of Experience by Painting — Monory*, ed. by Wilson, pp. 108–23.
26. Lyotard, 'Contribution des tableaux de Jacques Monory', pp. 174, 175–76.
27. Catherine Backès-Clément, 'L'Impossible Réel ou le leurre en vente', *Réalismes/2*, special issue of *Art vivant*, 37 (March 1973), 6–7 (p. 7).
28. Gérald Gassiot-Talabot, 'Le Double Sens des mythologiques quotidiennes', in *Mythologies Quotidiennes 2*, ed. by Gassiot-Talabot and others, [n.p]

29. Mária Minich Brewer's analysis of the work of Claude Simon, its rejection of the illusory order of narrative through what she calls 'narrativity', would be a pertinent example: 'The notion of narrativity without Narrative helps to make explicit the resistances that literary texts can offer to the hegemonic claims of today's master narratives', *Claude Simon: Narrativities without Narrative* (Lincoln, & London: University of Nebraska Press, 1995), p. xvii.
30. Jean-Christophe Bailly, 'Préface', in *Monory: noir*, exhibition catalogue (Paris: Galerie Lelong, 1991), pp. 3–29 (p. 8).
31. The phrase 'memento mori' means 'remember you must die', and the term refers to paintings that incorporate signs and symbols of mortality, such as a skull, hour glass or clock, guttering candle, etc.
32. 'En vieillissant, il se demande si la nouveauté de sa peinture ne venait pas d'un trouble de ses yeux, si toute sa vie n'a pas été fondée sur un accident de son corps', Maurice Merleau-Ponty, 'Le Doute de Cézanne', in *Sens et non-sens* (Paris: Nagel, 1948), pp. 15–49 (p. 16).
33. Sontag, *On Photography*, p. 15.
34. Roland Barthes, *La Chambre claire: note sur la photographie* (Paris: Gallimard, 1980), pp. 131, 149.
35. André Rouillé, *La Photographie: entre document et art contemporain* (Paris: Gallimard, coll. Folio Essais, 2005), p. 383.
36. Le Bot, 'Les Appareils du réalisme'.
37. Diana Knight, 'Roland Barthes, or, The Woman Without a Shadow', in *Writing the Image after Barthes*, ed. by Jean-Michel Rabaté (Philadelphia: Pennsylvania University Press, 1997), pp. 132–43 (p. 138).
38. See above, Chapter 2.
39. Duchamp is acknowledged in Monory's *Meurtre No 2* (*MM*, p. 161) with its visual recall of Duchamp's *Nu descendant l'escalier* in the repeated falling figure of Monory, as Vilar's text points out (*MM*, p. 158). Monory's painting also puns on the term for 'being shot': 'se faire descendre' (*MM*, p. 160).
40. The catalogue contains forty-four paintings of which fourteen were exhibited, and one photogram from Monory's 1968 short film *Ex*. Taking work from every decade, from 1966 to 2011, the catalogue is both a record of the exhibition and an overview of Monory's work.
41. Quoted in Pascale Le Thorel, 'Cinéma et roman noir', in *Jacques Monory*, ed. by Le Thorel, p. 149
42. See Wilson, *The Visual World of French Theory*, pp. 41, 42, for reproduction and description of the case and its contents. See Monory, *Écrits, entretiens, récits*, p. 344, for the photograph of the scene taken from the same angle as *Monet est mort*.
43. Jean-Jacques Beneix, Pascale Le Thorel, and Michel-Edouard Leclerc, 'Entretien', in *Jacques Monory*, ed. by Le Thorel, pp. 5–9.
44. Jean-François Vilar, 'Le Catalogue mondial des images incurables de Monory', *Rouge*, 904 (1–6 February 1980), 22. Vilar is combining here the publication details of the Bailly volume that includes virtually all Monory's paintings to that date, and the title of an earlier catalogue: Jean-Christophe Bailly, *Monory* (Paris: Maeght, 1979); Jacques Monory, *Les Premiers Numéros du catalogue des images incurables*, préface d'Alain Jouffroy (Paris: Centre national d'art contemporain, 1974).
45. Bill Readings, *Introducing Lyotard: Art and Politics* (London & New York: Routledge, 1991), pp. xxvi–xxvii.
46. H. G. Wells's story was first serialised in 1897.
47. 'Angèle' was the name of Monory's mother, and is the title of one of his novels.
48. Bailly, *Jacques Monory*, p. 74.
49. Cf also Vilar's short story, 'Terminus', in *La Vie du rail*, 2154 (21 July 1988), 46–49, with a very unpleasant tale of death and asphyxiation in the abandoned 'gare d'Avron'.
50. Lucien Vinciguerra, 'Comment inverser exactement *Les Ménines*: Michel Foucault et la peinture à la fin des années 60, des formes symboliques aux dispositifs', in *Le Moment philosophique des années 1960 en France*, ed. by Pierre Maniglier (Paris: Presses Universitaires de France, 2011), pp. 477–92 (p. 479).
51. Ibid., p. 497.

CONCLUSION

A large number of writers from the late 1960s onwards came from active political involvement to crime fiction with a common commitment to explore criminality, socially and politically as well as psychologically. They were a very diverse group, each forging a distinctive literary voice and body of work. Vilar's fictional and non-fictional writings share many things with Frédéric Fajardie, Didier Daeninckx, or Thierry Jonquet: plots that evolve in contemporary France, that deal with political protest, state killings, and state repression, both in France and abroad, as well as a political perspective on some of the key events of France's history such as the Algerian War and the Second World War. But his deployment of conceptual frameworks of political art and cultural criticism results in narratives that inflect the key markers of the genre in very particular ways. The city and the experience of the city are, for example, fundamental to the *néo-polar*; Vilar's city is certainly political, but it is distinctively Benjaminian and surrealist.[1] His main protagonist and narrator, Victor, draws on many established tropes of investigation — the *flâneur* as detective in the widest sense is a longstanding figure in critical literature on Paris — but he has a strong fictional presence with his political background, his intellectual pursuits, and his cultural references.

It has been argued that the transition from politics to literature and the creation of a distinctive literary field was accompanied by a certain de-politicisation, evident in the literary distancing of the ironic or rather detached treatment of political themes.[2] The undeniably ludic treatment of representation, the creation of Victor as a detached and ironic commentator, and the extensive use of history in some of the later novels would seem to justify the view that the political has been subordinated to the literary. Yet irony and detachment were powerful weapons in the political art of the 1960s and 70s; the past in these fictions is rigorously and dialectically captured in function of the political present, using Benjaminian perspectives; the pervasive themes of the Holocaust and the Latin American resistance struggles against murderous regimes are also profoundly political and never ironised; and the intricacies of the writing as textual practice should not be passed over since they are essential to any evaluation of the disruptive text and its politics.

Vilar's political background was one of full-time paid work — he was not just a committed member of La Ligue, participating in activities like demonstrations, but a full-time worker for at least eight years, involved in many aspects of the organisation, as a journalist, organiser, and political educator. And although May 1968 features regularly in his novels — usually through the Atelier des Beaux-Arts — which is not surprising since it was such an important political landmark in France for a good thirty years, he himself had been intensively committed to Trotskyist politics for a full thirteen years after 68 before turning to fiction. His comments that the failure of 68 hardly defines his politics are very convincing. He brings to his writing not only a continued commitment to political change, but a complex theorisation of political conflict, nationally and internationally. And the extensive deployment in his novels of the frameworks of analysis of contemporary philosophical, cultural, and art criticism and practice, clearly in part the result of the hundreds of articles he wrote on these topics in the 1970s and early 1980s, gives a conceptual coherence to the way these novels set every aspect of the fiction on a stage of theatricality, spectacle, and quotation as part of their political critique.

Vilar's plots are complex, even convoluted. His large casts of characters, the interlayering of multiple times and the elaborate citational techniques could be bewildering, yet there is poetic and rhetorical coherence too in the consistent use of the tropes of *noir* fiction and the key crime topoi of street and installation, which provide very strong fictional frames to each novel. The crimes at the centre of his narratives evolve across his novels. The first ones involve a very specific group of characters — Rose and the Bachelors, Locke and his circle of forgers and friends — and are extravagantly spectacular: a corpse acting out a Duchamp installation, the Centre Pompidou taken hostage, a video of a dramatic execution of a world-famous artist seen by millions. They are immediately situated as political crime novels, however, through a political context of police crimes, and the situating of characters in relation to their class and political backgrounds. Later crimes, of the Algerian War, of senior politicians, for example, are exemplary of political processes. At times the two have converged: the spectacular hostage-taking of Venice is inseparable from questions of extreme-left violence and the catastrophe of the Holocaust; in the extreme violence of the 1930s, or the apocalyptic vision of society in violent breakdown, the crimes are those of savage and powerful political movements, Nazism and Stalinism in *Nous cheminons*, and the new look neo-fascists in 'Memento mori'.

The nature of the psychological conflicts in the novels evolves too. Crime novels are novels of the extreme as well as of the mundane, and many of his characters carry out extreme actions because their obsessions have overwhelmed them psychologically. Rose in *C'est toujours les autres qui meurent*, Dennis Locke in *Passage des singes*, Anna Fried of *Les Exagérés*, are some of those described as mad at various points: the competing pressures are unresolvable, and these characters do not compromise. In the later novels, where it is the dynamic of utopias and betrayals going hand-in-hand that is dominant, the sense of melancholy and loss is in part explained by the difficulties of accepting compromise, capitulation, and betrayal. Driven by utopian beliefs, characters do dreadful things, including to those close to them. Or they betray the beliefs.

In *Jean-François Vilar: 95% de réel*, Vilar gave an insight into his approach to political fiction, in his emphasis on its engagement with reality (ninety-five per cent of the work), and the combination of avant-garde politics and avant-garde art. The meeting between Trotsky and Breton in 1938 was a chance for a new art and a new politics, one that was swept aside by Nazism, assassination, and exile: 'Ma capacité de parler avec mes contemporains repose sur ça' [My ability to talk with my contemporaries rests on that]. He also said, in the same film, that he wanted his novels to give a 'changement d'optique', a change of perspective, a change of viewpoint. His commitment to fiction as a continuation of his political activism never wavered; the disruptions of vision, of knowledge, and of the ideologically saturated everyday by the twentieth-century avant-gardes are no less vital in creating fictions to change our view of the world.

Notes to the Conclusion

1. See Jean-Noël Blanc, *Polarville: images de la ville dans le roman policier* (Lyon: Presses universitaires de Lyon, 1991).
2. See Collovald and Neveu, '"Le néo-polar"'. Philippe Corcuff and Lison Fleury make a similar point in relation to *C'est toujours les autres qui meurent* in 'Profondeurs du social et critique politique', *Le Polar entre critique sociale et désenchantement*, special issue of *Mouvements*, 15–16 (May–August 2001), 28–34, 30–31.

BIBLIOGRAPHY

A. Works by Jean-François Vilar

Novels

C'est toujours les autres qui meurent (Paris: Fayard, 1982; J'ai Lu, 1986)
Passage des singes (Paris: Presses de la Renaissance, 1984; J'ai Lu, 1985)
Etat d'urgence (Paris: Presses de la Renaissance, 1985; J'ai Lu, 1987)
Bastille-Tango (Paris: Presses de la Renaissance, 1986; Actes Sud, 1998)
Djemila (Paris: Calmann-Lévy, 1988)
Les Exagérés (Paris: Seuil, 1989; Seuil, coll. Points, 1990)
Nous cheminons entourés de fantômes aux fronts troués (Paris: Seuil, 1993)

Short Fiction

De parfaits petits crimes, illus. by Edmond Baudoin (Paris: Futuropolis, 1986)
Les Hiboux de Paris (Paris: Nathan, 1989)
La Grande Ronde du père Duchesne rue Saint-Antoine (Paris: Epigramme, 1989)
La Doublure (Paris: Nathan, 1990)
La Fille du calvaire (Paris: La Voûte, 1997)

Short Stories

'Tandem', *Tango*, 3 (July-September 1984), 32–37
'Cherie's Requiem', *ContreCiel*, 2 (June 1984), 61–65
'Dernières nouvelles de Fantomas', *Tango*, 4–5 (Spring-Summer 1985), 6–9
'Cher Nestor Burma', *Tango*, 4–5 (Spring-Summer 1985), 118–20
'La Tache de vin', in François Bon and others, *Café nocturne* (Paris: Harpo, 1985), 77–100
'En rade', *Après la plage*, 1 (Spring 1985), 10–16
'Ecran blanc, nuits noires', in *Mystères 86*, ed. by Jacques Baudou (Paris: Livre de poche, 1986), pp. 313–30
'Chapitre VIII', in *Agenda Polar 1986* (Paris: Eden, 1986), [n.p.]
'Le Dernier des Apaches', in *La Rue de Lappe* (Paris: Eden Galerie, 1987), pp. 75–100
'Karl R est de retour', in Frédéric Fajardie and others, *Black Exit to 68: 22 nouvelles sur mai* (Montreuil: La Brèche-PEC, 1988), pp. 61–81
'Terminus', *La Vie du rail*, 2154 (21 July 1988), 46–49
'Le Réveil du Golem', in *Métropolis: la ville est un roman 1841–1991* (Paris: Conseil Général Seine Saint-Denis and Denoël, 1991), pp. 20–21
'Rue de Prague', in *Octobre 1983/1993* (Paris: La Terrasse de Gutenberg, 1993)
'Je ne sais pas', in *Le Cinéma des écrivains: nouvelles*, ed. by Antoine de Baeque (Paris: Cahiers du cinéma, 1995), pp. 131–37
'Paris-Prague: aller simple et vague retour', *1968: le devenir de mai*, special issue of *Lignes*, 34

(1998), 82–98

Serial Fiction

'Paris d'octobre', *Le Matin de Paris*, 1–23 October 1985
'La Poupée phonographe', 1 October 1985, p. 19
'Lady L'Arsouille', 2 October 1985, p. 15
'Cadeaux volés', 3 October 1985, p. 20
'Etes-vous fou?', 4 October 1985, p. 13
'Le Calme de Stegosaure à l'heure du tabassage', 5–6 October 1985, p. 12
'Tête coupée et plomb dans l'aile', 7 October 1985, p. 14
'A bas le VIIe', 8 October 1985, p. 12
'Le Retour de la Joconde', 9 October 1985, p. 16
'"Flamber!", dit-elle', 10 October 1985, p. 19
'Canal Plus', 11 October 1985, p. 20
'"La Canaille? Eh bien j'en suis!"', 12 & 13 October 1985, p. 12
'Bercy, Bastille etc', 14 October 1985, p. 16
'Rififi rue Watt', 15 October 1985, p. 17
'Le Lion et l'oracle', 16 October 1985, p. 18
'Correspondances', 17 October 1985, p. 15
'Mort d'un pigeon', 18 October 1985, p. 24
'Gloire au 17e, bordel!', 19 & 20 October 1985, p. 14
'Je mourrai', 21 October 1985, p. 26
''La Descente de la Courtille', 22 October 1985, p. 15
'L'Arsouille, octobre et passé', 23 October 1985, p. 13

Text/Image

Paris la nuit, photographs by Michel Saloff (Paris: ACE éditions, coll. Le Piéton de Paris, 1982)
'Repérages pour un Paris des surréalistes et de quelques autres flâneurs', *Tango*, 4–5 (Spring-Summer 1985), 65–73
'Bastille-Opéra', *Tango*, 4–5 (Spring-Summer 1985), 132–33
'Poses', in Jacques Monory, *Come-back*, exhibition catalogue (Geneva: Galerie Sonia Zannettacci, 1990)
Sherlock Holmes et les ombres, photographs by Christian Louis (Paris: Du Collectionneur, 1992)
'Arch', in Jean-Paul Ruiz, *Moments noirs* (St Sornin-Lavolps: Jean Paul Ruiz, 1992), [n.p.]
[Untitled text, on Josef Kudek, 'Rêve de pierre (Prague 1953)'], Cahier I, in *Avant l'effacement*, ed. by Madeleine Millot-Durrenberger (Strasbourg: In Extremis, 1996–97), [n.p.]
[Untitled text], in Pierre Molinier, *La Grande Mêlée*, ed. by Madeleine Millot-Durrenberger (Strasbourg: In Extremis, 2001), [n.p.]
'Volver', in Antonio Seguí, *Seguí*, exhibition catalogue (Geneva: Galerie Sonia Zannettacci, 2009)
'Memento Mori', in Jacques Monory, *Memento mori*, exhibition catalogue (Geneva: Galerie Sonia Zannettacci, 2014)

Non-Fiction

'De Becassine à la reine Dahut', *Différences*, 5 (November 1981), 26–27
'Peer Gynt: la fuite vers soi', *Différences*, 5 (November 1981), 46
'La Parole à Jean-François Vilar: sous leurs pavés, notre histoire', *Différences*, 9 (March 1982), 48
'A Propos des "Maîtresses du Jeu de Maurice Périsset"', *Contreciel*, 1 (May 1984), 56–57
'Entretien avec Alexandre Trauner: propos recueillis par Jean-Louis Ducournau et Jean-François Vilar, *Tango*, 4–5 (Spring-Summer 1985), 10–17
'"Tango y Milonga": Munoz et Sampayo', *Tango*, 4–5 (Spring-Summer 1985), 98–99
'Entretien avec Léo Malet: propos recueillis par Jean-Louis Ducournau et Jean-François Vilar le 23 novembre 1984', *Tango*, 4–5 (Spring-Summer 1985), 121–25
'Les Pas perdus de Nestor Burma', *Le Monde*, 1 August 1986, p. 12
'Paris-énigmes', *Les Vacances*, ed. by Brigitte Ouvry-Vial and others, special issue of *Autrement*, 111 (January 1990), 19–21
'Paris désolé', in *Paris perdu: quarante ans de bouleversements de la ville*, ed. by Claude Eveno with Pascale de Mezemat (Paris: Carré, 1995), pp. 205–19
Les Fous de Chaillot (Paris: La Baleine, coll. Tourisme et Polar, 1997)
'Paris-Prague: aller simple et vague retour', *1968: le devenir de mai*, special issue of *Lignes*, 34 (1998), 82–98

Prefaces/Postfaces

'Introduction', in Joseph Périgot, *Le Dernier des grands romantiques, suivi de Vu, nouvelle par Marie-Dominique Arrighi* (Paris: Nouvelles éditions Oswald, 1984)
'Noir c'est noir', in Ernst Mandel, *Meurtres exquis: une histoire sociale du roman policier*, trans. by Marie Acampo (Montreuil: PEC, 1987)
'Postface', in Jan Valtin, *Sans patrie ni frontières*, trans. by Jean-Claude Henriot, rev. by Philippe Carella (Arles: Actes Sud, coll. Babel, 1997), pp. 873–94
'Preface', in Karel Pecka, *Passage*, trans. by Barbora Faure (Paris: Camourakis, 2013), pp. 9–11

Responses/Interviews in Magazines and Journals:

Lefebvre, Monique, 'Grand Prix du roman noir Télérama-Fayard: Jean-François Vilar', *Télérama*, 1673 (3 February 1982), 10
Brouillet, Christine, 'J-F Vilar de la nuit: entrevue de Jean-François Vilar', *Nuit blanche, le magazine du livre*, 26 (1986–87), 56–58 <http://id.erudit.org/iderudit/20641ac> [accessed 18 May 2020]
Simsolo, Noel, 'Jean-François Vilar tient le Hébert's fan club', *Politis*, 69 (7–12 July 1989), 60
'Des rapports amicaux', in 'Coulisses de l'édition: seize écrivains témoignent', *813 les amis de la littérature policière*, 33 (December 1990), 12
Bentolila, Eric, *Douze entretiens sur le polar français des années 80*, Temps noir la revue des littératures policières, 14 (2011), 10–69
Delouche, Hervé, and Alexis Violet [Jean-Michel Mension], 'Tapez "noir" pour mémoire' [interview with Jean-François Vilar], *Rouge*, 1538 (16 April 1993), 14
Violet, Alexis [Jean-Michel Mension], 'Série rouge' [interview with Jean-François Vilar], *Rouge*, 1170 (25 July to 22 August 1985), 27
'Jean-François Vilar: entretien', *Mic-mac*, 119 (October 1985), 55–58
Omar, 'Jean-François Vilar: sur les lieux du crime', *La Page*, 3 (May-June 1989), 6–7

Cited Articles in Rouge *by Jean-François Vilar*

'56 sardines, 30 puces, 50 pieds de vignes et 893 boîtes de foie gras', *Rouge*, 145 (6 September 1976)
'En attendant l'omelette campagnarde', *Rouge*, 150 (11–12 September 1976) 7
'Entre frites et affiches', *Rouge*, 151 (13 September 1976)
'Nouveaux juifs', *Rouge*, 885 (21–27 September 1979), 17
'Papon-Charonne', *Rouge*, 616 (6 April 1978), 3
'Juste des images : 'La Photographie' essai de Susan Sontag', *Rouge*, 896 (28 September-4 October 1979), 24
'Bercy-Chirac', *Rouge*, 891 (3–8 November), 19
'Les Porteurs de valise' [review], *Rouge*, 893 (16 November 1979), 16
'Essais', *Rouge*, 897 (14–20 December 1979), 20
'*Poésie sonore internationale*', *Rouge*, 890 (4–10 January 1980), 25
'Le Catalogue mondial des images incurables de Monory', *Rouge*, 904 (1–6 February 1980), 22
'Vichy Fictions' [review], *Rouge*, 941 (24–30 October 1980), 21–22
'L'Idéologie française selon B.-H. Lévy', *Rouge*, 955 (6–12 February 1981), 23
'A propos de "Vichy et les juifs" de Marrus et Paxton: la continuité du racisme d'état', *Rouge*, 970 (22–28 May 1981), 23
Jean-François Vilar, 'Paris mode d'emploi: "Les Passages couverts de Paris" ou "La Lumière de l'insolite"', *Rouge*, 974 (19–25 June 1981), 31

B. Other Works Consulted

ADAM, HÉLÈNE, and FRANÇOIS COUSTAL, *C'était la Ligue* (Tarbes & Paris: Arcane 17 & Syllepse, 2019)
ADES, DAWN, NEIL COX, and DAVID HOPKINS, *Marcel Duchamp* (London: Thames & Hudson, 1999)
ADORNO, THEODOR W., and WALTER BENJAMIN, *The Complete Correspondance 1928–1940*, ed. by Henri Loritz, trans. by Nicholas Walker (Cambridge, MA: Harvard University Press, 1999)
AGRET, ROLAND, *Coupable d'innocence* (Paris: Ramsay, 1984)
ALPHANT, MARIANNE, 'Vilar en flâneur noir', *Libération*, 7 March 1985, p. 28
AMBRE, JOANNÈS, and HENRI BAUDRY, *La Condition publique et privée du Juif en France (statut des Juifs): traité théorique et pratique* (Lyon: Joannès Devigne, 1942)
AMELINE, JEAN-PAUL, and BÉNÉDICTE AJAC, *Figuration narrative: Paris, 1960–1972* (Paris: Réunion des musées nationaux/Centre Pompidou, 2008)
[ANON.], 'Les Peintres contre l'expo Pompidou', *Rouge*, 146 (26 February 1972), 11
—— 'Les Mains sales', *Rouge*, 149 (18 March 1972), 5
—— 'A propos du FHAR', *Rouge*, 156 (6 May 1972), 4
—— 'Les États généraux du FAP', *Rouge*, 157 (13 May 1972), 7
——, LETTRE DU FHAR, *Rouge*, 159 (27 May 1972), 6
—— 'Algérie', *Rouge*, 166 (15 July 1972), 7
—— 'De Prinkipo à Cayoacan'', interview with Jean van Heijenoort, *Rouge*, 616 (3 April 1978), 11–12
—— 'Papon-Charonne', *Rouge*, 616 (6 April 1978), 3
—— [REVIEW OF *Djemila*], *Boum Boum*, 1–7 (April 1989), in 'Recueil Vilar: dossier de presse', Bibliothèque des littératures policières
ARAGON, LOUIS, *Le Paysan de Paris* (Paris: Gallimard, coll. Folio, 1978)

ARAMBASIN, NELLA, *Littérature contemporaine et histoires de l'art: récits d'une réévaluation* (Geneva: Droz, 2007)

ARNAUD, GEORGES, and JACQUES VERGÈS, *Pour Djamila Bouhired* (Paris: Minuit, 1957)

ARTIÈRES, PHILIPPE, and ERIC DE CHASSAY, eds, *Images en lutte: la culture visuelle de l'extrême gauche en France (1968–1974)* (Paris: Beaux-Arts de Paris, 2018)

ATACK, MARGARET, *May 68 in French Fiction and Film: Rethinking Society, Rethinking Representation* (Oxford: Oxford University Press, 1999)

—— 'From *Meurtres pour mémoire* to *Missak*: Literature and Historiography in Dialogue', *French Cultural Studies*, 12.3–4 (2014), 271–80

—— 'Streets and Squares, *quartiers* and *arrondissements*: Paris Crime Scenes and the Poetics of Contestation in the Novels of Jean-François Vilar', in *Crime Fiction in the City: Capital Crimes*, ed. by Lucy Andrew and Catherine Phelps (Cardiff: University of Wales Press, 2012), pp. 85–106

ATGET. EUGÈNE, *Atget's Paris*, intro. by Laure-Beaumont-Maillet, trans. by David Britt (London: Thames & Hudson, 1992)

AURON, YAÏR, *Les Juifs d'extrême gauche en mai 68* (Paris: Albin Michel, 1998)

BACKÈS-CLÉMENT, CATHERINE, 'L'Impossible Réel ou le leurre en vente', *Réalismes/2*, special issue of *Art vivant*, 37 (March 1973), 6–7

BAILLY, JEAN CHRISTOPHE, *Monory* (Paris: Maeght, 1979)

—— *Jacques Monory* (Neuchâtel: Ides et calendes, 2001)

—— 'Préface', in Jacques Monory, *Écrits, entretiens, récits*, (Paris: Beaux-Arts de Paris, 2014), pp. 9–10

—— 'Préface', in *Monory: noir*, exhibition catalogue (Paris: Galerie Lelong, 1991), pp. 3–29

BAMFORD, KIFF, *Lyotard and the Figural in Performance, Art and Writing* (London: Continuum, 2013)

BANCQUART, MARIE-CLAIRE, *Paris dans la littérature française après 1945* (Paris: La Différence: 2006)

—— *Paris des surréalistes* (Paris: La Différence, 2004)

BARTHES, ROLAND, *Essais critiques* (Paris: Seuil, coll. Points, 1981)

—— *La Chambre claire: note sur la photographie* (Paris: Gallimard, 1980)

—— *Mythologies* (Paris: Seuil, coll. Points, 1970)

BEAUVOIR, SIMONE DE, and GISÈLE HALIMI, *Djamila Boupacha* (Paris: Gallimard, 1962)

BENJAMIN, WALTER, *Paris, capitale du XIXe siècle: le livre des passages*, trans. by Jean Lacoste (Paris: Le Cerf, 1997)

—— *Petite histoire de la photographie*, trans. by Lionel Duvoy (Paris: Allia, 2012)

—— *Selected Writings*, ed. by Michael W. Jennings and others, trans. by Edmund Jephcott and others, 4 vols (Cambridge, MA, & London: Belknap Press, 1996–2003)

BENSAÏD, DANIEL, *Une lente impatience* (Paris: Stock, 2004)

BERMAN, MARSHALL, *All That is Solid Melts into Air: The Experience of Modernity* (London: Verso, 1983)

BIBLIOTHÈQUE DES LITTÉRATURES POLICIÈRES, 'Recueil Vilar: dossier de presse'

BLANC, JEAN-NOËL, *Polarville: images de la ville dans le roman policier* (Lyon: Presses universitaires de Lyon, 1991)

BRETON, ANDRÉ, *L'Amour fou* (Paris: Gallimard, coll. Folio, 1982)

—— *Nadja* (Paris: Gallimard, coll. Folio, 1964)

—— *Le Surréalisme et la peinture* (Paris: Gallimard, 1965)

BRIMO, NICOLAS, 'Papon: aide de camps', *Le Canard enchaîné*, 6 May 1981, p. 4

BROCHIER, JEAN-CHRISTOPHE, *Petits remèdes à la dépression politique* (Paris: Don Quichotte, 2017)

BUCK-MORSS, SUSAN, *The Dialectics of Seeing: Walter Benjamin and the Arcades Project* (Cambridge, MA, & London: MIT Press, 1991)

BUISINE, ALAIN, *Eugène Atget ou la mélancolie en photographie* (Nîmes: Jacqueline Chambon, 1994)
CAILLOIS, ROGER, *Le Mythe et l'homme* (Paris: Gallimard, 1972)
CALET, HENRI, *Le Tout sur le tout* (Paris: Gallimard, 1948)
CALLE, SOPHIE, *Suite vénitienne* (Paris: L'Étoile, 1983)
CAWS, MARY ANN, *The Art of Interference: Stressed Readings in Verbal and Visual Texts* (Cambridge: Polity Press & Basil Blackwell, 1989)
CHAMBARLHAC, VINCENT, 'Traces d'une œuvre: *Le Grand Méchoui* des Malassis en 1972', *Sociétés & Représentations*, 38.2 (2014), 281–94
CHEVALIER, LOUIS, *Histoires de la nuit parisienne: 1940–1960* (Paris: Fayard, 1982)
CLAIR, JEAN, 'L'Adorable Leurre', published in two parts: *Hyperréalisme 1*, special issue of *Art vivant*, 36 (February 1973), 4–5; *Réalismes/2*, special issue of *Art vivant*, 37 (March 1973), 4–6
—— *Art en France: une nouvelle génération* (Paris: Chêne, 1972)
—— *Marcel Duchamp ou, le grand fictif: essai de mythanalyse du grand verre* (Paris: Galilée, 1975)
—— *Marcel Duchamp: catalogue raisonné* (Paris: Centre Georges Pompidou, 1977)
CLAVEL, MAURICE, *Le Jardin de Djemila* [1958], in *Algérie: les romans de la guerre*, ed. by Guy Dugas (Paris: Omnibus, 2002), pp. 211–364
COHEN, MARGARET, *Profane Illuminations: Walter Benjamin and the Paris of Surrealist Revolution* (Berkeley, Los Angeles, & London: University of California Press, 1993)
COLLOVALD, ANNIE, 'L'Enchantement dans la désillusion politique', in *Le Polar entre critique sociale et désenchantement*, special issue of *Mouvements*, 15–16 (May-August 2001), 16–21
COLLOVALD, ANNIE, and ERIC NEVEU, '"Le néo-polar": du gauchisme politique au gauchisme littéraire', *Sociétés & Représentations*, 1 (2001), 77–93
COMPAGNON, ANTOINE, *La Seconde Main ou le travail de la citation* (Paris: Seuil, 1979)
CONLEY, KATHERINE, and PIERRE TAMINIAUX, eds, *Surrealism and its Others*, special edition of *Yale French Studies*, 109 (2006)
COOK, MARGARET, '*La Démolition* de Pierre Marcelle ou le crime du signe', *Tangence*, 38 (December 1992), 55–64 <https://doi.org/10.7202/025738ar38> [accessed 29 August 2019]
CORCUFF, PHILIPPE, and LISON FLEURY, 'Profondeurs du social et critique politique', *Le Polar entre critique sociale et désenchantement*, special issue of *Mouvements*, 15–16 (May-August 2001), 28–34
CORTÁZAR, JULIO, 'Les Fils de la Vierge', in *Les Armes secrètes* (Paris: Gallimard, coll. Folio, 1980), pp. 125–48
—— 'Hommage à une jeune sorcière', trans. by Isabelle Dessommes, with photographs of Rita Renoir, *Tango*, 3 (1984), 16–22
—— 'Manuscrit trouvé dans une poche', in *Octaèdre* (Paris: Gallimard, coll. Imaginaire, 2007), pp. 46–61
—— *Hopscotch*, trans. by Gregory Rabassa (New York: Pantheon Books, 1966)
DABIT, EUGÈNE, *Faubourgs de Paris* [1933] (Paris: Gallimard, coll. Imaginaire, 1990)
DAENINCKX, DIDIER, 'Archéologie du "un"', *Le Chroniqueur du cent-cinquantenaire*, p. 1, in *La Ville est un roman 1841–1991*, ed. by Hervé Delouche (Paris: Conseil Général Seine Saint-Denis & Denoël, 1991)
—— *Meurtres pour mémoire* (Paris: Gallimard, 1984)
DEBRAY, CÉCILE, *Marcel Duchamp: la peinture même*, exhibition catalogue (Paris: Centre Pompidou, 2015)
DEBRAY, CÉCILE, and OTHERS, *Le Nouveau Réalisme*, exhibition catalogue (Paris: Réunion des musées nationaux, 2007)
DELOUCHE, HERVÉ, ed., *La Ville est un roman 1841–1991* (Paris: Conseil Général Seine Saint-Denis & Denoël, 1991)

DEMURE, JEAN-PAUL, 'Écriture et dérision', in *Roman noir: pas d'orchidées pour les T. M.*, special issue of *Les Temps modernes*, 595 (August-October 1997), 157–63
DE QUINCEY, THOMAS, *On Murder Considered as One of the Fine Arts* [1827] (Richmond: Alma Books, 2016)
DÉSANGES, GUILLAUME, and FRANÇOIS PIRON, eds, *Contre-Cultures 1969–1989: l'esprit français* (Paris: La Découverte/La Maison rouge, 2017)
DUBOIS, CLAUDE, 'Requiem pour le musette', *Tango*, 1 (1983), 44
——*La Bastoche: une histoire du Paris populaire et criminel* (Paris: Perrin, 2011)
DUCHAMP, MARCEL, *Duchamp du signe* (Paris: Flammarion, 2013)
——*Manual of Instructions for Étant Donnés: 1° La Chute d'eau 2° Le Gaz d'éclairage* (Philadelphia: Philadelphia Museum of Art, 1987)
——*Marchand du sel: écrits de Marcel Duchamp* (Paris: Le Terrain vague, 1959)
——*La Mariée mise à nu par ses célibataires, même (La Boîte verte)* (Paris: Rrose Selavy, 1934)
DUCOURNAU, JEAN-LOUIS, 'Post scriptum', *Tango*, 4–5 (Spring-Summer 1985), 160
DUCREY, ANNE, 'Le Crime de Meursault: une machine à fictions', in *Romans du crime: littérature générale et comparée*, ed. by Karen Haddad-Wotling (Paris: Ellipses, 1998), pp. 61–85
DUHAMEL, MARCEL, 'Préface', in Raymond Borde and Étienne Chaumeton, *Panorama du film noir américain 1941–1953* [1955] (Paris: Flammarion, 1988)
DUVE, THIERRY DE, *Résonances du Readymade: Duchamp entre avant-garde et tradition* (Nîmes: Jacqueline Chambon, 1998)
ÉVRARD, FRANCK, *Fait divers et littérature* (Paris: Nathan, 1997)
Exposition internationale du surréalisme, janvier-février 1938 (Paris: Galerie Beaux-Arts, 1938)
FAJARDIE, FRÉDÉRIC, and OTHERS, *Black Exit to 68: 22 nouvelles sur mai* (Montreuil: La Brèche-PEC, 1988)
FARGUE, LÉON-PAUL, *Le Piéton de Paris, suivi de D'après Paris* (Paris: Gallimard, 1964)
Figurations critiques: 11 artistes des figurations critiques 1965–1975, exhibition catalogue (Lyon: ELAC, 1992)
FLEMING, JOHN, and HUGH HONOUR, *Marcel Duchamp: The Bride Stripped Bare by her Bachelors, Even* (London: Allen Lane, 1973)
FORSDICK, CHARLES, 'Direction les oubliettes de l'histoire: Witnessing the Past in the Contemporary French *polar*', *Crime and Punishment: Narratives of Order and Disorder*, ed. by Margaret Atack, special issue of *French Cultural Studies*, 12.3 (October 2001), 333–50
FRÉDÉRIC, MADELEINE, *La Stylistique française en mutation?* (Brussels: Académie royale de Belgique, 1997)
GALLET, PASCAL-EMMANUEL, ed., *Les Peintres-Cinéastes* (Paris: Ministère des relations extérieures, 1982)
GASSIOT-TALABOT, GÉRALD, 'De la Figuration narrative à la figuration critique', in *Face à l'histoire 1933–1996: l'artiste moderne devant l'événement historique*, ed. by Jean-Paul Ameline (Paris: Flammarion, 1996)
——*La Figuration narrative* (Paris: Jacqueline Chambon, 2003)
——*La Figuration narrative dans l'art contemporain*, exhibition catalogue (Paris: Galerie Creuze, 1965)
GASSIOT-TALABOT, GÉRALD, and OTHERS, *Mythologies quotidiennes 2*, exhibition catalogue (Paris: Musée d'Art Moderne de la Ville de Paris, 1977)
GASSIOT-TALABOT, GÉRALD, P. GAUDIBERT, and MARC LEBOT, eds, *Figurations 1960–1973* (Paris: Union générale d'éditions, coll. 10/18, 1973)
GENETTE, GÉRARD, *Palimpsestes: la littérature au second degré* (Paris: Seuil, coll. Points, 1992)
GODARD, JEAN-LUC, *Godard par Godard: les années Cahiers*, ed. by Alain Bergala (Paris: Flammarion, 1989)

GOLSAN, RICHARD J., 'Memory's *bombes à retardement*: Maurice Papon, Crimes against Humanity and 17 October 1961', *Journal of European Studies*, 28.1–2 (March-June 1998), 153–72

GORRARA, CLAIRE, *French Crime Fiction and the Second World War: Past Crimes, Present Memories* (Manchester: Manchester University Press, 2012)

—— *The Roman noir in Post-war French Culture: Dark Fictions* (Oxford: Oxford University Press, 2003)

GORRARA, CLAIRE, ed., *French Crime Fiction* (Cardiff: University of Wales Press, 2009)

GOULET, ANDREA, *Legacies of the rue Morgue: Science, Space and Crime Fiction in France* (Philadelphia: University of Pennsylvania Press, 2016)

GOULET, ANDREA, and SUSANNA LEE, eds, *Crime Fictions*, special issue of *Yale French Studies*, 108 (October 2005)

GULON, JÉRÔME, *Ernest Pignon-Ernest: le lieu et la formule* (Grenoble: Critères, 2012)

HILLAIRET, JACQUES, *Dictionnaire historique des rues de Paris*, 2 vols (Paris: Minuit, 1964)

HORSLEY, LEE, *Twentieth-century Crime Fiction* (Oxford: Oxford University Press, 2005)

HOUSE, JIM, and NEIL MACMASTER, *Paris 1961: Algerians, State Terror, and Memory* (Oxford: Oxford University Press, 2006)

HUTTON, MARGARET-ANNE, *French Crime Fiction 1945–2005: Investigating World War II* (Farnham, Ashgate, 2013)

JEIN, GILLIAN, '(De)Facing the Wall: The Traditions, Transactions and Transgressions of Street Art', *Irish Journal of French Studies*, 12 (2012), 83–111

JONQUET, THIERRY, *Rouge c'est la vie* (Paris: Seuil, 1998)

JOPPOLO, GIOVANNI, 'Petits crimes quotidiens et anonymes: Marc Petitjean', *L'Art Hors Sur Dans Contre La Ville?*, *Opus International*, 65 (Winter 1978), 45–47

JOUFFROY, ALAIN, *Les Pré-voyants* (Brussels: La Connaissance, 1974)

KAFKA, FRANZ, 'The Cares of a Family Man', in *The Complete Short Stories*, ed. by Nahum N. Glatzer, trans. by Willa and Edwin Muir (London: Vintage, 2005), pp. 427–29

KNIGHT, DIANA, 'Roland Barthes, or, The Woman Without a Shadow', in *Writing the Image: After Roland Barthes*, ed. by Jean-Michel Rabaté (Philadelphia: University of Pennsylvania Press, 1997), pp. 132–43

KRACAUER, SIEGFRIED, *Le Roman policier*, trans. by Geneviève and Rainer Rochlitz (Paris: Payot & Rivages, 2001)

KRASNY, JOSEPH [EDWY PLENEL], 'Algérie', *Rouge*, 166 (15 July 1972), 7

KRAUSS, ROSALIND E., *Bachelors* (Cambridge, MA, & London: MIT Press, 2000)

—— *The Optical Unconscious* (Cambridge, MA, & London: MIT Press, 1993)

KRAUSS, ROSALIND, and JANE LIVINGSTON, *L'Amour fou: Photography & surréalisme* (New York: Cross River Press, 1985)

LAMÉ, LOUISE, and CORSAIRE SANGLOT, *Passage Jean-François Vilar* <http://passagejfv.eklablog.com> [accessed 1 June 2020]

LANZMANN, CLAUDE, *Un vivant qui passe: Auschwitz 1943-Theresienstadt 1944* (Paris: Gallimard, coll. Folio, 2013)

LE BOT, MARC, 'Les Appareils du réalisme', *Hyperréalisme 1*, special issue of *Art vivant*, 36 (February 1973), 6–8

LEQUENNE, MICHEL, 'L'Art du régime et le régime de l'art', *Rouge*, 158 (20 May 1972), 6

—— 'Bide noir pour Pompidou', *Rouge*, 159 (27 May 1972), 7

LE THOREL, PASCALE, ed., *Jacques Monory*, exhibition catalogue (Landerneau: Fonds Hélène & Edouard Leclerc, 2014)

LIGUE COMMUNISTE RÉVOLUTIONNAIRE, *Ce que veut la ligue communiste: manifeste du Comité Central du 29 et 30 janvier 1972* (Paris: François Maspero, 1972)

LITS, MARC, *Le Roman policier*, 2nd edn (Liège: Le Céfal, 1998)

LŒILLETON, FERNAND, 'La Mémoire courte ou les dents longues?', *Rouge*, 145 (19 February 1972), 16
LYOTARD, JEAN-FRANÇOIS, *The Assassination of Experience by Painting — Monory. L'Assassinat de l'expérience par la peinture — Monory*, ed. by Sarah Wilson, parallel trans. by Rachel Bowlby (London: Black Dog, 1998)
—— *L'Assassinat de l'expérience par la peinture, Monory. The Assassination of Experience by Painting, Monory*, ed. by Herman Parret, parallel trans. by Rachel Bowlby (Leuven: Leuven University Press, 2013)
—— 'Contribution des tableaux de Jacques Monory à l'intelligence de l'économie politique libidinale du capitalisme dans son rapport avec le dispositif pictural, et inversement', in *Figurations 1960–1973*, ed. by Gérald Gassiot-Talabot, P. Gaudibert, and Marc Lebot (Paris: Union générale d'éditions, coll. 10/18, 1973), pp. 154–238
—— 'Esquisse d'une économique de l'hyperréalisme', *Hyperréalisme 1*, special issue of *Art vivant*, 36 (February 1973), 9–12
—— '*Étant donnés*: inventaire du dernier nu', in *Marcel Duchamp: abécédaire: approches critiques*, ed. by Jean Clair with Ulf Linde (Paris: Musée national d'art moderne, 1977), pp. 86–109
—— *The Lyotard Reader*, ed. by Andrew Benjamin (Oxford: Basil Blackwell Ltd., 1989)
—— *Récits tremblants*, illus. by Jacques Monory (Paris: Galilée, 1977)
MACCHIA, GIOVANNI, *Paris en ruines*, trans. by Paul Bédarida with Mario Fusco (Paris: Flammarion, 1988)
MAILLARD, ROBERT, ed., *25 ans d'art en France: 1960–1985* (Paris: Larousse, 1986)
MAJASTRE, JEAN-OLIVIER, *Approche anthropologique de la représentation: entre corps et signe* (Paris: L'Harmattan, 1999)
MANDEL, ERNEST, *Delightful Murder: A Social History of the Crime Story* (London: Pluto Press, 1984)
MARCELLE, PIERRE, *La Démolition* (Paris: Denoël, 1985)
—— 'Last Exit from Bercy', *Tango*, 4–5 (Spring-Summer 1985), 47–48
MARX, KARL, and FRIEDRICH ENGELS, *The Communist Manifesto*, intro. by A. J. P. Taylor, trans. by Samuel Moore (Harmondsworth: Penguin Books, 1967)
MATHEY, FRANÇOIS, ed., *72: douze ans d'art contemporain en France*, exhibition catalogue (Paris: Réunion des musées nationaux, 1972)
MELLIER, DENIS, and GILLES MENEGALDO, eds, *Formes policières du roman contemporain* (Poitiers: La Licorne, 1998)
MENSION, JEAN-MICHEL (Alexis Violet), *Le Temps gage: aventures politiques et artistiques d'un irrégulier à Paris* (Paris: Noésis, 2001)
—— *The Tribe: Conversations with Gérard Berréby and Francesco Milo*, trans. by Donald Nichelson-Smith (London: Verso, 2002)
MERLEAU-PONTY, MAURICE, 'Le Doute de Cézanne', in *Sens et non-sens* (Paris: Nagel, 1948), pp. 15–49
MICHA, RENÉ, 'Étant donné *Étant donnés*', in *Marcel Duchamp: tradition de la rupture ou rupture de la tradition*, Colloque de Cerisy, ed. by Jean Clair (Paris: Union générale d'éditions, coll. 10/18, 1979), pp. 177–80
MINICH BREWER, MÁRIA, *Claude Simon: Narrativities without Narrative* (Lincoln & London: University of Nebraska Press, 1995)
MONORY, JACQUES, *Écrits, entretiens, récits*, ed. by Pascale Le Thorel (Paris: Beaux-Arts de Paris, 2014)
—— *Les Premiers Numéros du catalogue mondial des images incurables*, préface d'Alain Jouffroy (Paris: Centre national d'art contemporain, 1974)
MOULIN, RAYMONDE, 'Vivre pour vendre', in Jean Cassou and others, *Art et contestation* (Brussels: La Connaissance, 1968), pp. 121–36

MÜLLER, ELFRIEDE, and ALEXANDRE RUOFF, *Le Polar français: crime et histoire*, trans. by Jean-François Poirier, preface by Frédéric H. Fajardie (Paris: La Fabrique, 2002)

MUNRO, JANE, ed., *Silent Partners: Artist and Mannequin from Function to Fetish* (Cambridge: Fitzwilliam Museum; New Haven, CT, & London: Yale University Press, 2014)

NEWMAN, MIKE, 'Odradek and the Rethinking of Political Method in the Work of Art' <https://research.gold.ac.uk/21412/1/Newman-Benjanin%20Brecht%20Wall%20and%20Odradek%20for%20Oxford_rev.pdf> [accessed 7 May 2020]

NIZAN, PAUL, *Aden Arabie* [1931], intro. by Jean-Paul Sartre (Paris: Maspero, 1960)

NOGUEZ, DOMINIQUE, 'Sur le réalisme', *Art vivant*, 36 (February 1973), 32

Opus International, '68–78', 66–67 (May-June 1978)

—— *Duchamp et après*, 49 (March 1974)

—— *Écrire sur l'art*, 70–71 (Winter 1979)

—— *L'Art Hors Sur Dans Contre La Ville?*, 65 (Winter 1978)

—— *Monory*, 134 (Autumn 1994)

PELLETIER, ROBERT, and SERGE RAVET, *Le Mouvement de soldats: les comités de soldats et l'antimilitarisme révolutionnaire* (Paris: Petite collection Maspero, 1976)

PEREC, GEORGES, *Je me souviens* (Paris: Hachette, 1978)

PLATTEN, DAVID, *The Pleasures of Crime: Reading Modern French Crime Fiction* (Amsterdam & New York: Rodopi, 2011)

—— 'Reading-glasses, Guns and Robots: A History of Science in French Crime Fiction', in *Crime and Punishment: Narratives of Order and Disorder*, ed. by Margaret Atack, special issue of *French Cultural Studies*, 12.3 (October 2001), pp. 253–70

PLENEL, EDWY, 'Jean-François Vilar: étoile filante du roman noir', *Mediapart* <https://blogs.mediapart.fr/edwy-plenel/blog/221214/jean-francois-vilar-etoile-filante-du-roman-noir> [accessed 23 December 2014]

—— *Secrets de jeunesse* (Paris: Stock, 2001)

POLLOCK, GRISELDA, and MAX SILVERMAN, eds, *Concentrationary Imaginaries: Tracing Totalitarian Violence in Popular Culture* (London: I. B. Tauris, 2015)

—— *Concentrationary Memories: Totalitarian Terror and Cultural Resistance* (London: I. B. Tauris, 2014)

POUY, JEAN-BERNARD, with STÉFANIE DELESTRÉ, *Une brève histoire du roman noir* (Paris: Seuil, coll. Points, 2016)

PRADEL, JEAN-LOUIS, *La Figuration narrative: des années 1960 à nos jours* (Paris: Gallimard, 2008)

—— 'Instrument critique d'un système global du visible', in Gérald Gassiot-Talabot and others, *Mythologies quotidiennes 2*, exhibition catalogue (Paris: Musée d'art moderne de la Ville de Paris, 1977), [n.p.]

PRANVILLE, PIERRE-MICHEL, 'Le Néo-polar est-il un avatar littéraire de Mai 68?', *Carnets*, 2nd ser., 16 (2019) <https://journals.openedition.org/carnets/9785> [accessed 4 February 2020]

PRONIER, RAYMOND, 'Les Finances à Bercy', *Le Matin de Paris*, 14 October 1985, p. 16

—— 'Les Petites gens et la rénovation', *Le Matin de Paris*, 16 October 1985, p. 18

RABATÉ, JEAN-MICHEL, *Etant donnés: 1. L'Art, 2. Le Crime: la modérnité comme scène du crime* (Dijon: Presses du réel, 2010)

RAGON, MICHEL, *25 ans d'Art vivant, chronique vécue de l'art contemporain: de l'abstraction au pop art 1944–1969* (Paris: Galilée, 1986)

RAYNAL, PATRICK, 'Le Roman noir est l'avenir de la fiction', *Roman noir: pas d'orchidées pour les T.M.*, special issue of *Les Temps modernes*, 595 (August-October 1997), 88–99

READER, KEITH, *The Place de la Bastille: The Story of a Quartier* (Liverpool: Liverpool University Press, 2011)

READINGS, BILL, *Introducing Lyotard: Art and Politics* (London & New York: Routledge, 1991)
RENOIR, RITA, 'Pour Julio mon corps sans hasard', *Tango*, 3 (1984), 15
RESTANY, PIERRE, *Le Nouveau Réalisme à Paris et New York* (Paris: Galerie Rive Droite, 1961)
—— *Les Nouveaux Réalistes*, preface by M. Ragon (Paris: Planète, 1968)
RESTELLINI, MARC, ed., *Le Pressionnisme 1970–1990: les chefs-d'œuvre du graffiti sur toile de Basquiat à Bando* (Paris: Pinacothèque de Paris, 2015)
REUTER, YVES, *Le Roman policier* (Paris: Nathan, 1997)
RICHARD, DENIS, and ELISABETH CARRIÈRE, eds, *Le Procès de Draguignan*, illus. by Cabu (Monaco: Le Rocher, 1975)
RIVIÈRE, FRANÇOIS, 'Léo Malet: un noir jeu de l'oie', *Magazine Littéraire, Le Paris des écrivains*, 332 (May 1995), 61–63
Roman noir: pas d'orchidées pour les T.M., special issue of *Les Temps modernes*, 595 (August-October, 1997)
ROLLS, ALISTAIR, 'Paris as Rewrite: Getting Away with it in Léo Malet's XVe Arrondissement', in *Rewriting Wrongs: French Crime Fiction and the Palimpsest*, ed. by Angela Kimyongür and Amy Wigelsworth (Newcastle upon Tyne: Cambridge Scholars Publishing, 2014), pp. 81–94
ROSS, KRISTIN, *May 68 and its Afterlives* (Chicago & London: University of Chicago Press, 2002)
—— 'Parisian noir', *Literary History*, 41.1 (Winter 2010), 95–109
ROTHBERG, MICHAEL, *Multidirectional Memory: Remembering the Holocaust in the Age of Decolonization* (Stanford, CA: Stanford University Press, 2009)
ROUILLÉ, ANDRÉ, *La Photographie: entre document et art contemporain* (Paris: Gallimard, coll. Folio Essais, 2005)
SAINT, NIGEL, 'Space and Absence in Sophie Calle's *Suite vénitienne* and *Disparitions*', *Esprit créateur*, 51.1 (Spring 2011), 125–38
SALLES, JEAN-PAUL, *La Ligue communiste révolutionnaire (1968–1981): instrument du Grand Soir ou lieu d'apprentissage?* (Rennes: Presses universitaires de Rennes, 2005)
SARTRE, JEAN-PAUL, *L'Imaginaire: psychologie phénoménologique de l'imagination* (Paris: Gallimard, 1940)
SAUVAGEOT, PIERRE-ANDRÉ, DIR., *Jean-François Vilar: 95% de réel* (1997)
SCHAEWEN, DEIDI VON, 'Murs', *L'Art ~~Hors~~ ~~Sur~~ ~~Dans~~ ~~Contre~~ La Ville?*, *Opus international*, 65 (Winter 1978), 13
SCHOOF, KERSTIN, 'Les Photos dans les polars de Jean-François Vilar', trans. by Michel Marx, <http://pagesperso-range.fr/arts.sombres/polar/8_dossiers_article_kertin_schoof_fr.pdf> [accessed 25 April 2010]
SCHULMAN, PETER, 'Paris en jeu de l'oie: les fantômes de Nestor Burma', *The French Review*, 73 (May 2000), 1155–64
SCHWEIGHAEUSER, JEAN-PAUL, *Le Roman noir français* (Paris: Presses universitaires de France, coll. Que sais-je?, 1984)
SHERINGHAM, MICHAEL, *Everyday Life: Theories and Practices from Surrealism to the Present* (Oxford: Oxford University Press, 2006)
SILVERMAN, MAX, *Palimpsestic Memory: The Holocaust and Colonialism in French and Francophone Fiction and Film* (New York & Oxford: Berghahn Books, 2013)
SONTAG, SUSAN, *On Photography* (London: Penguin Books, 1979)
STAFFORD, ANDY, *Phototexts: Contemporary French Writing of the Photographic Image* (Liverpool: Liverpool University Press, 2010)
STEFANICH, FERNANDO, 'Crime and the *Figuration narrative* Movement: The Case of Jacques Monory', in *New Approaches to Crime in French Literature, Culture and Film*, ed. by Louise Hardwick (Oxford: Peter Lang, 2009)

STIERLE, KARLHEINZ, *La Capitale des signes: Paris et son discours*, trans. by Marianne Rocher-Jacquin (Paris: La Maison des sciences de l'homme, 2002)

TRONCHE, ANNE, 'Anne et Patrick Poirier ou l'espace-temps conditionné', *L'Art ~~Hors Sur Dans Contre~~ La Ville?*, *Opus International*, 65 (Winter 1978), 34–38

—— 'Pignon sur rues', *L'Art ~~Hors Sur Dans Contre~~ La Ville?*, *Opus international*, 65 (Winter 1978), 13–16

VASSEUR, BERNARD, *Monory* (Paris: Éditions Cercle d'art, 2012)

VERNET, MARC, '*Film noir* on the Edge of Doom', in *Shades of Noir*, ed. by Joan Copjec (London: Verso, 1993), pp. 1–32

VINCIGUERRA, LUCIEN, 'Comment inverser exactement *Les Ménines*: Michel Foucault et la peinture à la fin des années 60, des formes symboliques aux dispositifs', in *Le Moment philosophique des années 1960 en France*, ed. by Pierre Maniglier (Paris: Presses universitaires de France, 2011), pp. 477–92

WALKER, DAVID H., *Outrage and Insight: Modern French Literature and the 'fait divers'* (Oxford & Washington, DC: Berg, 1995)

WENDERS, WIM, *The Logic of Images: Essays and Conversations*, trans. by Michael Hofman (London: Faber & Faber, 1991)

WILSON, SARAH, *The Visual World of French Theory: Figurations* (New Haven, CT, & London: Yale University Press, 2010)

INDEX

A.D.G. 21, 26 n. 53, 87, 92 n. 24
Ackendengué 12
Adorno, Theodor W. 53, 109, 112 nn. 30 & 31
Agret, Roland 11, 25 n. 14
Aillaud, Gilles 37
Ajac, Bénédicte 27 nn. 71, 72 & 76
Alphant, Marianne 86, 91 n. 12, 92 n. 21
Ambre, Joannès 14
Ameline Jean-Paul 27 nn. 71, 72 & 76
Apostrophes 1, 6 n. 3, 21, 27 n. 65
Aragon, Louis 43, 49, 69
Arambasin, Nella 44 n. 21
Arbus, Diane 12, 55
Arley, Catherine 21
Arman 22
Arroyo, Eduardo 37
Atget. Eugène 2–3, 29, 30, 39, 40–41, 47, 49, 55, 75, 83, 84
Auron, Yaïr 25 n. 32

Bacall, Lauren 21, 26 n., 40, 53
Backès-Clément, Catherine 117, 129 n. 27
Bando 79, 90 n. 1
Barthes, Roland 23, 39, 42, 45 n. 36, 74, 92 n. 18, 116, 121–22, 130 n. 34
Baudelaire, Charles 20, 45 n. 38, 47, 48, 116
Beauvoir, Simone de 92 n. 23
Benaquista, Tonino 114
Ben Barka, Mehdi 18, 62 n. 42
Benjamin, Walter 2–3, 29, 39, 45 n. 38, 53, 61 n. 7, 62 n. 24, 72, 75, 76 nn. 11, 12, & 20, 77 n. 22, 82, 95, 108, 111 n. 12, 112 n. 30, 129 n. 17
Bensaïd, Daniel 13, 14, 15, 25 n. 24, 26 n. 36, 31, 44 n. 12, 85, 102–03, 104, 111 n. 21, 112 n. 27
Berman, Marshall 94, 111 n. 8
Blanchot, Maurice 23
Blue, Sugar 12
Bogart, Humphrey 20, 21, 26 n. 40, 83
Boileau, Pierre, 21
Borges, Jorge Luis 4, 16, 126
Bouhired, Djamila 87, 92 n. 23
Boupacha, Djamila 87, 92 n. 23
Brando, Marlon 55
Brassaï, 3, 111 n. 23
Breton André 2, 17, 19, 20, 49, 52, 95, 100, 103, 105, 108, 132

Amour fou 52, 103, 111 n. 23
 Nadja 36, 52, 67, 73, 103, 110, 112 nn. 25 & 29, 116, 129 n. 15
Brochier, Jean-Christophe 1, 6–7 n. 5, 11, 25 n. 10
Brouillet, Christine 24 n. 2, 43 n. 10
Burroughs, William 12, 43, 105

Caillois, Roger 48, 61 n. 9
Calet, Henri 48, 55
Calle, Sophie 81, 91 n. 13
Camus, Albert 4, 16
Carrière, Elisabeth 24 n. 4
Caws, Mary Ann 42, 45 n. 42
Chabrol, Claude 20
Chambarlhac, Vincent 44 n. 26
chance 4, 29, 57 71
 chance and necessity 4, 33, 69, 71
 chance encounters 49 50
 computer game 71
 games of chance 4
  chess 33, 42, 44 n. 18
  jeu de l'oie/goose game 4, 17, 18, 50, 71
  hasard objectif/objective chance 4, 41, 71, 75, 100, 105
  tarot cards 4, 54, 73
Chandler, Raymond 23, 81
Chéreau, Patrice 83, 92 n. 19
city 2, 3, 4, 9, 17, 41, 42, 48, 67, 73, 75, 82, 86, 89, 97, 106, 122. 124, 125, 128, 131
 and art 6, 79, 81, 105
 architecture 3, 48, 68, 82, 113
 Beirut 101
 Buenos Aires 31, 57, 58, 59, 80
 and crime fiction 2, 4, 9, 19, 21, 23, 131
 and death 81, 82, 83, 84, 86
 Djemila 2, 6, 43, 79, 86–90, 110
 dream city 100, 106, 109
 imaginary city 47–77, 83, 84, 85, 89
 labyrinth 71, 81
 London 6, 69, 93, 96, 97, 98
 maps 17, 18, 49, 58, 59, 69, 105, 106
 palimpsest 97
 and photography 3, 39, 41
 and politics 50–51, 57, 79. 131
 Prague 1, 2, 6, 21, 43, 85, 93, 96, 97, 98, 100. 101, 102, 104, 106–10
 as puzzle 48, 71, 106

reading the city 54, 55, 56, 71, 81
and signs 48, 54
spaces 48, 52, 79, 105, 106
as theatre 3, 6, 79, 85
underground 21, 49, 84, 97, 106, 109, 110
Venice 2, 6, 43, 79, 81–86, 90, 110, 132
  canals 79, 81, 82, 84, 85, 86
and violence 21, 79, 80, 81, 83
see also Paris
Clair, Jean 44 n. 29, 45 n. 43, 116, 129 n. 15
Clavel, Maurice 88
Cohen, Margaret 95, 103, 111 n. 12, 111 n. 24
Collovald, Annie 2, 7 n. 9, 26 n. 53, 43 n. 7, 113 n. 2
Compagnon, Antoine 42, 45 no. 40, 75, 77 n. 21
Conan Doyle, Arthur 69, 96, 97, 111 n. 15
  'A Scandal in Bohemia' 93, 95, 96, 98, 99
  Sherlock Holmes 69, 93, 95–96, 97, 98, 99
Cook, Margaret 91 n. 11
Cook, Robin, 114
Corcuff, Philippe 133 n. 2
Cortázar, Julio 2, 4, 16, 26 n. 43, 52, 53, 55, 62 n. 39, 71, 72, 73
Courbet, Gustave, *L'Origine du monde* 32
Coustal, François, 25 n. 22
Crepax, Guido 31
crime fiction 1, 2, 4, 5, 9, 18 20, 31, 33, 41, 48, 87, 97, 98, 99, 131
  crime scene 3, 39, 42, 48, 51, 52, 54, 65. 72, 75, 79, 86, 89, 90, 107
  detective 3, 17, 18, 23, 29, 43 n. 8, 72, 74, 126, 131
  fait divers 11, 36, 41, 42, 83, 87, 89
  and history 1, 9, 18, 48, 73, 99, 111 n. 18
  néo-polar 18–19, 20, 27 n. 65, 73, 74, 131
  polar 6, n. 3, 18, 21, 26 n. 50, 27 n. 66, 87, 93
  and politics 2, 3, 6, 9, 18, 24, 29, 30, 37. 57, 73, 93, 99, 101, 110, 131, 132
  roman noir 1, 2, 3, 5, 9. 16, 17, 18, 19, 20, 21, 22, 23, 24, 27 nn. 71 & 79, 38, 41, 48, 49, 53, 54, 56, 57, 63 n. 44, 67, 71, 73, 75, 81, 86, 99–100, 122, 123, 125, 128, 132
  Série noire 9, 16, 20
theatre of crime 2, 3, 6, 48, 65, 79, 86
Czechoslovakia 30, 79, 93, 98, 99, 102, 108, 100, 110
  International Students Day 101, 109
  Munich Agreement 30, 98, 100, 109
  Prague *see* city
  Soviet invasion 30, 101, 102
  Velvet Revolution 30, 101

Dabit, Eugène 48
Daeninckx, Didier 1, 12, 27 nn. 67 & 68, 51, 62 n. 20, 74, 87, 114, 132
Dard, Frédéric 18
Debray, Cécile 44 n. 20
Deleuse, Robert 27 n. 67
Delouche, Hervé 21, 27 nn. 67 & 68, 111 nn. 3 & 13

Delvaille, Bernard 49
Delvaux, Paul 105, 106
Demure, Jean-Paul 19, 27 n. 57
Désanges, Guillaume 62 n. 16
Döblin, Alfred 12
Doisneau, Robert 16, 17, 49
Dragan 21
Dubois, Claude 16, 26 n. 42, 62 n. 36
Duchamp, Marcel 1, 2, 5, 23, 24, 29, 30, 31, 32–33, 34, 35 36, 37, 39, 41, 42, 43, 43 n. 3, 44 nn. 18, 20 & 28, 45 nn. 31 & 33, 54, 62 n. 18, 89, 92 n. 27, 100, 113, 115, 116, 122, 123, 124, 130 n. 39, 132
  Etant donnés/Given 32, 33 35, 41, 42, 43, 44 n. 18, 71, 75, 79, 82, 83, 84, 89, 113, 122
  Le Grand Verre/The Large Glass 30, 32, 33, 35, 44 nn. 17 & 18
  LHOOQ 33, 54
Ducournau, Jean-Louis 15, 17, 26 n. 44
Ducrey, Anne 4, 7 n. 20
Dufrêne, François 22, 91 n. 6
Duhamel, Marcel 20, 27 n. 64
Dunaway, Faye 53
Dürer, Albrecht 32, 115, 116, 122

Engels, Friedrich 94, 111 n. 7
everyday/everyday life 3, 9, 11, 12, 20, 22, 23, 42, 73, 80, 81, 82, 83, 96, 106, 112 n. 31, 126, 128, 133
Évrard, Franck 41, 45 nn. 36 & 37

Fabre-Luce, Alfred 15
Fajardie, Frédéric 1, 7 n. 11, 12, 24 n. 2, 26 n. 5, 131
Fantomas 54, 55
Fargue, Léon-Paul 47, 49, 61 n. 3
Feuillade, Louis 20
Fleury, Lison 133 n. 2
Forsdick, Charles 74, 76 n. 17
Frédéric, Madeleine 7 n. 7, 44 nn. 21 & 22
Fromanger, Gérard 23
Front des Artistes Plasticiens (FAP) 34, 44 n. 25
Front Homosexuel d'Action Révolutionnaire (FHAR) 10, 25 n. 9
Fuller, Samuel 55, 82

Gassiot-Talabot, Gérald 22, 27 n. 74, 117, 129 nn. 12 & 28
Genette, Gérard 42, 45 n. 41
Godard, Jean-Luc 20, 22, 23, 27 n. 73, 48, 82
  Michel Poiccard 20, 43, 73
Golsan, Richard J. 74, 76 n. 17
Goodis, David 20
Gorrara, Claire 26–27 n. 54
Goulet, Andrea 26 n. 54, 97, 98, 111 nn. 15 & 16
Gracq, Julien 81
Grass, Günther 12
Guédon, Henri 12

Hains, Raymond 22
Halimi, Gisèle 92 n. 23
Hallyday, Johnny 16, 17, 26 n. 50
Hammett, Dashiell 1, 2, 6 n. 4, 19, 21, 23, 94, 95
Hayworth, Rita 53
Hébert, Jaques-René (le père Duchesne) 66, 68, 69, 70
Highsmith, Patricia 39
Hillairet, Jacques 69, 76 n. 2
historiography 6, 48, 66, 67, 68, 69, 73, 75, 94, 100
history 1, 2, 6, 9, 12, 13, 14, 15, 18, 51, 57, 60, 67, 69, 72, 73, 74, 76, 93, 95, 99, 100, 102, 103, 104, 108, 110, 117, 125, 131
   1930s 1, 2, 17, 20, 21, 27 n. 63, 29, 40, 93, 94, 95, 101, 104, 105, 110, 115, 132
     Anschluss 30, 100
     Kristallnacht 30, 40, 100, 101
     Moscow show trials 6, 29, 94
   Algerian War 1, 6, 9, 12, 13, 25 n. 21, 56, 59, 75, 79, 86, 87, 90, 131, 132
     Charonne 12–13, 25 n. 27, 51, 80
     Organisation de l'Armée secrète (OAS) 12, 87, 89
     17 October 1961 12–14, 51, 74
   Commune 1, 12, 49, 50, 51, 74, 75, 80, 91 n. 7, 127
     Semaine Sanglante 51, 74
   Fall of the Berlin Wall 30, 101, 108
   French Revolution 6, 9, 30, 65, 66, 68, 73, 74
   German Occupation of France 1940–1944 1, 12, 14, 15, 18, 31, 40, 54, 59, 56, 73, 74, 93, 101
     deportations of Jews 13, 14, 15, 59, 74
     Drancy 15, 21, 59, 72, 76 n. 8, 79, 102, 103
     resistance 6, 15, 18, 87, 88, 89, 102, 107
     Vélodrome d'hiver/Vél d'hiv 6, 5, 14, 18, 76 n. 8, 79, 102, 107
   Hiroshima 125, 128
   Holocaust 12, 15, 18, 23, 40, 70, 74, 84, 85, 89, 93, 110, 131, 132
     Auschwitz 51, 79, 92 n. 22, 102, 103, 107, 125
     concentration camps 6, 15. 35. 45 n. 34, 70, 79, 85, 98, 104
     concentrationary 40, 45 n. 34, 84
     Terezin 79, 85, 98, 110
   May 68: 2, 9, 10, 13, 30, 31, 35, 79, 87, 101, 102, 108, 131
     Atelier des Beaux Arts 22, 35, 79, 131
   and memory 2, 6, 12, 65–77, 68, 69, 102, 110
   Spanish Civil War 101, 102
Hitchcock, Alfred 20, 82
Hopper, Edward 105, 125
Horsley, Lee 19, 27 n. 61
House, Jim 25 nn. 20 & 25
Hugo, Victor 3, 20, 49
Hutton, Margaret-Anne, 27 n. 54

Jein, Gillian 91 n. 5
Jonquet, Thierry 1, 12, 131
Joppolo, Giovanni 80, 91 n. 9

Jouffroy, Alain 91 n. 6, 114, 115, 128 n. 4, 129 n. 11, 130 n. 44

Kafka, Franz 19, 85, 108
   'Cares of a Family Man' 108
   Odradek 108–09, 110, 112 n. 31
Kagan, Elie 13, 34, 44 n. 25
Kienholz, Edward 12
Klement, Rudolf 12, 25 n. 19, 100, 103, 108
Knight, Diana 122, 180 n. 17
Kracauer, Siegfried 27 n. 55
Krasny, Joseph *see* Plenel, Edwy
Krauss, Rosalind E. 5, 7 n. 21
Krivine, Alain 10, 13, 14

Lang, Fritz 20, 21
Lanzmann, Claude 91 n. 4
Lautréamont, comte de 30
Léautaud, Paul 49
Le Bot, Marc 117, 122, 129 n. 22, 130 n. 36
Lee, Suzanna 26 n. 54
Lefebvre, Henri 23
Lefebvre, Monique 43 n. 2, 92 n. 25
Lenin 55, 73, 100
Lequenne, Michel 44 n. 25
Lesage, Alain-René 84
Le Thorel, Pascale 128 n. 1, 129 n. 10, 130 nn. 41 & 43
Lévy, Bernard-Henri 15
Lœilleton, Fernand 25 n. 31
Louis, Christian 7 n. 24, 96, 97, 111 n. 17, 113
Lyotard, Jean-François 6, 35, 36, 44 n. 29, 113, 115, 116, 117, 118, 122, 126, 128, 129 nn. 12, 13, 14, 16, 17, 18, 19, 20, 25 & 26

Macchia, Giovanni 47, 61 n. 4
MacMaster, Neil 25 nn. 20 & 25
Majastre, Jean-Olivier 7 n. 7, 44 nn. 21 & 22
Malassis, La Collective des 34, 44 n. 25
Malet, Léo 2, 16, 17, 21, 26 n. 45, 43 n. 8, 48, 51, 53, 54, 58, 62 n. 29, 72, 75, 76 n. 8
Manchette, Jean-Patrick 1, 18, 20, 21, 26 n. 53, 27 n. 65
Mandel, Ernest 5, 7 n. 22
Marcelle, Pierre 62 n. 17, 79, 80, 81, 91 n. 11
Marrus, Michael 15, 26 n. 37
Marville, Charles 47, 49
Marx, Karl 21, 94, 111 n. 7
Maspero, François 48, 111 n. 20
Mathey, François 44 n. 23
Mellier. Denis 26 n. 54
Menegaldo, Gilles 26 n. 54
Mension, Jean-Michel (Alexis Violet) 7 n. 19, 11, 12, 13, 15, 25 nn. 12, 25 & 29, 26 nn. 33 & 52, 43 n. 6, 111 nn. 3 & 22
Mercader, Ramón 100, 101, 105
Merleau-Ponty, Maurice 121, 130 n. 32

Micha, René 45 n. 43
Michals, Duane 12
Millot-Durrenberger, Madeleine 128 n. 1
Minich Brewer, Mária 130 n. 29
Mitterrand, François 34
Modiano, Patrick 1
Molinier, Pierre 113, 114, 128 n. 3
Monory, Jacques 1, 2, 5, 6, 8 n. 25, 12, 22, 23, 25 n. 18, 27 n. 71, 30, 43 n. 6, 113–30
Montigny, Serge 21
Moro, Aldo 81, 85, 91 n. 17
Moulin, Raymonde 37, 44 n. 30
Müller, Elfriede 26 n. 53
Munro, Jane 76 n. 1, 82, 111 n. 19
museums/galleries 5, 35, 36, 37, 58, 80, 89, 99, 118, 113, 122
    Beamish 99
    Grand Palais 22, 34
    Madame Tussaud's 69, 93, 99
    Musée Grévin 36, 40, 66, 67, 68, 69, 70, 71, 109, 129 n. 15
    Museum of Modern Art 32, 34
    Natural History Museum 97, 98
    Pompidou Centre/Beaubourg 27 n. 71, 32, 34, 36, 47, 58, 80, 132

Narcejac, Thomas 21
Nerval, Gérard de 30, 53
Neveu, Eric 2, 7 n. 9, 43 n. 7, 133 n. 2
Newman, Mike 112 n. 31
Nizan, Paul 101, 111 n. 20
Nogrette, Robert 13
Noguez, Dominique 23, 27 n. 77
narration 6, 30, 31, 36, 81, 93, 107, 109, 113, 117, 123
    allusion 2, 29, 42, 55, 83
    citation/citational 2, 6, 24, 29, 36, 38, 42, 43, 56. 71, 75, 118, 132
    fictionality 36, 110, 118, 122
    fragments 57, 71, 73, 75, 122, 126
    narrating the past 6, 14, 23, 65–77, 87, 90, 93, 94–95, 102–03, 103–04, 110, 131
    palimpsest 42, 74, 75, 97
    puzzle 23, 29, 38, 66, 71, 73, 75
    reference/referential 1, 2, 5, 18, 20, 31, 32, 33, 37, 42, 52, 53, 54, 55, 56, 62 n. 29, 62, 72, 74, 75, 80, 81, 83, 87, 98, 99, 105, 122, 123, 126, 131
    reflexivity 1, 31, 34, 69, 115, 122, 127
noir/le noir 5, 6, 7, 18, 20, 21, 23, 27 n. 63, 51, 52, 53, 57, 81, 93, 95, 114, 118, 124, 125, 127, 128
    film noir 2, 3, 5, 6, 9, 20, 21, 22, 26 n. 40, 27 n. 63, 83, 112 n. 31, 122, 125
    gothic 3, 5, 19–20, 21, 52, 67, 84, 95, 97, 99, 100, 128
        gothic novel 9, 19, 82, 86
    labyrinth/labyrinthine 5, 19, 20, 23, 34, 57. 69, 71, 81, 95, 98, 99, 106, 109
    roman noir see crime fiction

Oulipo (Ouvroir de littérature potentielle) 33, 45 n. 41

Papon, Maurice 13–14, 15
Paris 1, 2, 3, 4, 5, 6, 12, 13, 14, 16, 17, 18, 21, 22, 23, 30, 31, 33, 38, 40, 43, 47–63, 65–77, 79, 80, 81, 82, 84, 86, 87, 88, 89, 93, 95, 100, 103, 105, 106, 108, 109, 125, 131
    badaud 32, 41–42, 83
    boulevard du crime 48, 53, 55, 69, 73
    canals 16, 21, 34, 48, 50, 53, 55, 58, 75, 107
    demolitions 17, 50, 56, 58, 79, 80, 81
    flâneur 2, 3, 7 n. 12, 17, 32, 41, 47, 48, 72, 73, 93, 131
    history and memory 3, 6, 50–51, 65–77
    as imaginary city 47–63
    as imaginary object 3, 47
    and the night 17, 18, 47, 48, 49–52, 57
    passages/arcades 7 nn. 12 & 13, 18, 32–33, 39, 40, 49, 50, 54, 57, 58, 72, 73
    Père Lachaise cemetery 50. 51. 53, 54
    photographer as *flâneur* 3, 49, 73
    place de la Bastille 26 n. 42, 56, 57, 58, 59, 79, 80
    rue de Lappe 57, 58, 62 n. 37, 63 n. 44
    rue Watt 51, 55, 56, 75–76
    Sacré-Cœur, église de 50, 91 n. 7
Paxton, Robert 15, 26 n. 37
Pelletier, Robert 24 n. 4
Perec, Georges 1, 21, 23, 24, 45 n. 41, 49, 70, 76 n. 3
Petitjean Marc 80, 91 n. 9
Pignon-Ernest, Ernest 80, 91 nn. 7 & 8
Piron, François 62 n. 26
Platten, David 26 n. 54, 27 n. 63, 111 n. 15
Plenel, Edwy (Joseph Krasny) 13, 15, 24 n. 1, 25 n. 22, 26 n. 39
Poe, Edgar Allan 3, 19, 20, 21, 97, 123, 124, 126
political movements:
    anti-semitism 14, 15, 40, 98
    communism/communist 10, 11, 15, 19, 44 n. 25, 86, 87, 94, 99, 100, 101, 102, 104, 105, 107, 108, 110, 111 n. 20
    nazism 20, 37, 40, 74, 85, 93, 99, 101, 104, 110, 132, 133
    Red Brigades 6, 79, 81, 84, 91 nn. 2 & 17
    Socialist party 35, 42, 88, 89
    stalinism 10, 15, 19, 30, 74, 92 n. 22, 93, 101, 102, 104, 132
    trotskyism 2, 5, 9, 13, 15, 24, 29, 30, 34, 35, 74, 93, 95, 100, 101, 108, 110, 132
        Ligue communiste/Ligue communiste révolutionnaire 9–10, 11, 13, 14, 15, 24 nn. 4 & 5, 25 n. 22, 26 n. 35, 131
    and Jewish militants 14–15
    Rouge, newspaper of the *Ligue communiste révolutionnaire* 5, 7 n. 16, 9–15, 24 n. 4, 25–26, 34, 43 nn. 6 & 7, 44 n. 25, 45 nn. 34 & 43, 49, 57, 74, 85, 125, 130 n. 44
terrorism 1, 6, 11, 18, 42, 83

politics 1, 2, 3, 6, 9–15, 18, 22, 24, 29, 30, 31, 34, 35, 37, 38, 50, 57, 68, 73, 93, 101, 110, 131, 132, 133
   avant-garde in politics 10, 95, 110, 132
   class 10. 23–24, 48, 49, 82, 93, 132
      working-class 5, 10, 14, 16, 25 n. 9, 48, 50, 57, 75, 82, 86, 94, 95, 127
   elections 6, 30, 35, 42, 88
   extreme-left 13, 18, 23, 91 nn. 2 & 17, 132
   extreme-right 10, 12, 24 n. 5, 26 n. 53, 40, 81, 86, 87, 88, 89, 91 n. 17
   immigration/immigrant 10, 11, 51, 70, 87, 89
   internationalism 10, 15, 24, 25 n. 22, 57, 95
      anti-colonialism 10, 13, 15
      Argentina 5, 48, 56, 57, 59, 60, 62 n. 38
      colonialism 10, 13, 23
      East Timor 10
      independence struggles / wars of independence 10, 15
      Latin America 16, 38, 57, 131
      Vietnam War 10, 22, 36, 40, 125
Pouy, Jean-Bernard 111 n. 1, 27 n. 69
Pradel, Jean-Louis 22, 27 n. 74, 91 n. 7
Pronier, Raymond 53, 56, 62 n. 32

Rabaté, Jean-Michel 32, 44 nn. 15 & 16
Rancillac, Bernard 23
Ravet, Serge 24 n. 4
Ray, Man 30, 43, 105, 106
Raynal, Patrick 111 n. 18
Reader, Keith 61, 62 n. 34
Readings, Bill 126, 130 n. 45
Recalcati, Antonio 22, 37
Renoir, Rita 16, 26 n. 43
representation 1, 2, 22, 23, 24, 29, 35, 36, 61, 66, 68, 99, 110, 113, 114, 115–16, 117, 119, 121, 126, 131
   artifice 29, 55, 95, 96, 115
   illusion 5, 31, 94, 96, 116, 117–18, 125, 129 n. 15
   model/mannequin 5, 21, 31–32, 33, 36, 42, 54, 66, 67, 68, 69, 70, 71, 72, 73, 99, 100, 105, 106, 109, 128, 129 n. 15
   model/maquette 83–84, 90
   simulacrum 5, 69, 70, 99, 108, 110
   spectacle 14, 37, 38, 40, 48, 66, 67, 69, 82–83, 85, 104, 125, 132
   theatre/theatricality 1, 35, 36, 48, 66, 79, 85, 88, 89, 90, 109, 117, 126, 127, 132
   trompe l'œil 5, 24, 29, 36, 67, 107, 108
Restany, Pierre 22
Restellini, Marc 90 n. 1
Restif de la Bretonne 53
Reuter, Yves 26 n. 54
Richard, Denis 24 n. 4
Rieti, Fabio 83, 91–92 n. 18
Rivière, François 26 n. 46
Robbe-Grillet, Alain 12
Roché, Henri-Pierre 29

Rodanski, Stanislas 123
Ross, Kristin 2, 7 n. 8, 73, 76 n. 9
Rothberg Michael 74, 76 n. 19
Rouge, newspaper of the *Ligue communiste révolutionnaire* 5, 7 n. 16, 9–15, 25–26, 34, 43 nn. 6 & 7, 44 nn. 24, 25 & 26, 45 nn. 34 & 43, 49, 57, 61 n. 14, 74, 85, 111 n. 3, 125, 130 n. 44
Rouillé, André 121, 130 n. 35
Rousset, Pierre 10, 45 n. 34
Rousso, Henry 74
Ruiz, Jean-Paul 114, 128 n. 2
Ruoff, Alexandre 26 n. 53

Saint, Nigel 91 n. 14
Salles, Jean-Paul 11, 14, 24 n. 4, 25 nn. 10 & 11
Saloff, Michel 1, 6 n. 1, 49, 51, 52, 62 n. 22, 113
Sartre, Jean-Paul 16, 24, 41, 47, 111 n. 20, 117
Sauvageot, Pierre-André 1, 26 n. 49, 30, 110
Schaewen, Deidi von 80, 91 n. 10
Schulman, Peter 26 n. 46
Schweighaeuser, Jean-Paul 18, 26 n. 51, 27 n. 56
Seguí, Antonio 1, 44 n. 13
Semprun, Jorge 1
Sheringham, Michael 23, 24, 27 nn. 75 & 81, 45 n. 36
Silverman, Max 74, 45 n. 34, 76 n. 18
Simsolo, Noel 55
Siné 21
Siniac, Pierre 1
Siodmark, Robert 20
Sontag, Susan 3, 7 nn. 16 & 17, 121, 130 n. 33
Spoerri, Daniel 22
Stierle, Karlheinz 48, 61 n. 8
St. Phalle, Niki de 22
Sue, Eugène 3, 17. 20, 48, 53
surrealists/surrealism, 2, 3, 4, 5, 9, 17, 20, 21, 30, 41, 47, 48, 62 n. 8, 71, 72, 95, 99, 100, 103, 105, 106, 109, 131
   1938 Exhibition 76 n. 8, 100, 105, 111 n. 19

Tango art and literary magazine 5, 9, 15–18, 20, 24, 26 n. 41, 48, 52, 57, 63 n. 43, 80, 113
Tardi 21
Tierney, Gene 21
Tour de France 16
Trauner, Alexandre 17, 26 n. 45
Tronche, Anne 80, 81, 91 nn. 8 & 15
Trotsky, Leon 2, 12, 15, 55, 73, 95, 100, 103, 105, 109, 112 n. 28, 132
Truffaut, François 20

Ubac, Raoul 105

Vailland, Roger 18
Valtin, Jan 94, 104, 111 n. 5, 112 n. 26
Van Heijenoort, Jean 12, 25 n. 19, 112 n. 28

Vasseur, Bernard 128 n. 1
Vergès, Jacques 92 n. 23
Vernet, Marc 27 n. 62
Vian, Boris 12, 51, 55, 75
Vilar, Jean-François:
    biography 9–10, 24 n. 3, 30
    contributions to artist books 113–14
    on crime fiction 18–24
    exhibition catalogues 2, 6, 96, 113
        'Memento Mori' 2, 6, 113, 118, 122–28, 132
        'Poses' 113, 118–22, 128
        'Volver' 31, 44 n. 13
    non-fiction:
        '"Tango y Milonga"' 17
        'Bastille-Opéra' 80, 81, 17, 63 n. 43
        'Cher Nestor Burma' 17, 72, 75–76
        'Noir c'est noir' 18, 19, 26 n. 50, 27 n. 59
        'Paris désolé' 56, 76 n. 10, 80
        'Paris énigmes' 48–49
        'Repérages pour un Paris des surréalistes et de quelques autres flâneurs' 17
        Les Fous de Chaillot 93
        Postface to Jan Valtin, *Sans patrie ni frontières* 93–94, 94–95, 112 n. 26
    novels:
        Bastille-Tango 2, 5, 17, 18, 30, 31, 48, 56–61, 68, 71, 80
        C'est toujours les autres qui meurent 1, 2, 5, 14, 15, 29, 30, 31–36, 37, 40, 41, 43 n. 3, 113, 132, 133 n. 2
        Djemila 6, 30, 31, 79, 81, 86–90
        Etat d'urgence 1, 6, 79, 81–86, 113
        Les Exagérés 2, 5, 6, 30, 31, 40, 65–71, 93, 103, 132
        Nous cheminons entourés de fantômes aux fronts troués 6, 7 n. 24, 12, 30, 93, 95, 99–110, 132
        Passage des singes 1, 5, 29, 30, 31, 36–41, 43, 92 n. 26, 132
    other fiction:
        'Arch' 114
        'Le Réveil du Golem' 21
        'Tandem' 16, 30, 48, 52–54, 55, 73
        'Terminus' 130 n. 49
        Agenda Polar 1986 21
        'Paris d'octobre' 7 n. 5, 48, 53–55, 56

photobooks 2, 49, 113
    Paris la nuit 1, 5, 47, 48, 49–52, 56, 61 n. 13
    Sherlock Holmes et les ombres 6, 93, 95–99, 110
    and *Rouge* 5, 9–15
    and *Tango* 5, 15–18
Villéglé, Jacques 22
Vincent, Gene 16
Vinciguerra, Lucien 128, 130 n. 50
Violet, Alexis, *see* Mension, Jean-Michel
visual arts 9, 113, 117
    art 1, 2, 3, 5, 6, 16, 17, 21, 22, 23, 29–45, 48, 50, 54, 57, 58, 75, 79–92, 101, 113–30, 131, 132
    affichistes 22, 80, 127
    art and politics 1, 5, 12, 22, 30, 34, 37, 39, 79, 101, 110, 131
    art history 22, 35, 47, 113, 115
    art market 5, 30, 37, 80
    Art vivant 22, 116, 129 n. 15
    avant-garde art 1, 5, 11, 29, 61 n. 6, 95, 110, 113, 122, 128, 132, 133
    contestation in art 1, 2, 5, 9, 11, 22, 34, 37, 39, 79
    figuration narrative 2, 5, 22–23, 34, 39, 79, 114, 122
    Malassis, collective des 34, 44 n. 25
    nouveau réalisme 22, 34, 37, 79, 80, 122
    Opus international 22, 80
    Pop Art 22, 37, 115
    street art 7 n. 5, 79–80, 83
    film 1, 6, 7 n. 24, 13, 17, 20, 22, 23, 36, 39, 41, 49, 52, 56, 68, 69, 70, 72, 76 n. 6, 48, 55, 60, 65, 66, 67, 82, 84, 86, 98, 102, 113, 114, 115, 122, 124, 125, 130 n. 40, 133
    film noir see *noir/le noir*
    iconography 18, 21, 95
    photography 1, 2, 3, 6, 12, 15, 16, 17, 18, 21, 22, 29, 30, 31, 37, 38, 39, 40–41, 42, 48, 49–52, 72, 80–81, 95–99, 113, 114, 115, 116, 117, 118–22

Waits, Tom 16
Wallace, Richard 55
Warhol, Andy 22, 29, 36, 37, 49
Weegee 3, 41
Wenders, Wim 48, 82, 84, 92 n. 20
Wilson, Sarah 23, 27 n. 78, 91 n. 18, 115, 129 nn. 6, 9, 12, 13, 16, 18, 19, 20 & 25, 130 n. 42

www.ingramcontent.com/pod-product-compliance
Lightning Source LLC
LaVergne TN
LVHW061252060426
835507LV00017B/2042